CREATING THE UPSIDE DOWN ORGANIZATION:

Transforming Staff to Save Troubled Children

By: Andrew L. Ross, Ph.D., LCSW-C
Gary L. Grenier, BA
Frank J. Kros, MSW, JD

Creating the Upside Down Organization

Published by The Children's Guild, Inc., Baltimore, MD

Printed in the United States of America by Victor Graphics, Inc.

Address requests for information to:
    Andrew L. Ross
    The Children's Guild
    6802 McClean Boulevard
    Baltimore, Maryland 21234

Includes Bibliographical references

Typesetting and Book Design by Momi Antonio
Cover Design by Michael Diliberto

ISBN 1-931596-02-6

FIRST EDITION

Organizational Literature

Emotional Disturbed and Behavior-Disordered Children

WHO SHOULD READ THIS BOOK?

This book has been written for professionals in child-serving organizations. We define child-serving organizations as schools and institutions, such as nonpublic schools, residential treatment centers, group homes therapeutic foster care homes, delinquency institutions, day treatment programs and like organizations involved in the care, education and re-socialization of emotionally disturbed and behavior-disordered children. While we believe the principles apply to any organization attempting to change the mindset and behavior of the people it serves, we have limited the examples to our experience in nonpublic schools, group homes and residential treatment centers.

A THUMBNAIL SKETCH OF TRANSFORMATION EDUCATION

Definition

Transformation Education is an organizational philosophy that guides the creation of a culture to transmit the values and life skills necessary for a successful life. The basic premise of this philosophy is that life is a journey of personal growth and enlightenment that comes from the continuous struggle and search for meaningful responses to life's challenges. Transformation Education embraces the journey experience of the individual and incorporates it into the culture of an organization as the operative reality.

How It Works

Transformation Education uses the power of integrated messages to create a culture of pro-social values, thinking and behavior that is transmitted through the organization's employees, operational systems, physical environment and curriculum/program. Children immersed in this culture mimic, idealize and internalize these cultural messages and cues. Transformation Education is inherently value-based. Consequently, the design and implementation of Transformation Education begins with the organization's identification of its beliefs, values and understanding of the purpose of life that it wants to transmit to the children in its care. To do this, the organization must first struggle with identifying and understanding its beliefs, values and concept of the purpose of life.

Belief

Organizations do not have a "culture"; organizations *are* a culture. Cultures, which are simply organized differently, become organizations. Transformation Education places culture at the center of organizational design instead of at its periphery.

The Social Problem Transformation Education Is Attempting to Solve

The vast majority of child-serving organizations* are designed and operated to be staff-centered rather than child-centered.

Impact of This Social Problem on Society

The staff-centered approach yields schools that can't teach, repeated movement of children in and out of foster homes and group care, growing numbers of children diagnosed with mental health problems, increases in youth violence and school dropout rates. A study conducted by Dartmouth Medical School in 2003 evaluated hundreds of research studies on how children develop the patterns of thinking and behavior that lead to healthy, as well as unhealthy, emotional development. They found that although increased dollars are spent on programs to help troubled youth, the number of children suffering from emotional and behavioral problems continues to increase.

The Idea to Impact the Social Problem

Transformation Education is the vehicle for motivating the restructuring of child-serving organizations from adult-centered purveyors of disparate professional services into integrated, child-centered organizations that help troubled children experience and internalize the connectedness and meaning essential to adopt pro-social values and behavior. Therefore, by establishing a movement to adopt Transformation Education and to study and refine it, child-serving organizations will be able to more effectively serve the needs of emotionally and socially disadvantaged children.

Transformation Education's Innovativeness

- It emphasizes changing the mindset of the organization and the staff it employs to socialize and educate behavior-disordered children.
- It integrates theories and research from multiple fields into an understandable and practical organizational approach to increase the service effectiveness of child-serving organizations.
- It brings the physical environment, the way the program is transmitted and how the staff responds to the child into alignment with how a child's brain operates.
- It uses the force that created the troubled child's mindset, culture, to transform it.

DEDICATION

Those who provided me with the tenacity, passion and skills to write and question assumptions made my contribution to this book possible. First among those is my writing teacher, spouse and major support in life, Dianne Ross. There were also those who transformed me from a concrete to a critical thinker: Drs. Arthur Blum and Tom Holland of Case Western Reserve's Mandel School of Applied Social Sciences Doctoral Program. Everyone needs encouragement to publish their work. Mine came from the late Dr. Fritz Mayer, former Executive Director of Bellefaire Jewish Children's Bureau in Cleveland, Ohio. It took 13 years of wrestling with these ideas to write this book. I would have given up long ago if it were not for my first teachers in life who modeled the perseverance and work ethic it takes to complete a task, my parents–Vinnie and Rae.

Andrew L. Ross

For my father, Bernard, and his love of intellectual debate, my mother, Fern, and her creativity, and for my wife, Jennifer and our three sons, Aaron, Trevin and Paul, who have taught me most of what I know. And for those children and youth who are non-traditional learners…those whose voices are seldom heard by the right-side-up organization.

Gary L. Grenier

This book is dedicated to those child-care workers who truly taught me the craft: Ed Shobe, Mark Brown, Noreen Harrington, Gavino Saldivar, Bob DiBlasi and the countless other dedicated professionals with whom I've been blessed to work. Special thanks to my wife, Shawn Reagle Kros, the finest child-care professional I've ever known.

Frank J. Kros

CONTENTS

ACKNOWLEDGEMENTS

If the essence of life is found in the struggle, we certainly found it! This book has emerged from a long and arduous journey that has transformed our lives personally and professionally.

The ideas for this book emerged in 1982 but were first attempted to be expressed in writing in 1992. Gary and Andy's children were in elementary school. Since then they have been asking, "Hey Dad, are you done with the book yet?" It has taken 13 years to give an affirmative answer. It has been a struggle to find the time to write, the clarity to express the ideas and to overcome the complexity of the intellectual property issues.

Along the way to completion of the book we encountered much help. John Adams, our CFO at Children's Square U. S. A., helped us plan and express the workplace expectations and some of the management principles. Help and encouragement also came from Mike Clark, a retired journalist from the *Baltimore Sun*, who edited the book and is a true soul brother. This book would never have been published without his involvement. Then there was Suzanne Molino Singleton and Michelle Kramer, proofreaders, who spent days examining every word and sentence. The transformation of the project from a manuscript to a book was the result of the creative talent of our book designer, Momi Antonio.

The aforementioned effort resulted in one book ready for publication. However, to make this book available to those who are interested in transforming child-serving organizations, it took Alfred Moses of McClean, Virgina, and Amalie Cass of Lincoln, Massachusetts. We thank Alfred and Amalie for believing in this project and honoring their mother, Helene Moses, one of the first Board Chairs of The Children's Guild, through providing the funds to expedite its publication. Their help has provided the major tool needed to launch the Institute for Transformation Education and for improving the lives of thousands of disadvantaged children.

ABOUT THE AUTHORS

The authors have spent the past 20 years reflecting on, designing, field testing and conceptualizing the use of organization and culture to resocialize and educate behavior-disordered and emotionally troubled children and youth.

Andrew L. Ross, Ph.D., LCSW-C is currently the president of The Children's Guild in Baltimore, Maryland, which provides special education and child mental health services to emotionally disturbed children. Dr. Ross has worked with emotionally disturbed children and their families since 1969. He has served two other multiservice organizations as chief executive officer and has also worked as program director, supervisor and social worker. He has published 12 articles on working with children in group care and led and authored a national study on preventing child abuse in child-serving institutions.

Dr. Ross received his doctorate in social welfare administration and his master's degree in social work from Case Western Reserve University, and his bachelor's degree in psychology from Thiel College.

Gary Grenier, BA is an educator with 27 years of experience in elementary education, educational television and special education and has worked as an educational consultant to the Educational Information Resource Center in New Jersey. He is currently the executive director of The Lincoln Center, which operates schools for nontraditional learners in the Philadelphia area. He has served in key administrative positions in three child welfare organizations prior to assuming his current post with The Lincoln Center and is an innovator in the creation of learning environments for children.

Frank Kros, MSW, JD joined The Children's Guild as executive vice president of programs in 2000. Prior to this, Mr. Kros practiced law with Luce, Forward, Hamilton & Scripps in San Diego, California, where his practice focused on children's issues. He has also served as vice president for curriculum and training at Children's Square USA in Council Bluffs, Iowa, a child abuse service officer for the Douglas County Juvenile Court in Omaha, Nebraska, and a family teacher at Father Flanagan's Boys Home (Boys Town).

Mr. Kros received his law degree magna cum laude from Notre Dame Law School in 1993 where he served on the Notre Dame Law Review. He also holds a master's degree in social work from the University of Nebraska at Omaha and a bachelor's degree in psychology from Creighton University.

INTRODUCTION

Most Programs Cannot Execute Service at the Level They Advertise.

In our 93 years of combined experience working with troubled youth, we have found few instances when child-serving organizations worked well. Despite their promises, they were not able to deliver what their brochures marketed. Even our own services were inconsistent with what we promised. In the last 25 years, we have learned how to organize and deploy the systems needed to provide an integrated holistic learning environment that expresses the values we propose and are compatible with how the brain learns and functions.

Our Workforce Needs to Be Trained to Carry Out the Mission.

The present-day reality of group care and special education is that both fields are experiencing a serious manpower shortage. Employers are not able to recruit a sufficient number of experienced and effective practitioners who can educate and socialize emotionally disturbed children. Colleges and universities do not adequately prepare students to work with these youth. Even if they did, staff salaries are extremely low for the skill and knowledge it takes to work effectively with this challenging population. Recruiting a sufficient number of talented and experienced direct care staff and teachers is a major problem. Despite these drawbacks, we believe this handbook offers a methodology that enables the available workforce to carry out effectively what is being proposed.

There Is a Vital Need to Change Our Social Environments.

Illustrative of the dysfunctional nature of many of the institutions designed to serve children is the undeniable fact that instead of helping children with emotional disabilities, the opposite happens despite an increase in programs and funds to serve at-risk youth. This is pointed out in a 2003 study jointly published by the YMCA of the USA, Dartmouth Medical School and the Institute for American Values, titled *Hardwired to Connect: The New Scientific Case for Authoritative Communities* (p. 9). This report acknowledges a "crisis" faced by children and adolescents in the United States, citing a study estimating that 20% of today's youth are suffering from mental illness, emotional distress and behavioral problems.

Neuroscience Has Uncovered an Essential Truth: Our Children's Brains Are Hardwired to Seek Connection with Others and for Understanding Moral Purpose and Ultimate Meaning. But for that to Happen We Need a Receptive Social Environment.

The *Hardwired to Connect* study found that "Social environments matter. They can impact us at the cellular level to reduce genetically based risks and help to transform such risks into behavioral assets. They can also help substantially raise intelligence and measures of intelligence" (*Hardwired to Connect* , 2003, p.21). . . . The new scientific findings indicate that ". . . (the) social environment can change the relationship between a specific gene and the behavior associated with that gene. Changes in social environment can thus change the transcription of our genetic material at the most basic cellular level" (*Hardwired to Connect* 2003, p. 19).

The study discusses how the brain is hardwired to connect to other people and to moral meaning. Meeting the brain's basic need for this connectedness is essential to health and human flourishing. If the child-serving institutions are organizationally dysfunctional (i.e., lack connectedness and a spiritual component), they will not meet the children's need for connectedness and cannot effectively serve them. What is required for children, who do not get this need met in their family or school is an organization that lives out the types of connectedness that the children have been deprived of experiencing.

Therefore, we came to realize that the philosophy and the designed organizational model will have a significant impact on a large portion of America's vulnerable children. The neuroscience research is clear – it is important to design or redesign child-serving organizations to meet more fully the needs of the children we serve.

A Working Philosophy Is Essential to Motivate the Transformation of the Emotionally Disturbed Child and Rekindle the Child's Interest in Learning.

We have developed a working philosophy and a practicing model of Transformation Education at The Children's Guild in Baltimore. Those who would like to view this approach in action are welcome to visit. While we have achieved progress in implementing our philosophy, we have not maximized the results we can, and will, obtain. However, the *Hardwired to Connect* study made us realize that we now have research support for our philosophical approach and have a responsibility to share our results.

Where We Began

Transformation Education – as an approach to teaching values and life skills to emotionally disturbed children – began in 1981 with our work at a multiservice agency for children. We realized from the outset that we were designing an organizational culture to generate personal growth and transformation. More specifically, the culture was purposely designed to transform those youth with whom the traditional educational and social institutions have experienced the least success. These are the youth who are expelled or quit, and who "fail" in the human service institutions the state has set up. Often these youth die an early drug-afflicted death on city streets or end up in prison ironically called "a corrections facility."

In our traditional but errant ways, we were teaching youth that we could make them "well" if they agreed they were "sick." We could make them "good" if they agreed they were "bad." We continuously emphasized our power over them as a means to empower them. It was a model of social control that did not make sense. We chose to create a system that would hold true to the goal of empowering, aware that our ideas would not be gladly received, as we began to question the authority and moral basis of the existing social service system, its operation, methodology and cultural role.

Along the way, we were also led to question the impact of other non-human service organizational cultures on our society's children and youth. As we began to understand the role organizations can play as agents of transformation and change, we came to a new understanding of the role corporations play in our culture. We realized organizations have become powerful parental influences in our society and have a significant responsibility for modeling cultural values and setting cultural expectations.

Where We Arrived

After 25 years of attempting to acculturate a child-serving organization with the Transformation Education philosophy, we have achieved a greater understanding of the beliefs and assumptions needed to design and operate an organization that fosters change and growth. In addition, we have developed many, though not all, of the systems needed to transmit these beliefs to the children and the employees who work with them. We found that success was not dependent on 100% deployment of Transformation Education. An earnest attempt to create a culture of learning where troubled children can discover connections that reveal a sense of meaning, healthy relationships and life purpose generated better outcomes than traditional approaches.

The statements that undergird our organizational philosophy and mission were not developed at the outset of our journey. We present them in their completed state as a guide to the reader.

Culture as an Effective Agent of Transformation

Once we grasped the importance of culture, we came to understand the reason culture is so effective as an agent of transformation. Our understanding resulted from exposure to the latest developments in neuroscience and brain-based education. We came to realize that by integrating concepts from anthropology, education, social work, neuroscience, organizational theory, crisis and chaos theory into an integrated and systematic approach, we had developed a systematic philosophy we call Transformation Education. By demonstrating our philosophy and mission in an existing working organizational model, we believe we can motivate transformation in other child-serving organizations. The work in progress over the past 25 years has gone beyond theory to practical application that is supported by an abundance of research.

The Purpose of Transformation Education

This book is a practical guide about how to transform the antisocial behavior of emotionally disturbed and behavior-disordered children and youth into prosocial behavior. That is accomplished by intentionally changing the mindset of child-serving organizations and the staff they employ.

We begin by discussing why child-serving organizations play a critical role in reversing the deteriorating mental health of our children. We trace what has happened in our culture over the last 50 years that has weakened our collective ability to grow and nurture children into healthy adults.

In line with the neuroscience research, the primary theme is the concept of "connectedness." Connectedness describes the essential needs our children have for intimate relationships with others and for deep understanding of the moral and spiritual meaning of their lives (*Hardwired to Connect,* 2003, p.5). It is our opinion that it is society's declining ability to meet the connectedness requirements of its children that has most directly led to the increasing numbers of children suffering from mental illness. We must restructure our organizations to meet an emotionally disturbed child's need for connectedness and meaning. Transformation Education is the vehicle we have developed for converting child-serving organizations from purveyors of disparate professional services into integrated institutions that help children experience and internalize the connectedness essential for healthy development and interpersonal change and growth.

By "transformation" we mean a fundamental change in the nature, function and condition of the child-serving organization and the children it serves. By "education" we mean the knowledge, thinking and behavior the organization and the children internalize as a result of immersion in a specially designed culture. Transformation Education is intent on "changing the organization" into a wise, warm, value-laden culture and immersing the child into it.

Changing an organization is a formidable task, especially when the historic lens through which the organization views itself must be replaced with a new looking glass. The distinctive feature of Transformation Education is that it fundamentally changes the focus of the child-serving organization from the troubled child to the supervising adults.

Traditionally, child-serving organizations have applied philosophies inspired by the medical model. Consequently, the child and, more accurately, the child's pathology, is the cornerstone on which traditional child-serving institutions are built. Under this traditional model, the organization is a "container" for the various professionals gathered together to treat the pathology and "fix the child."

However, as research in neuroscience is demonstrating more clearly each day, children do not thrive in environments driven by pathology. Moreover, promoting connectedness is clearly not the priority in organizations designed as forums in which physicians, therapists, psychiatrists, social workers and others gather to practice their individual crafts. Rather, the new research confirms the ancient wisdom that children will reflect the cultural values, behaviors and problem-solving methods of the integrated, collective environment in which they are immersed.

Based on our observations over a quarter century, children thrive and grow in a culture of adults who model the positive values, meaningful relationship skills and effective problem-solving methods necessary for hope, happiness and success. Children learn these "connectedness" traits through immersion in a culture where adults actually believe and behave in ways consistent with these traits. The adults convey these beliefs through actions, words and the operating systems of the organization. When children are immersed in this culture, growth and change is inevitable. It is how human beings are made.

The Notion that It Is the Adults Who Will Grow and Change When They Come to Work for the Children's Agency Is Not Initially a Popular One.

Change is difficult. And new perceptions and understandings are essential in times of crisis. Let us not kid ourselves. This is a time of crisis for American youth experiencing "rising rates of depression, anxiety, attention deficit, conduct disorders, thoughts of suicide and other serious mental, emotional and behavioral problems" [The Commission on Children at Risk: *2003, p.5*].

Abraham Lincoln realized in the early stages of the Civil War that "the dogmas of the quiet past are inadequate to the stormy present. . . . As our case is new, so we must think anew, and act anew. We must disenthrall ourselves. . . . " To move ahead with Transformation Education, our child-serving organizations and their staff members need to understand that there is a major shift in thinking required.

It is much more popular to be "child focused" in the modern parlance of social work and education. Unfortunately, being child focused often means a concentration on pathology. We contend that a consideration of a child's pathology is necessary, but never sufficient for producing success. As we will share in the following pages, staff resistance to creating a culture in which they are personally expected to grow and change is persistent and, at times, passionate. However, once created, this newly designed organizational culture is the most powerful tool we know of for changing the minds and characters of children. The most joyful stories to tell are always those of transformation. Children's stories almost always begin with their experience with adults who transformed their lives.

This book will provide you with the transformational tools to turn your organization into a more effective force for meeting the needs of emotionally disturbed and behavior-disordered children seeking connectedness and meaning. In the process of erecting the essential organizational scaffolding, we are confident that you and your colleagues will find a deeper meaning and purpose in your work, individually and collectively.

In writing this book, we have grown tremendously in our knowledge and experience in furthering the theory and the practice of this methodology. Our sense of discovery and wonder is ongoing. There is no end to the new insights all of us will experience as we develop a connective culture.

While we will provide many of the "how to's," we cannot present each "how to" in its entirety.

Many could be a book in, and of, themselves. What follows is theory and research that draws on real-world examples and practices that are applicable to schools and group care organizations. This book is designed to meet your need for practical, hands-on advice to improve a child-serving organization.

SECTION I

Transformation Education: The Conceptual Foundation

This section provides an understanding of the powerful nature of culture and its ability to shape and change our fundamental values, beliefs and assumptions through the transmission of messages and expectations. This understanding allows us to utilize organizational culture to acculturate children with prosocial values and skills in a way that is compatible with how our brains operate.

CHAPTER 1
The Importance of Organizations

Principle: A social environment can change the relationship between a specific gene and the behavior associated with that gene.

> *The hope of Transformation Education has nothing to do with fixing children, but rather about healing the organizations that prevent children from overcoming the obstacles they encounter to learn and grow. —Andrew L. Ross*

Transformation Education is designed as a model for child-serving organizations. By child-serving organization, we mean any group of adults who gather for the purpose of caring for or educating children who suffer from emotional/behavioral problems or who are cared for outside the immediate or extended family. Child-serving organizations exist in an enormous variety of sizes and structures. At its core, the child-serving organization exists to serve children with special mental health needs and risks.

As noted in the Introduction, the needs of these children are, for the most part, not being met. Despite phenomenal increases in knowledge, technology and material resources, our children's mental health is deteriorating. This is not to say there have been no improvements. In the last 50 years, our knowledge, technology and resource boom has had a substantial positive impact on children in several areas. For example, the rates of death for children due to unintentional injury ("accidents") fell by 47 percent, cancer death rates fell by 60 percent and overall childhood death rates fell by 53 percent.

But in the same 50-year period, suicide rates among our children increased a staggering 137%, and homicide rates rose 133%. The current rate of serious, impairing disorders in children hovers between 10 and 12%. Thirteen percent of children ages 9-17 have a diagnosed anxiety disorder, 6.2% have a mood disorder, 10.3% have a disruptive behavior disorder and 2% have a substance abuse disorder [The Commission on Risk, 2003 p. 76]. Regarding children traditionally cared for by child-serving organizations, a growing body of research finds children entering out-of-home care are more disturbed than in the past.

In light of these alarming statistics, it is obvious that child-serving organizations, as a whole, are currently not meeting children's needs for the care and guidance necessary for sustained mental health and happiness. This is not to say that child-serving organizations are responsible for the worsening mental health of our children. Nor do we suggest that child-serving organizations are not providing value and benefit to the children they serve.

Troubled children's suffering has reached a level at which we must admit that our current organizational structures and practices do not work well enough to stem the tide of skyrocketing psychosocial problems. Is it realistic to believe that child-serving organizations can reverse the rising trends in emotional and behavioral problems in youth? We are confident that they can, but only if they are reconstituted to address the unmet needs of children; most notably, the need for connectedness and meaning.

Our confidence is rooted in two primary constructs: our own experience working in and with such organizations and the explosion of research in neuroscience that confirms the theoretical foundations of Transformation Education. Fundamental to the Transformation Education approach is the belief that organizations matter. As the American family has struggled with stability, child-serving organizations have stepped in to provide a crucial societal role as the surrogate parents and extended family for the children in their care.

Once a child is labeled as "troubled," "special needs," "at risk" or a similar diagnostic term, child-serving organizations become a primary player in the care and development of these children. Child-serving organizations wield powerful influences on children in need. Moreover, they exercise a strong impact on the families of these children and the communities in which they live.

In this role, child-serving organizations provide a critical prevention function by educating and guiding families out of maladaptive ways of living. They have the ability to marshal the resources and systems necessary to implement models of care to create an impact on large numbers of children. In our experience, child-serving organizations are uniquely positioned to have immediate and widespread impact on changing the way children with emotional disturbance and other special needs receive care.

The fact that child-serving organizations can have significant influence on the children in their care may not seem at first blush to be a radical thought. Our contention is that this influence is far greater than most organizations recognize or appreciate. In our view, so great is the influence of child-serving organizations, that they have the power to change children at the cellular level and influence how genetic traits are expressed. Recent findings in neuroscience support this groundbreaking fact.

In other words, the Nature vs. Nurture Debate is irrelevant. One does not dominate or control the other. To the contrary, genetic predisposition can influence the quality of the social environment. Just as important, the social environment can influence genetic expression.

Organizations Impact Children at the Cellular Level

The Commission on Risk's *Hardwired to Connect* study, reports that effective care giving and enriched environments have an impact on children at the cellular level. Research by Larry Young at Emory University, Mary Carlson, Felston Earls, Stephen Suomi of the National Institute of Child Health and Human Development, and others, support these findings. *Hardwired* outlines several studies in which the genetic predisposition of offspring is altered – positively or negatively – by the type and consistency of care provided by the caregiver's behavior. Simply put, social contexts can alter genetic expression. Quoting the conclusions of the commission:

> *A social environment can change the relationship between a specific gene and the behavior associated with that gene. Changes in social environment can thus change the transcription of our genetic material at the most basic cellular level . . . the various social environments that we create or fail to create for our children matter a great deal, for good or for ill . . . these hard facts tell us that the environments we create influence our children's genetic expression.*

We cannot fathom a more exciting or sobering finding. Once a child is referred to a child-serving organization, the organization will provide a significant part of the social environment that actually influences the child's cellular structure and, as a result, the genetic structure of future generations.

The opportunity and responsibility inherent in this realization are equally inspirational and terrifying. Organizations do matter. We can hardly imagine how they could matter more. This is one of the reasons why we are so excited about the promise of Transformation Education. Nature has given us the chance to create change for the better.

If the social environment (i.e., organizational culture) has this much influence on both behavioral outcomes and the way the brain is configured to think, then we must take a serious look at how the cultures of child-serving organizations are organized. In our experience, child-serving organizations are traditionally set up on three basic but flawed assumptions.

Assumption #1: There Is No Relationship between How Organizations Are Designed and How the Brain Operates.

This is an erroneous assumption that leads many organizations to ignore the fundamental needs of the children they serve. The *Hardwired to Connect* study points out that the brain is designed to connect to other people and to connect to moral meaning. This desire to connect with other people and have meaningful experience is not just a need of the child's brain, it is also the need of the staff's brain. Therefore the culture of the organization needs to be designed to promote the connection among the children, among the staff and the children, and among the staff, and do so in a way that fosters meaningful experiences.

Assumption #2: The Organization's Culture Is Functional and Therefore More Healthy than the Dysfunctional Culture that Has Created the Social Behavior and Emotional Problems the Child Is Experiencing.

This is only partially true. The organizational culture in child-serving organizations and schools designed to serve emotionally disturbed children is an improvement over the dysfunctional culture the children come from – yet it still has many dysfunctional elements. The children often receive inconsistent messages from staff, and their constant turnover results in policies and procedures not carried out in a consistent way. The philosophy may speak of caring and nurturance, but systems and staff mindsets espouse social control.

The organization speaks of a child-centered approach but often practices a staff-centered one. This incongruity is more than problematic. It results in reinforcing the very cultural messages and mindset of dysfunction, power and control that brought the child to the child-serving organization initially. It affirms the child's worldview regarding adults, peers and education.

These child-serving organizations are far from being as effective as they could be. The need is for a re-tooled organization designed with more understanding of its cultural importance and power to promote change and growth in children. But many of these organizations are unwilling to spend the time needed to connect their mission to every aspect of their organization. Without an integrated approach, fragmentation, dysfunction and inefficiencies result. Management spends far too much of its time and resources resolving crises rather than providing the necessary organizational support that the staff needs to promote change and growth in the children.

Assumption #3: The Culture of an Organization Designed to Serve Emotionally Disturbed Children Should Focus on Treatment.

In reality, the staff needs to focus on teaching values and life skills. This assumption emanates from the understanding that the children are "at risk," and therefore vulnerable and in need of special instruction, medicine and counseling. It takes specialists to provide the special instruction (special education teachers), medicine (nurses and psychiatrists) and counseling (social workers, psychologists, speech/language therapists). The organization is viewed as a container to hold these professionals and provide the supports they need to "fix" the child.

This focus is necessary but not sufficient. It does not account for the fact that the professional staff spends little time with emotionally disturbed children. The children spend most of their time with untrained care givers: child care workers, teaching assistants or young professionals who lack the experience and training to understand and effectively deal with the aggressive and challenging behavior the children exhibit. Instruction takes a backseat to efforts to control behavior. Correcting these erroneous yet fundamental assumptions is a key task in the implementation of Transformation Education.

The Neuroscience Revolution

In her seminal work *Brain Matters*, author and educator Patricia Wolfe notes that we can literally look inside a brain and see which areas are most active while the person is engaged in various mental activities. The advent of technology has so greatly improved brain research that Wolfe accurately claims: "We've learned more about the brain and how it functions in the past two decades than in all of recorded history." The creation of P.E.T. scans, the functional MRI and S.P.E.C.T. scanners has taken us into the deepest, most mysterious regions of the human mind and permitted us to emerge with astounding new insights into the most complex organ in the known universe.

The implications of this explosion in understanding how our brains function, learn and develop have revolutionary repercussions for mental health professionals. The brain is the epicenter of our work with children. To say that we do not need to understand the brain to be able to heal it would be like saying a physician does not need to understand the body to treat it. Every child-serving organization must develop an intimate familiarity with this research so that methods in designing programs to serve children are based on accurate understandings of the structure and functions of their brains. The best child-serving organizations of the future will be those that commit to accessing, analyzing and putting into practice the "applied research" of modern neuroscience.

Transformation Education establishes a moral imperative for a new professional standard: If you serve children with emotional problems then you must understand the brain, how it is assembled, how it functions and what interventions are effective in healing it.

The *Hardwired to Connect* study brought together a commission of doctors, research scientists, and mental health and youth service professionals to investigate the science related to the current mental health condition of our children. As part of their investigation, the commission conducted an in-depth study of the research available on how children develop the patterns of thinking and behavior that lead to healthy—as well as unhealthy—emotional development. The majority of this research is from the burgeoning field of neuroscience. The findings cited in *Hardwired to Connect* and similar brain research provided solid support for the theoretical foundations of Transformation Education.

The findings from applied brain research are both electrifying and affirming. They confirm the ancient wisdom on the makeup of the human mind and soul. Most significant to us, the implications of these findings illuminate how and why Transformation Education works.

Children Learn Through Mirroring Culture

Following the foundational concept that organizations have profound impacts on the children they serve is the equally important concept that children are hardwired to learn patterns of thinking and behavior by observing, modeling and responding to the adults in their environment. This "mirroring" process is particularly strong in children's development of moral thought and behavior.

The framework for moral thought and behavior is initiated through the adult-infant bond. Even before language and complex conceptual ideas are capable of being understood, human infants have the capacity to "read" the culture surrounding their relationship with a caretaking adult. Based on the infant's reading of caretaker cues, s/he begins to establish constructs in the brain around "right" and "wrong" behavior according to whether that behavior is pleasing or displeasing to the caretaker. The infant's quest for caretaker approval is the foundation for the emergence of conscience. Researcher Barbara Stilwell describes this early moral development as follows:

> *Very early in development, infant attachment and parental bonding interact to form a security-empathy-oughtness representation within the child's mind. Physiological feelings associated with security and insecurity combine with intuitively perceived, emotionally toned messages that certain behaviors are parent pleasing or non-pleasing; prohibited, permitted or encouraged; while other behaviors gain no attention at all. A bedrock value for human connectedness guides the child's readiness to behave in response to parent wishes and attentiveness.*

Thus, the child's biological need for connectedness with others is at the heart of developing a strong sense of right and wrong. This moral development process continues to be shaped by relationships with adults throughout childhood. Children begin to idealize both persons and ideas as they grow and mature through adolescence. This idealization results in mirroring behavior by the child, attempting to recreate within them the idealized person or virtue they have identified as worthy.

Hardwired to Connect states: "Because of the 'idealizations' to which we humans are perhaps distinctively prone, we clearly tend to imitate–in moral terms, we tend to become–those whom we admire, whether those persons wish it or not. Accordingly, the challenge for civil society is to expose young people to morally admirable persons."

Children learn moral thinking and behavior by reading the cues and messages in their environment and by idealizing persons and ideas they find attractive. This is an example of how brain research confirms ancient wisdom. If children are provided social environments in which caretakers are warm, nurturing, attentive, have clear boundaries, set high expectations and exhibit prosocial values and thinking, they will respond positively to these relationships and environmental cues.

Children will respond by idealizing the thoughts and people in the culture and internalizing over time, the values, patterns of thinking and behavior reflected by the caretaking culture. We have known about and even understood this moralization process. However, we have not fully focused our energies on building the very caretaking cultures we want children to mirror.

Another critical confirmation of the *Hardwired to Connect* study is the strong human desire for asking ultimate questions about the purpose of life. The drive to find the answer to this ultimate question has a physiological basis in the brain. Moreover, the study concluded that children need to connect to ultimate meaning and to the transcendent "… is not merely the result of social conditioning, but is instead an intrinsic aspect of the human experience." In particular, the teenage years propel children toward a "particularly intense searching for, and openness to, the transcendent." Researcher Lisa Miller of Columbia University concludes:

> *A search for spiritual relationship with the Creator may be an inherent developmental process in adolescence. Our experience with children leads us to agree with the implications of this research. Children have spiritual needs that must be addressed. To ignore the spiritual quest in each child's life is to risk creating a void that may be filled by other forms of searching and satisfaction seeking.*

Creating a Culture that Expresses Social Values and Skills

It follows then that the most effective method of resocializing and educating behavior-disordered youth is through designing a culture that radiates messages expressing prosocial values and skills to children through the operating systems, employees, physical environment and its program/curriculum. The emphasis of Transformation Education is not on changing the child but on changing the staff mindsets to be congruent with the organization's expressed values and beliefs. When that happens, the children experience the connectedness and sense of meaning they lack.

Behavior-disordered children strongly hold their beliefs valid and their own view of reality as accurate. They have learned their mindset from the experience of living in their personal culture. They have established a mindset regarding reality and the principles used to manage it, and behave in accordance with those principles. Consequently, Transformation Education acculturates children to values, beliefs and skills that transform their world view and places them on the path of being successful in their personal and academic lives.

The major priorities of Transformation Education emphasize:

- Values over treatment
- An integrated curriculum/program that incorporates the arts
- A stimulating learning environment that challenges the intellect, touches the emotions and excites the senses
- Changing staff attitudes and behaviors rather than those of the child
- Experiential learning, contextual thinking, concepts over facts, questions over answers, and process over knowledge
- A philosophy that is child-centered, family focused and community based
- Norms over rules

SECTION 2
Foundations of Transformation Education

The chapters in this section assist the reader in understanding the basic principles and beliefs management must instill in the culture of an organization to foster transformation in troubled children and the organizational agility to adapt to the dynamism of the political, market and service environment.

CHAPTER 2
Understanding Culture as Transformation Methodology

Principle: Culture is the most powerful force available to child-serving organizations for transmitting prosocial values and transforming one's mindset.

> *Culture penetrates and shapes every human life, engulfs each person totally, overwhelmingly. Yet, people are seldom aware of its existence. They do not understand its effect upon their lives and their behavior. But they believe they act out of their own private independent volition, out of whims and fantasies and their own individuality. Culture has been misunderstood, . . . confused with customs and traditions, folkways or mores, its significance has been concealed and its role in human life overshadowed by the emphasis on psychological processes. —Charles Case*

Culture as an Elemental Force

Perhaps the best way to understand the impact organizational culture can have on youth is to understand the dynamics and power of culture. It will help if we consider culture as an elemental force. Like gravity, culture cannot be seen, smelled, tasted, felt or heard, but its effect on us is profound and continuous. It is precisely this characteristic that makes it so easy to overlook. Few of us think of gravity on a daily basis. We most often discuss it in terms of science and space. Yet, it is what provides the very air we breathe, holding our atmosphere to the surface of the earth. Gravity affects every aspect of our daily living from why milk pours to how our hair behaves, yet we seldom give gravity a conscious thought. We accept it as a static condition rather than a dynamic force. So it is with culture.

"It is whAT IT is"

Culture is most often relegated to the science of anthropology and thought of as a word describing how the ancients lived. Culture by anthropological definition is: the sum total of attainments, behavior patterns and ways of living built up by a group of human beings and transmitted from one generation to another. The implication is that someone created culture and we are its recipients. This definition is helpful in that it summarizes culture, but is of little help in thinking of it as something we can consciously create and develop. The best definition and understanding of culture that we found was presented by Charles Case in *Culture: The Human Plan.* [Case: 1977]

In a very fundamental sense, culture is the most human part of man's existence. It encompasses those aspects of being that are learned, those regularities that are acquired, as things that are gained through association with other humans. It is the social heritage that has developed out of the biological responses in the life process. It is the web of relationships holding people together in various viable groups. It is the structure of predictability in the behavior of the members of society, which tells each person who he is and who other people are. It provides the techniques for dealing with life's problems, and for directing the shape of one's existence. . . . Culture . . . is a guiding system, a behavioral map, a grammar of behavior that leads one to places unsuspected, by paths unknown and perhaps even against one's will. It is constantly present working to shape behavior in its outward form.

How Cultural Messages Are Learned

The process an individual, family or organization experiences in adopting the beliefs, values, traits, behaviors and social patterns of a culture is called "acculturation." We refer to this method of education and organizational design as the cultural model or more exactly, the "acculturation model." Let's explore in greater detail how acculturation actually works.

In staff workshops, we use the following exercise to demonstrate the subtle yet profound effect culture has on us. We ask the who speaks English, how many are wearing shoes and if anyone is wearing nontraditional clothing. We ask: Why? Why not a sarong? Why not barefoot? Why not speak Chinese?

There is usually embarrassed laughter. Discussion quickly reveals that they learned such patterns of behavior by growing up in American culture. The following axiom illustrates the obvious yet profound nature of cultural power: No one will ever grow up German if they are born of Chinese parents, grow up in China, eat Chinese food, dress Chinese and live the Chinese experience. Instead, they will be Chinese.

Culture must be learned, but it is not consciously taught. It is commonly known that infants do not arrive in the world knowing the rules of a culture. All infants must learn the rules and meanings of their culture and shape their behavior accordingly. They have the capacity to incorporate all the messages to which they are exposed, whether or not we intend this to happen.

This point was well made by a statement in a church bulletin entitled: "Your Home is Bugged!"

In every home, there are two microphones per child. There is one in each ear. These highly sensitive instruments pick up ordinary conversation, incidental remarks, types of language, a variety of words, intensities of sound, off-hand comments, table prayers, Scriptures read, hymns sung. These all-absorbing microphones transmit all that they hear to highly impressionable minds. These sounds then become the vocabulary of the child and the child's basis for values, priorities, action and reaction. Some psychologists say that a child's values and standards are well established before that child enters school. This is a frightening, but also a heartening thought. It relates to what the ancient Hebrews discovered and expressed in one of the Proverbs 22:6: "Instruct a child in the way he should go and when he grows old he will not leave it."

Integration Is Our Sixth Sense

Learning one's culture comes from the input received through senses as well as the *sixth sense*, which we are defining as the integration of sensory input. Virtually everyone is familiar with the senses of taste, sight, hearing, smell and touch. Historically, these five senses have been viewed as part of a child's physical development.

RADAR

Approaching the senses as physical phenomena is like discussing radio channels without listening to the music. Of prime importance is not the mechanics or logistics by which music is transmitted from a radio station to our ear. What is of utmost importance is the effect of the sound on our emotions, our behavior, our understanding of culture and our relationships.

Our senses are carriers of messages both individually and in combination. When drinking hot chocolate our senses integrate the experience: the sweet chocolate taste, the heat on our tongue, the feel of the cup, the warmth as we swallow, the smell that enhances the taste and the visual sight of chocolate liquid. Together these senses integrate in our brain with our current environment and past experiences and stimulate a *sixth sense*.

This *sixth sense*, we believe, is one of the most critical senses we have, especially in developing an understanding of cultural messages and nuance. It is the central sense we use to interpret context and symbolic meaning.

How Culture Is Transmitted

We might think of the means by which culture is communicated by comparing it with the transmission of television messages. We seldom stop to think that we are living in a sea of air and in a sea of energy waves. We are immersed in an atmosphere filled with TV signals being "broadcast." While we cannot see, hear, taste, smell, or touch them, we can detect and interpret them as video and audio through use of an antenna and a TV. Cultural messages, like broadcast television messages, are transmitted continuously and fill our environment.

When it comes to culture, we are all endowed with extraordinary fine antenna and receivers. Our senses act as the antenna and our brain as the receiver. In the real world, we are subject to more than TV signals. We are continuously bombarded by numerous energy waves (heat, light, magnetic, electrical, etc.) acting upon us at the same time. Culture is made up of numerous forms of transmitted messages.

Through our *sixth sense*, we convert, integrate and decode the messages. Our children have the most sensitive antenna, keenly receiving and interpreting the cultural messages we transmit. We do not claim to have a complete understanding of all of the various cultural transmitters or messages. But we have developed a framework for understanding how such messages are transmitted.

Through many hours of intense organizational debate and years of organizational design and development, we have found the primary organizational transmitters to be: systems, people, physical environment and program/curriculum.

Based on our observation, our youth responded to a series of core messages transmitted by our educational setting and the larger organizational culture. Increasingly, they acted in accord with these beliefs and values, assumptions about reality (or the nature of life's journey) and expectations of life.

Build Relationships
Teach skills

We came to realize that an organization has a powerful teaching culture when the organizational systems, environment and staff reflect what the organization believes. A major part of our current cultural dysfunction is that our operating systems (organizations) and environment are inconsistent with the culture's expressed beliefs and values. In designing an organization with integrity, it must deliver what it promises. It is not essential that all of the cultural transmitters or systems proceed at the same time and rate to ensure integrity. Given the scope of organizational change required, this is seldom possible or even desirable.

Our employees, the community and our youth dealt with the disparity in messages between what we had achieved and what we had yet to accomplish once they believed in our "intentionality" to achieve our stated goals. We also had to acknowledge up front that our goals and actions were discordant with the culture we were intent on establishing.

Capturing the messages of an organization must begin with the assumptions, values and beliefs of the chief executive as the head of the culture. There is no quick fix. It cannot be accomplished by tampering with the organizational chart, constructing a new physical plant or altering what one delegates to a group or an individual.

As aforementioned, one of the most helpful books we read was *Culture: The Human Plan* by Charles Case. Case used the term "nomeme" to define the smallest meaningful unit of cultural communication. *"Nomemes are the enduring self-instructions that enable a person to behave and which give the individual's activity consistency and group behavior its commonality. . . ."*

Culture, viewed in this perspective, is equivalent to DNA, the code inherent in biology. It is probably the most complex of all the codes, as it provides individuals in society general and detailed instructions for enacting concrete behavior.

For our purposes, we define the word "nomemes" to mean "messages."

The Emphasis of Culture over Therapy

Our most fundamental purpose is to empower children and youth with the moral values and life skills necessary to live meaningful lives. By teaching children morality combined with life skills, successful behavior results. By morality, we mean a way of thinking about one's self, others and the purpose of life.

What we saw in practice in many institutions were methodologies we considered abusive. Most glaring was the use of negative labels for children: conduct disordered (the psychiatric term) behavior disordered (the behaviorist term), emotionally disturbed (the educational term) and juvenile delinquent (the criminal justice term). These labels are exclusively pathology based and attempt to change children who are, "thought disordered," those who have "wrong" thoughts and therefore wrong behaviors. These organizations attempt to modify children's behavior by rewards (activities typically) and punishments (locked in isolation cells euphemistically referred to as "time out" rooms) and modify thoughts by using psychotherapy focused on the children's identified pathologies.

Behavior Modification Approaches Seemed to Us Culturally Acceptable, but Morally Bankrupt.

Children are taught to behave in an appropriate way to obtain personal gain (profit) or avoid personal punishment (loss). The cultural message is "Do the right thing!" because it is a benefit to you, not because "It's the right thing to do."

The problem is, in a culture that reinforces selfishness, we are attempting to get the individual to buy into the culture of "meism," only at a more sophisticated and socially accepted level. The only meaningfulness is self-gratification by "playing by the rules" to get there.

The psychotherapy approach, on the other hand, is supported by cultural authority, which we have ascribed to the medical community. However, it considers "wrong thinking" a mental illness or at least "sick" and can only operate within the medical paradigm.

It also assumes that "right thinking" is simply a matter of "talking it out" even though "thought-disordered" youth are the least amenable to thoughtful insight and suggestions. Without alternative paradigms, additional medications and psychotropic drugs are needed to control behaviors. The fallacy stems from the medical belief that the individual in our society has dominance over the influence of culture.

The psychotherapy approach does not have a significant track record of substantial success. In fact, recent research on the structure and function of the emotional centers of the brain implies that some traditional psychotherapeutic treatments may be doing more harm than good.

The Brain's Gatekeeper – The Amygdala

The limbic system is that area of the brain housing the neurological hardware of our emotions exerting enormous control over our thoughts and behavior. Central to this influence is the role played by the amygdala, two almond-shaped organs deeply embedded in the center of our brains, one in each hemisphere.

The amygdala serves as the security guard responsible for screening the sensory information sent to the brain for processing. Without exception, every stimulus flowing through our neurons gets the once-over from the amygdala. The amygdala's function to the operation of our brain and body is so important that it is one of the few organs in the human species that is completely mature at birth.

If uncertainty is detected, the amygdala bears down on the new data to determine if it poses a physical or psychological danger. Intricately wired to every other organ in the brain, the amygdala can dispatch urgent requests for information about the threat.

Should the amygdala be satisfied with the information received about the stimulus in question, it passes it on for further processing and response. If, however, the alerted amygdala is not calmed or soothed by the information received, it moves to secrete hormones in the body designed to protect us from the perceived physical or emotional danger.

Chief among these hormones is cortisol, commonly known as the stress hormone. The injection of cortisol into the bloodstream is designed to put us on alert by quickening our heartbeat, increasing our blood pressure, speeding our breathing and sharpening our senses. Cortisol commands the body and the mind to give attention to the object of the amygdala's concern.

Once the concern is addressed and the amygdala convinced that threat no longer exists, cortisol secretions cease, and the cortisol is eventually flushed from the body. If the amygdala's perceived threat is not addressed, cortisol continues to course through the body, and other catecholamines (e.g., adrenaline) are secreted to further enhance the capacity of the brain and body to escape, avoid or successfully confront the danger. The amygdala's function as the "security guard in our brain" is the human hardwiring for avoiding physical and emotional danger and enhancing survival.

Key to this survival function is the fact that the amygdala never forgets. Once a pattern of stimulus trips the uncertainty switch and rises to the level of danger in the amygdala, the same or similar pattern of stimulus will have the same result in the future. It is biological. With few exceptions, there is no known way to eliminate or erase amygdala memories. Instead, the cortical regions of our brains must be trained to "sit on" these amygdala alarms by sending calming messages to the amygdala once the stimulus triggers the amygdala's memory and associated stress response.

The psychotherapeutic approach will either enhance or inhibit cortisol secretion by exciting or calming the amygdala. Psychotherapeutic approaches focused on accessing the cortical regions of the brain responsible for problem solving, creativity, organization and planning will help these cerebral regions mollify the amygdala's reaction to the sensory memory. These therapies focus on building strengths, rehearsing skills and enhancing existing assets.

If the therapy seeks to "relive," "process" or otherwise "deal with" the trauma that trips the amygdala, cortisol production will likely increase. In other words, the therapy itself may intentionally cause a biological stress reaction by consciously requiring the child to recall (and therefore relive) the danger-activating experience, thereby dumping cortisol into the bloodstream. Overstimulation of the amygdala and excess secretion of cortisol can result in serious negative repercussions.

Cortisol destroys the cells of the brain's chief memory processor, the hippocampus. Also located in the limbic system, the hippocampus is essential to the creation and storage of long-term conscious memory. When excess cortisol is present in the brain, the resulting destruction of hippocampus cells not only interferes with the memory-making process (i.e., learning) but also may erase existing memories. Excess amounts of cortisol can inhibit a child's access to the regions of the brain essential for effective problem solving.

Chronic biological stress weakens the immune system and makes the body and mind vulnerable to disease and disorder. Thus, despite well-intentioned and even honorable attempts to help children overcome trauma, traditional psychotherapeutic approaches may trigger the very automatic biological responses the therapy is designed to overcome by revisiting and/or reliving traumatic emotional or physical events.

The Biology behind Resistance to Change

Children hold their beliefs valid and their own view of reality as accurate. They have learned this mindset from the experience of living in their personal culture, the one in which they grew up. They have established a mindset regarding reality and the principles used to manage it, and have behaved in accordance with those principles. Their amygdala functions perfectly and they are consciously and unconsciously hardwired to survive in their particular culture. This does not make them "wrong thinking" and certainly not "sick."

The Deep Entrenchment of this Cultural Learning Is the Biological Process of How Children Learn.

To create a memory, the brain undergoes actual physical change. In its simplest sense, learning is the creation of stored memories that can be retrieved and applied in reaction to emotional or sensory stimulus. The physical changes occurring in the brain as these memories are manufactured provide important insight into the power of culture for establishing patterns of thinking.

Our brains are predominately made of nerve cells called neurons. It is estimated that the human brain contains tens of billions of neurons. These abundant neurons communicate with each other by releasing molecules known as neurotransmitters. Most learning occurs through neuron-to-neuron communication via the discharge and reception of neurotransmitters between neurons.

A neuron consists of three primary parts: the cell body, the dendrites and the axon. The cell body produces the neurotransmitter molecules and determines the molecular response to stimulus inputs received by the cell. Surrounding the cell body are tubular extensions called dendrites. These fingerlike structures are studded with receptors that receive the neurotransmitters secreted by other neurons. The axon is a single, longer extension that carries the cell's own neurotransmitters to other neurons. An axon will typically branch out at the end to enable it to send neurotransmitters to a number of other neurons. At the very tip of each axon branch is a terminal where the neurotransmitters are stored for release in tiny holding glands called vesicles.

Neurons communicate by secreting neurotransmitters from vesicles at the tip of the axon across a narrow gap to the receptors on the dendrites of another neuron. This narrow gap between the axon of one neuron and the dendrites of another is known as the synapse.

When a neuron is stimulated, it sends an electronic message out from the cell body and down the axon. When this electrical impulse reaches the axon terminal, the vesicles open to release specified neurotransmitters into the synapse. Scientists have identified more than 50 neurotransmitters. The specific neurotransmitters released by the vesicles are determined by the impulse sent down the axon by the cell body.

The neurotransmitters communicate messages based on the combination of molecules secreted.

Just like a 26-letter alphabet can create hundreds of thousands of words, 50 neurotransmitter molecules can create vast combinations to communicate unique cell-to-cell messages.

After being released into the synapse, the neurotransmitters are picked up by the receptors on the dendrites of the receiving cells. This, in turn, stimulates the cell body in the receiving neuron to send an impulse down its own axon, and the neuron-to-neuron communication process continues. As the same message is passed on from cell to cell, a circuit is formed from the connection of multiple neurons communicating the message.

In addition to neurons, another type of cell found in the brain is the glial cell. Glial cells perform several important functions in support of the neurons. One of these functions is to form a layer of insulation around the axon, much like the insulation placed around an exposed pipe to keep it from freezing in the winter. This insulation around the axon is known

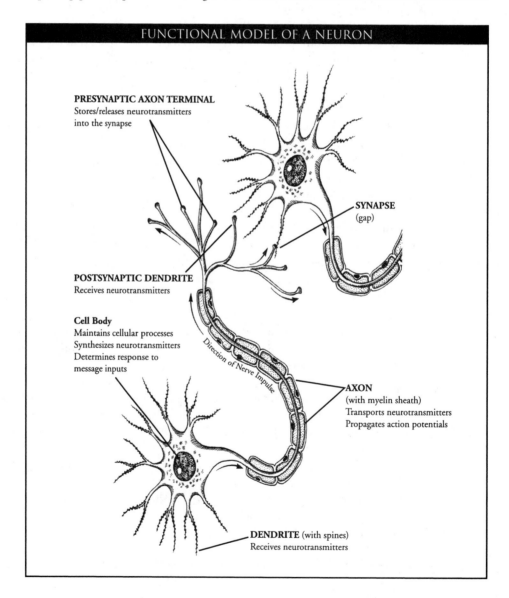

FUNCTIONAL MODEL OF A NEURON

PRESYNAPTIC AXON TERMINAL
Stores/releases neurotransmitters
into the synapse

SYNAPSE
(gap)

POSTSYNAPTIC DENDRITE
Receives neurotransmitters

Cell Body
Maintains cellular processes
Synthesizes neurotransmitters
Determines response to
message inputs

Direction of Nerve Impulse

AXON
(with myelin sheath)
Transports neurotransmitters
Propagates action potentials

DENDRITE (with spines)
Receives neurotransmitters

as the myelin sheath. The myelin sheath thickens as the neuron circuit is used to transport the same messages. The thickening of the myelin sheath is similar to the construction of a superhighway in that it increases both the speed and accuracy of the objects traveling across it. A circuit of neurons frequently carrying the same or similar messages will form a formidable superhighway with heavily insulated myelin sheaths to process impulses through the circuit with lightning speed and substantial power.

These "neural networks" are the foundational structures through which our brain processes new events or objects. The establishment of these neural networks literally changes the physical composition of our brains. Once established, these powerful networks combine to process all new information coming into the brain from the outside world by relating the new information to the memories or learning constructed in the neural networks.

Children have powerful neural networks that reflect their adaptation to their own culture. Since the chief concern of childhood is physical and emotional survival, children are particularly attentive to cultural messages and construct strong neural networks as they learn to navigate the values, expectations and behaviors modeled in the culture.

Children's brains are hardwired to their culture; they have physically adapted by forming neural networks based on their perception and interpretation of the specific cultural demands placed on them. The deep entrenchment of the beliefs, values and behavior of their respective culture is as biological as it is psychological.

The Biology behind Change

The biological hardwiring of neural networks reflecting cultural adaptation presents two similar yet competing themes. The brain physically changes to form powerful neural networks as cultural beliefs, values and behaviors are learned. As a result, children's beliefs, values and behaviors undergo change and will eventually dismantle maladaptive networks. Completely new networks are created. This reconstruction will take time, consistency and patience.

By immersing children in a prosocial environment, the brain's remarkable capacity to learn and adapt can result in substantial, long-lasting and positive change. The brain has the ability to change its physical structure to accommodate new information. The children's adherence to their mindsets suggests that if culture and cultural messages are so strong a force, and so compatible with how the brain functions, then it is logical to harness this force and use it to create a prosocial environment.

What Message Should We Send?

The central question becomes: Toward what end should this force be used? Like nuclear energy, exploiting its power is not enough. We must determine whether to use it for good or for evil. Quite naturally, it was also this question that began our investigation into what successful living means. If we are creating a culture that is effective at changing mindsets and empowering children, what are the beliefs, values, reality assumptions and purpose of life we are fostering?

CHAPTER 3
The Values Expressed by a Transformational Culture

Principle: Life is a journey of personal growth ascending from a focus on self to a focus on family, community and world.

> *More important than either capital goods or skills is the power to determine the behavior messages of the society. What happens in most societies is that some people come to have a determining influence over the message-making and message-enforcing capacity in a society. When a group gains control over the message making and the enforcing agent of the society, they strive to structure the messages to their advantage. This generally produces both a new kind of society . . . and a different kind of individual. –Charles Case*

An Organization's Values

The cornerstone question every child-serving organization needs to ask itself is, "What are we growing?" The query determines how the organization will operate and the kind of messages that will radiate from its structure, systems and employees. The values inculcated into the structures, systems and employees of an organization are what radiate from the organization and are received by the children. For this reason it is important for executive management and the board of trustees to take the time to struggle with the question.

The answer for child-serving organizations should be: "We are in the business of growing intelligence and citizenship." Knowing that the brain is hardwired to seek and make connections with other people and to seek meaning, the concept of organization should aim to foster the growth of dendrites for this purpose. The messages in the Transformation Education organization focus on expressing commitment to community and a cause larger than one's self, i.e., citizenship.

The collective wisdom gathered across time and cultures is centered on the idea that life is a journey of personal growth, as we move from self-centeredness to selflessness. We draw on the writings of the late Joseph Campbell, who revealed the power of myth that is expressed in cultures.

The diagram below suggests three aspects of the journey of personal growth: 1) there are various paths to move toward selflessness; 2) the journey has its ups and downs; and 3) our personal journey toward selflessness is not linear. We both progress and regress. We began exploring the journey of personal growth as a means of understanding how we teach our youth. Our goal is personal growth and empowerment—not social control and behavioral subjugation. Most importantly, the organizational assumptions, beliefs, values, expectations and operations must be congruent with its teachings.

THE JOURNEY OF PERSONAL GROWTH

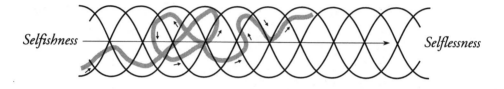

Selfishness   *Selflessness*

As described in earlier chapters, it is through exploration and observation that we came to recognize:

1. The power of culture as a primary influence on a children's existing beliefs
2. The opportunity to utilize this force as a means of developing and changing mindsets
3. The role of the organization and its leadership in establishing the cultural beliefs
4. The critical importance of organizational integrity in harnessing the power of culture

In exploring the concept of personal growth toward selflessness, we developed three critical questions:

- What are the central values needed to access personal growth?
- What is the process through which growth occurs?
- What are the skills needed to achieve growth?

Answers took several years and thousands of hours of debate to articulate, and emerged as nine core principles. These "Wisdom Principles," as we call them, serve as our guides, the foundation for our organizational belief system. They are not the source of truth, but they are of tremendous assistance in shaping our organizational culture, its values and processes. These principles gave us clarity in achieving organizational integrity.

The first question, "What are the central values needed to access personal growth?" is the central moral question. What do we hope to achieve and what do we want our children to become? All decisions are based on one's values and have outcomes that are personal and moral. As an organization we must embody these values and ensure that our decisions and operations reflect their light.

The Wisdom Principals

The Values Comprising the Wisdom Principles

1. The Principle of Caring
   Child-serving organizations need to be caring.

The real question now becomes: What does it mean to be caring? Far too often in educational and human service organizations, it is assumed by the public and administration that by definition, they are a caring organization. Yet, it is often these organizations that have the most difficult time responding to change for the sake of the children. They dislike the accompanying pain it causes–despite the potential for improving the quality of service.

Caring is not static but dynamic in its meaning. It calls upon us to alleviate suffering. It also calls upon us to endure suffering. Caring means to care about one's self and others.

The word "caring," like "love," has come to have little meaning. Perhaps in its most destructive form, "caring" means never hurting anyone or anything. While this is an often-expressed sentiment, it is unrealistic and negative in its outcome.

We grow through a process that has at its very core the experiencing of pain. Moving from selfishness to selflessness is not easy. We must change our mindsets and give up ways of operating if we are to progress. It is perhaps the most painful thing we will experience in life.

We must also broaden our perspective of caring to include the reality that we constantly hurt others. Whether it is simple pain of receiving a tetanus shot or complex pain such as open-heart surgery, we regularly subject ourselves to physical pain. And we pay doctors and nurses to inflict it! This, of course, is acceptable. We realize it is for long-term gain of our physical health.

When it comes to caring for other life forms, we do not hold to the idea that caring is never hurting anything. On a daily basis, we kill animals and plants, and even worse, we do so to eat them! It is this dichotomy that children run up against. We say, "Don't hurt anything," and yet we kill to live. We impose decision after decision, but from a child's perspective, it is hurtful. The problem with an overemphasis on avoiding pain and keeping everyone safe is that on the surface, it appears to lead toward wellness. But personal growth sometimes happens at the risk of experiencing pain.

To care means that accepting the difficulties in life can assist us in gaining deeper personal meaning and growth. Caring is not to prevent struggle or pain but to assist in guiding children and others to understand painful experiences and draw meaning from them.

To be supportive is not to fight the problem for someone, nor to remove him from the battle. Caring is to affirm the "okayness" of the struggle and the principles for which he struggles. Love is more than simply being open to experiencing the anguish of another person's suffering. It is the willingness to live with the helplessness of knowing that we can do nothing to save the other from his pain. [Kopp, 1972]

2. The Principle of Contribution

Child-serving organizations need to be contributors.

This does not simply refer to the idea that corporations need to contribute money to good causes. It is the realization that caring does not exist without performing action. Contribution is the demonstration of caring. We act out our belief in caring at the organizational level. Caring is the idea. Contribution is the enactment.

As an organization you may agree with our beliefs and understanding of caring, but without putting it in action, it remains an intellectualism. It is only as we make caring a core value that we experience the agony and exhilaration of actually attempting to do the right things. With Transformation Education, the beliefs, decision-making process and outcomes of the organization are reflective of its values. The Holy Teachings of Vernalahicti indicate:

"Man grows when action is performed as sacrifice free from attachment to results: Be intent on action, not on the fruits of action; avoid attraction to the fruits and attachment to inaction."

To care exclusively about one's self, in total selfishness, at six months old is normal. It is precisely what is required for the young child's survival in society. To live in this mode when one is 50 years old is not normal. Such selfish behavior is destructive to one's self and to society, as the individual is not contributing back to the very life process through which he has benefited. At its most mature level, contribution is the concept of giving of one's self (and self interest) for the greater good of the larger community. It is giving without regard for a direct selfish return.

3. The Principle of Commitment

An organization must reflect commitment.

Commitment is contribution over time. It is the continuous dedication to grow in one's ability to care and contribute. It is to live with the constant awareness that every decision is personal and every choice is moral.

The Growth Process in Transformation Education

"What is the process through which growth occurs?" This is by far the most difficult process to articulate and accept and the most serious challenge to organizational growth and development. We refer to the principles of this process as struggle, transformation and enlightenment. Most staff readily accepted this as the process our youth go through to change. On a personal level, they found it less comfortable to accept. We found most staff members believe themselves to be whole and complete and that further personal growth is not necessary.

This is the result of the linear mindsets we developed while achieving in the educational systems and work world. As staff, we graduated and/or received promotions to supervisor or administrator. These rituals recognized our growth in knowledge and competency. Perhaps we gained in hubris, but not in wisdom. The Circle of Life: Rituals From The Human Family Album states:

> *Throughout the world, societies both modern and traditional celebrate our journey through life with astonishing rites of passage. Elaborately beautiful, deeply heartwarming, shocking, even life threatening, these rituals distill the wisdom of the ages into comprehensible dramas.*

The path leading to wisdom is lost in the dark woods of our culture. Few go there. The concept is in stark contrast to the linear mindset that we believe in as the organizational model. The dark woods are full of uncertainty. We bump into trees and are haunted by the screech of the owl. We are outside our comfort zone. Transformation Education accepts the chaotic as normative. The howls you hear are the reactions employees express for management practices that are not traditional or comfortable.

It is during the development and implementation of Transformation Education's growth process and principles that we come face to face with the organization, not the individual, as the mentor of the cultural values.

For the organization to accept its mantle as mentor of the values means it must engage in the process of growth. The organization supplants the exclusive domain of the individual. It is threatening. It forces all of us to acknowledge the power that organizations play in our lives and our own subservient role. It is a rude and difficult awakening for all of us.

An understanding of the process emerged after we recognized that the journey and resulting growth is a continuous life process. We reach new levels of understanding as we proceed through the moment-by-moment challenges of living. Personal growth is the result of embarking on an inward journey where there will be many obstacles, challenges and experiences. For organizations, the inward journey of organizational self-examination and exploration is equally challenging.

Life's journey, if it is to be meaningful, is the constant search for truth. By seeking truth, we discover that it is not found in an organizational manual but revealed. Those who go through life looking for dogmatic truth face pitfalls and dangers that stultify personal growth. They either fritter away their lives, never finding what they are looking for, or become dogmatic and fixated on a specific set of external rules. They become rigid and inflexible in their perceptions and abilities. We must prepare our minds before the search. In our culture of organizational values, how are we trained to look for truth?

We adapted former baseball player Yogi Berra's quote to assist us in working with staff who become frustrated as they attempt to understand an organizational culture that operates in a "bumper car" metaphor – "You won't know what you don't know until you know it!" Yogi recognizes that meaning is learned over time, through the process of struggling with the choices in life.

4. The Principle of Struggle

A child-serving organization needs to embrace the idea that struggle is good.

Struggle is the prerequisite to growth and is life enhancing, not life defeating. Struggle results from the continuous state of tension that exists between what is familiar and what is new. It is this crisis that brings with it the opportunity to change.

Humanistic psychologist and anthropologist Jean Houston puts it this way, "Tension is what shines the soul. One cannot get smart unless you fight someone or some thing." Management expert for the social sciences, Mary Parker Follet [Follet: 1982] describes it in this way:

As conflict is here in the world, as we cannot avoid it, we should, I think, use it. Instead of condemning it, we should set it to work for us. Why not? What does the mechanical engineer do with friction? Of course, his chief job is to eliminate friction but it is true that he also capitalizes on friction. The transmission of power by belts depends on friction between the belts and the pulley. The friction between the driving wheel of the locomotive and the track is necessary to move the train. All polishing is done by friction. The music of the violin we get by friction.

The major struggle we must endure concerns the actual living and dying of our ideas, our beliefs and in some ways our very image of self. This is what growing up is all about. This struggle is emotionally and spiritually difficult. Our life journey is an adventure in learning how to die and renew. It is coming to grips with this fundamental principle that is so difficult.

The concept of struggle and its importance in growth is illustrated by the *Dungeons and Dragons* game that was so popular in the early 1980's. The beginning of the game immediately gives you choices. The best choice, however, is not necessarily the option that appears to give you the quickest "win," e.g., the gold is recovered or the maiden rescued. While these may be objectives, the primary purpose is the growth and development of the individual seeker.

Your character in the game has very little experience, knowledge or wisdom. You are forced into making decisions, some of which can be harmful and deadly. As the game progresses, you gradually learn to make decisions that are more knowledgeable; your warrior gains strength and wisdom. This process, however, does not occur without many of your characters being destroyed. It is only after many deaths and lengthy periods of playing the game that one can achieve a seeker who has great wisdom.

The myths tell us that it is only through engaging the beast in struggle that you will learn what you need to know about yourself, the beast, the mission, the door beyond, the light and the nature of struggle. It is this same lesson we must learn as organizations.

The current controversy over children and video games might decrease if we understood the importance of struggle from the perspective of a cultural myth. They parallel the growth process that leads to wisdom. The problem comes when children follow the existing organizational norms of our culture and come to believe that winning is the object of the game; that living the game vicariously is actually living.

They are trapped into believing that the games are the struggle. They lose the meaning and do not make the translation that struggling to overcome their opponent, trying again and again, using new techniques and developing new methods, is the same as struggling to understand their math at school or facing the myriad challenges they must deal with in daily life.

Teaching with video games can be positive if the true lessons of growth and development are drawn from them. In other words, certain video games themselves are not inherently bad, if they are viewed from a story perspective. The meaning of the games needs to be understood by parent and child before the games can become effective teachers.

5. Principle of Transformation

> *To grow, a child-serving organization must accept the death of existing roles and ideas.*

Transformation is the act of becoming, by letting go of one's former mindset and emerging as a new self, with greater understandings. It is letting go to move on.

The process of letting go of a former mindset or idea deals with eliminating barriers that we have constructed. Scott Peck, self help author and psychiatrist, refers to this process as "emptying." To empty oneself we need to be willing to go into the unknown. The price of admission is to empty one's mind of expectations and preconceptions of the unencountered experience.

For example, the current practice in composing living units in group care is homogeneous groupings, i.e., younger boys with younger boys, girls with girls and older boys with older boys. We attempted to move to heterogeneous groupings in a new living unit we were building, but the idea was met with resistance. What we heard was: "The older ones will prey on the younger ones!" "The referral workers will not approve!" and "It is too hard for the staff to program for diverse groups!" With this mindset, there is little room for even trying heterogeneous groupings.

The preestablished thinking precluded any new opportunities for enhancing the personal growth and development of the youth. Obviously in real life, children will have many opportunities to interact with youth of all ages.

In a segmented, isolationistic and negative world, where children are feared and seen as diseased perpetrators, it makes sense to isolate and contain the spread of the "infection." In a culture where adults do not fear youth but are confident of their values and the strength of their culture, it is of key importance to allow for interaction as a means of developing wellness.

The idea that the "rotten apple will spoil the barrel" is another linear progression. Taken in the context of apples, it may be true. In the context of human beings, it does not allow for transformation. In Transformation Education, it is our belief that the good barrel heals the spoiled apple!

One's willingness to transform oneself is the key indicator of a psychologically and spiritually mature adult. Scott Peck [Peck: 1985] writes:

> *We come now to still another interesting paradox: it is the most psychologically and spiritually mature among us who are the least likely to grow old mentally. Conversely, much (not all, there are biological factors involved) of what we call senility is a fatal end-stage form of psychological and spiritual immaturity . . . true adults are those of us who have learned to continually develop and exercise their capacity for transformation. Because of this exercise, progress along the journey of growth often becomes faster and faster the further we proceed on it. For the more we grow, the greater becomes our capacity to empty ourselves of the old so that the new may enter and we may therefore be transformed.*

All of us, even those who have chosen to play out the roles prescribed by others, feel within our innermost selves that we are meant for something more in this life than simply eating, sleeping, watching television and going to work five days a week. The "something else" is the experience of becoming more fully human.

As practitioners of Transformation Education, we model this most difficult of life processes. We do not mean simply trying it on so that others might see how transformed we are; we mean internalizing it as a central understanding and belief. This is how we can move to a new level of awareness and understanding of our role as mentors of cultural values. Organizational integrity about our operating system is essential. Every decision is communicated to our children. If we are a caring organization, we are no longer simply the host for their services.

6. The Principle of Enlightenment

> *A child-serving organization can expect to achieve new insight and awareness if it searches for ways to apply its values to the everyday challenges and decisions it encounters.*

Enlightenment is a new state of awareness, a higher level of consciousness, a greater acceptance of one's responsibility and moral obligation. The state of enlightenment, however, is transitory. Like the horizon, it is always before you. The next state after enlightenment is struggle, with the cycle continuously repeating itself, as one transcends into an ever-greater awareness of selfhood and community. Sociologist Karlried Druckheim points out:

> *Enlightenment eliminates the fear of growing old. For age should bring more growth and enlightenment. Therefore, our future is not narrowed but extended, as we grow older. We are old when we have no future life.*

The Skills Needed to Promote Growth in Transformation Education

The third question: "What are the skills needed to achieve growth?" forces us to consider what skills an individual needs to understand what engages us in the process of growth. These skills are expressed through the principles of vision, courage and will.

7. The Principle of Vision

> *A child-serving organization needs to develop the ability to envision the possible.*

Vision is the ability to see beyond your present situation or self to what you can become. It is opening our minds to a new picture of reality, to new levels of caring, contribution and commitment. It is also seeing the process that one must go through for growth to occur. It is seeing with the mind what is invisible to the eye. It is the ability to discern the greater good.

8. The Principle of Courage

> *A child-serving organization needs to exhibit courage.*

Courage is demonstrated by risking to achieve one's vision. It is the act of making one's self vulnerable enough to face the unknown and to be open to struggle. Courage is to risk making bad judgments. To use an old adage: "Good decisions come from experience . . . experience comes from having made bad decisions."

To become a champion wrestler takes more than knowing about wrestling, reading about wrestling, practicing moves and watching wrestling. One must actually wrestle. You not only have to wrestle, but you have to make yourself vulnerable. You likely will have to struggle long and hard and lose many times before you can be a champion wrestler. Without courage, there is no meaningful change.

9. The Principle of Will

> *A child-serving organization needs to develop the strength to persevere.*

Will is courage over time. It is the continuing effort made to live in a state of awareness, risking for growth in a search for meaning. It is the perseverance to believe in and strive toward living out the wisdom principles mindful of the risks.

CHAPTER 4
Defining the Organization's Basic Cultural Beliefs and Life Expectaions

Principle: Chaos is the norm, not the exception, in a child-serving organization. The key to managing it is to embrace it, not fight it.

Don't fight forces, use them! – Richard Buckminster Fuller

If we are to accept Transformation Education as the imprimatur of our organizational culture and prime educational methodology, we need to express a set of assumptions. These assumptions will be used throughout the organization and will be consistent with our beliefs and the organization's mission. As we explored various conceptual worldviews, "Life is a Journey" clearly fit as our metaphor.

The Importance of Beliefs

Why the emphasis on beliefs? Defining the beliefs inherent in how an organization operates and makes decisions is critical for several reasons:

- It is important to have alignment among the organizational policies and procedures that reflect our core beliefs. This is essential to ensure clear communication and minimize confusion for employees and the children.
- Burnout occurs when the staff operates in ways that are inconsistent or contrary to the realities of organizational life.
- A great deal of organizational inefficiency results when employees are at odds with the operating beliefs of the organization. This often results in long meetings, venting of feelings, disciplinary write-ups and high staff turnover

An organization's expectations should be overt. Employees bring with them from their work experience expectations of how an organization should operate. If their previous places of employment were unionized, they will tend to limit the scope of their responsibilities to their job functions. If they come from organizations that provided a holiday bonus or turkey, they will expect a similar treat. If people left exactly at quitting time, they will expect to leave exactly at quitting time. If staff worked in a company ruled by intimidation and fear, they will fear management. Expectations of organizational life are the everyday norms that express the beliefs of an organization.

Life Is a Journey

What does it mean—life is a journey? It means personal growth and enlightenment come from the unending struggle and search for meaningful responses to life's challenges. Avoid the journey and you get arrested growth, stagnation and personal rigidity. Scott Peck in *The Road Less Traveled* puts it this way: ". . . those who try to avoid truth risk mental illness and unhappiness."

Yet, it is not simply the knowledge of truth that we seek. As Joseph Campbell suggests, simply knowing truth is neither satisfactory nor satisfying. Truth can be found in many ways. Instead, it is the search for having a meaningful life experience . . . it is the search for life itself for which people hunger, not the knowledge of it. It is this search, which is an ever-continuing process as the context of our lives change.

Great movies and literature are tales of "journey" and of the principles learned. Life-giving principles of giving, searching, caring, selflessness, sacrifice, brotherhood, community, tolerance and honesty. We discover, too, the principles of arrested development—selfishness, pride, hatred, prejudices, covetousness and hypocrisy.

We can, of course, decide not to journey (knowing that we may be hurt or even killed) and not face the struggles, challenges and obstacles that will confront us. We often think we can keep ourselves from emotional and physical harm by isolating ourselves from life's dangers. We do so at the grave risk of killing the spirit. The result is worse than death. We languish in a state of mindlessness. In the words of Shakespeare:

> *"There comes a tide in the affairs of men which taken at the flood lead on to fortune. Omitted, all the rest of their voyage is bound in shallows and in miseries."*

The myths, Joseph Campbell tells us, demonstrate over and over the importance of undertaking the journey. He points out that heroes, those who come to symbolize the values in a culture, have a moral objective, e.g., saving people, a person or an idea. The hero is willing to sacrifice him/herself for others. We should not revere existing life (the status quo) so highly as to worship it as the goal in and of itself.

As a society, we have become bound by our beliefs that individuals are the conveyers of cultural values. The challenge that child-serving organizations face is whether to embark on the hero journey or hold on to the status quo. The journey metaphor is a clear alternative. Its path leads to a culture that is full of promise.

The Journey Experience . . . Life as a Bumper Car Theory of Reality was best described by Dr. Jean Houston.

> *We journey towards selflessness in a world of chaos continuously bumping up against situations where we must decide what is the moral choice. It is the constant tension between our selfishness and our call to selflessness that hones the spirit. And it is the struggle to do the right thing, which shines the soul.*

The three metaphors for experiencing the journey in a child-serving organization are: the tank, the sailboat and the bumper car. In each model, we visualize ourselves as the navigator/pilot i.e. the Tank Commander, Sailboat Captain or Bumper Car Driver.

The Tank

This model illustrates the linear thinking of the industrial and scientific systems of which we are all products. To achieve life's goal in this model you adhere to the principle that the "shortest distance between two points is a straight line," a well-known mathematical principle we have all been taught. Symbolically, it stands for the ideal in efficiency and effectiveness.

As in all journeys, there will be many difficulties and obstacles to overcome and many personal dangers. Individuals or organizations that operate from this worldview are risk aversive.

The perfect vehicle for such a journey is a tank. It will keep us physically safe and is superb at keeping "on track." It rolls over or through most obstacles and features a handy cannon. Such weaponry can ward off any unwanted attacks and intimidate others whose cannons 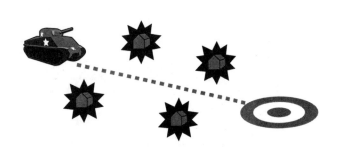 are smaller. A good commander can spot obstacles and blast them before they interfere with progress. This is why strategic planning is so critical in the tank model. If things go wrong, it is the planning that is at fault. Tank commanders don't like surprises.

We have all received excellent training as tank commanders. Think of how our education is organized for us. Our schools are organized on linear tracks: K through 12. As are our universities. Grading is linear: A, B, C, D, E/F. Our organizations follow business plans that delineate goals. The goals are broken down into objectives; objectives are stripped down to step-by-step action plans. Before anything happens, hierarchy approves the battle plan. Organizations do not like "surprises" either. Every effort is made to plan and prevent anything from occurring spontaneously or interfering with progress toward the goal.

Management works with the employees to set objectives. This approach had great credibility during the 1980's. It is known as "Management by Objectives." If you achieve the objectives in the time allotted, you're rewarded. If not, your supervisor, as a team manager, reviews the objectives once more with a critical eye. Naturally, if you still can't meet the objectives you are terminated as a failure, and the organization continues on its efficient path.

This model is excellent at achieving bottom-line production goals. It is an excellent way of communicating directional "information" rapidly. It is long on efficiency but short on exploration, which is the foundation of growth and development.

One major problem of a tank is when the terrain changes and the tank commander is suddenly confronted with a new environment—a new reality. When a tank is faced with a lake, it is effectively paralyzed. We now need a boat.

The Sailboat

In this journey metaphor, our environment is now a lake and we are confronting a body of water with a sailboat. We have shifted our operational paradigm to fit the existing environment. We need wind. Like the tank, we will also meet some resistance along the way. Lets start with a wind of 20 knots blowing in the direction of the large arrow. How do we reach our goal?

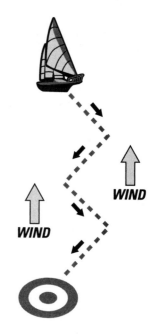

When given this illustration in a workshop we asked "sailors" (those who know something about sailing) not to respond immediately. The ensuing conversation among the "tank commanders" varied from: "It's impossible to sail against the wind" to "Get out and swim." The most telling commentary came from a young man who growled, "Start the outboard motor!" Ah, the true technocrat!

For those familiar with the dynamics of sailing, the answer is simple yet amazing. You can sail against the wind! Using a procedure called tacking, you sail at an angle 45 degrees to the right of the wind, then "come about" and sail 45 degrees to the left of the wind. By "tacking" back and forth, you can reach your destination even with the wind blowing directly opposite from where you want to go. Even more fascinating is that the harder the wind is blowing against you the faster you will get there!

The object here is to illustrate that as the conditions change so do the operating guidelines. Where once a tank was the best vehicle given the perception of the environment, it would sink to the bottom if we tried to cross the lake. Even with access to a sailboat, to attempt to get to our destination by using the old rules (straight line, shortest route between two points) is not only inefficient, it is impossible!

If our environment has changed so will the nature of the journey. This strikes at the very heart of an organization's cultural mindset and modus operandi. If the chief executive or the governing body are tank commanders, and the environment has changed to a lake, the organization will be unable to effect a change in values or the culture. What is needed is a change in their operational beliefs.

Imagine a tank commander watching the sailboat from shore. Heading for one side of the lake, the sailboat now nears the rocky shore. The tank commander attempts to warn the boat. Not knowing the procedures for tacking and the rules of sailing, the tank commander assumes the boat is in danger and will continue straight onto the rocky shore.

"You're heading for the rocks!" the commander yells. The boat veers off at the last second. The commander feels good that he saved the boat from destruction. To his surprise, however, he now watches the boat near the rocks on the far shore. "What the hell is wrong with that guy?" Again, he yells out a warning. And again, the boat turns away. The commander feels good but is angry that the captain has put the boat in jeopardy again. He begins to think the captain is a lousy commander. As the boat once again heads for the rocks, the commander gives a halfhearted yell and then says. "Screw 'em! If they're that dumb, let 'em hit the rocks!"

This is akin to the situations we face in our organizations when new leadership is intent on changing the culture of the organization but the Board of Directors maintains the existing attitudes and organizational mindset. Whether an individual is a member of the governing board or an employee, if they have a tank commanding mindset, they are going to think that the chief executive, acting as a sailboat captain, is crazy. The old adage of "lead, follow or get out of the way" is applicable to an organization undertaking the transformation of a culture.

The Bumper Car

The metaphor that we feel most accurately reflects the reality of the life journey is the bumper car. In this model, we start with the initial intent of reaching the destination or goal. As you head for it via the straight-line method, another bumper car (increased mortgage rates) heads at you from the side. You collide, and like billiard balls, both bounce off each other and head in a new direction. Just about the time you get your bearings and readjust your course, another blow (you decide to get married again) blasts you off in a different direction. But what's this? Just as you move into position to shoot the gap, you are squeezed out and hit from behind! As you steer right and hit the accelerator you career off the wall

and bypass the hopelessly jammed up cars that squeezed you out moments earlier.

Finding your bearings, you are moving fast in the opposite direction from which you initially started, but the scenery here isn't so bad, and the ride is exhilarating. Let's not go to the mountaintop, let's head for the shore!

The bumper car metaphor illustrates a dynamic and rapidly changing environment where you are neither entirely in control nor out of control. Control is not the central issue. Control is a concept arising from the linearity of the industrial age. When we ask for a definition of the zigzag in the sketch, invariably we get the response: "CHAOS!"

Life is chaotic! We cannot predict when we are going to be bumped, nor can we, in many cases, do much about it. This is not to resign ourselves to fate. Our sense of reality shifts.

After determining that our journey appears chaotic, i.e., having the *appearance* of chaos (which is quite distinct from being in chaos), the next question is: "What are the factors that keep it from being chaotic?" Could it be that this model leads us to a purposeful meaning?

Let us examine this bumper car excursion. First, there is a goal. It is not the one we started with at the top of the illustration. Has the bumper car driver discerned a different goal on the way? In undertaking the challenging, dizzying journey, did the driver find a moral purpose?

Finding a moral direction means we must face the varied situations life presents us. How we exercise judgment and hone our values are the keys to personal, spiritual growth. The bumper car model illustrates the type of journey we take to maximize our personal growth and development and the organizational model that best prepares troubled children for life.

To the tank commander, the bumper car administrator will be regarded as downright crazy and incomprehensible. It is always the case when a new reality is described. Copernicus was scorned and excommunicated. Christ was crucified. Martin Luther King was assassinated. When leaders attempt to take organizations in new directions, there probably will be criticism and hostility.

Chaos Is the Norm

In organizations where life is a bumper car journey, the seemingly chaotic is the norm, not the exception. Life is supposed to be this way! The key is to embrace it, not fight it. It is the *pain of living*. Life is a happening, an evolving situation filled with emotions that range from agony to ecstasy. We are not separate from life but a sojourner in it.

Several years ago, a champion kayaker was interviewed before a historic run down ferocious rapids. The kayaker was running it without a paddle. When asked why he responded, "I have run many rapids. On numerous occasions, I have been forced to abandon my kayak in order to save myself. Invariably, I would have to clamber down to the bottom of the rapids to retrieve my boat. After doing this a number of times, I asked myself why I can't make it down but my boat can?" The thought occurred that perhaps I was doing something that prevented me from being successful. I began to observe myself and realized that whenever there was a chaotic situation, I would attempt to brace myself with the paddle as I had been taught. I began to wonder if, in trying to protect myself, I was, in fact, creating the very situation I was trying to avoid. And so, I began to kayak without a paddle."

When the time came for the historic attempt, the cameras rolled and the kayaker started smoothly. Halfway down he flipped and was unable to right himself, so he bailed out. When he returned to the head of the rapids, the TV crew swarmed to him. What went wrong? Was the river too wild? Was the kayak not suitable? Did he need a paddle? Was it the wrong time of day? His response was simple yet amazing. "There is nothing wrong with anything. It's to be expected if you are going to kayak. I was simply overwhelmed by the ferocity of the water and momentarily became afraid. My thoughts became focused on me. I was no longer one with the river."

What an extraordinary statement about life's journey. Everything is okay. The level of chaos is high, the pace is frenetic, everything is constantly in a state of flux. It is dangerous and there is a risk of injury and even death. To survive the journey and enjoy the ride, you must become one with the river of life. Undertake the journey.

There is much unexpected order amid the chaos. This is revealed when the attributes of a chaotic system are plotted on a graph. The system will reveal an elegant geometric pattern. These characteristic forms demonstrate an underlying order that can be used to understand systems once considered random. The hidden order cannot be guessed by studying a system's parts. It appears only as a property of the whole. This is becoming as evident in the social sciences as in the physical sciences. It is becoming increasingly apparent that we cannot change behavior of individuals or systems by focusing on specific behaviors. [Gleick: 1987, Murray: 1989, May: 1989, Percival: 1989, Savit: 1990]

Life reflects the systems of the universe. Life is consistent, yet dynamic and ever changing, and is in its own way chaotic. It is a mistake to regard chaos as bad or to mean "opposite of order." Chaos and order exist at the same time. To function without a stable external frame of reference, we need to have a strong internal system of beliefs and values with which to navigate.

Shades of Gray

In every decision, there is a "light" side and a "dark" side, and that's the difficulty. In virtually every choice, there is a moral dilemma. We must attempt to discern which, out of all the options, is the best moral alternative.

There are seldom situations in which there are only two alternatives with absolute moral clarity between them. If this were the case, life would indeed be simple as well as unchallenging. We would also be unable to produce moral and spiritual growth. It is precisely in the continuous effort of attempting to apply our values to the situations we face (choosing based on our analysis, living with the choice and then reevaluating) that we refine and hone our moral sensibility and set of values. This is the essence of shades of gray. We are faced with thousands of possibilities and hundreds of choices every day that are neither black nor white, but gray.

One of the fascinating aspects of most organizations is the wealth of informational materials they produce. For instance, say you are having a document printed. It will not be long before you are confronted by this question from your design firm or printer: "What color paper and ink do you want?" Through experience we learned that even white is not white. There are hundreds of shades of white! Eggshell, bone, cloud, snow, ivory, chalk, daisy, rabbit, etc., each with its own variations. And to assist in determining how light or dark you want a photograph to appear (screened), they have a helpful device called the gray scale. Between black and white, incremental shades of gray are presented. From a general perspective, it is normal to think in terms of 10% increments, e.g. 10% black, 60% black, etc. Designers however, think and specify in 1% increments. In reality, the variations are infinite.

Joseph Campbell, in his book the *Power of Myth* suggests that all decisions and actions have both a positive and an adverse effect. It is seldom that you can do good 100% of the time. Rain may bring welcome relief to the farmer but dampen the spirits of the 4th of July parade. In making organizational decisions, what should tip the scales once the economic, political and social options are weighed? Let's choose the side that is the most moral and with the greatest symbolic impact. Certainly, this is idealism. By placing these ideals at the center of our organizational decision-making, it will restore a culture of meaning.

Organizations can no longer ignore how they communicate values. As organizations, we must become adept at designing cultural messages and be aware of their nuances. In a bumper car world, you are required to determine if the decision is the one that leaned "toward the light" as Joseph Campbell suggests. If a better course of action arises or you realize that the choice made is not the best alternative, you simply do a midcourse adjustment and change your direction. You are not "retreating." Nor have you gone from black to white. You simply have moved to a different position, to a different shade of gray. You have not failed. Life is operating just as you might expect.

Crisis Is Inevitable; Crisis Is Opportunity

As the ancient Greek philosopher Heraclitus said: "You cannot put your hand in the same river twice," with the implication that by the time you put your hand in the second time, the river has changed. We would update this statement to say: "You cannot put your hand in the same river once." The river is changing even as you immerse your hand. One of the assumptions of the bumper car journey reality is that change is a constant and crisis is positive. It is impossible and even unhealthy to avoid change.

Let's face it. We regard change as hostile. It is programmed into most of us not to accept change as a normal state. In boardrooms across the land, you will hear the words, "We don't like surprises." We asked, why? We were often criticized for "surprising" staff and board with changes. Tank commanders don't like the unexpected. Bumper car drivers expect and revel in it.

It seems strange that a fear of change is manifest, when it's quite clear that change is so basic to life. Clearly, everyone accepts the notion that our bodies are changing moment by moment as we age and grow toward death. And it seems to be general knowledge that the universe is in a constant state of change.

Our children come to us having experienced the stress of living in an unpredictable, inconsistent and constantly changing environment. There exists a pervasive belief that we must protect our youth from this unpredictability. We attempt to remedy this by providing predictability through routine, e.g., scheduled meals, bedtime, activities, etc. The danger is that we isolate our children from the normal emotional stress of living. In essence, we are teaching them to be risk aversive.

In reality, we want the opposite. We want them to take the risk of accepting unpredictability as a normative expectation of life. How is it that we demand children to make fundamental change in their constructs of reality, when simultaneously we shield them and ourselves from experiencing the natural dynamics of normal, everyday life?

Psychiatrist and creator of Reality Therapy, William Glasser has another view. He believes that people do not act irresponsibly because they are ill; but rather they are ill because they act irresponsibly. [Glasser: 1965] Crisis is the stimulus that creates the need to make the decisions that lead to change and growth. Growth comes as children and staff struggle to master crises and solve problems. It is the positive force through which we develop wisdom. Good decisions come from experience. Experience comes from making bad decisions and being willing to learn from them!

Everything Is Connected

When we think of joy or bliss, we seldom think of work. Instead, we project ourselves into an escape fantasy that removes us from the toils and tribulations of life. This becomes a problem if it begins to dominate our journey mindset and we search for an idealized reality in which there is no tension.

Fantasy behavior has taken over the existing mindsets of many organizations that see reality as the tank metaphor. Wouldn't it be nice if we could eliminate the struggle and constant battling. Another, euphemistic reference to the frustration of the organizational problems are oft spoken references to the organization's leaders, need to plan ahead, and needing better communication.

In our culture, we expect organizations to be tank organizations with a linear approach. We only allow for black and white results. We are either going forward, stalled or retreating. Going forward is good. Stalled out or retreating is considered bad. "Going ahead or falling behind" is often cited in today's businesses. This mindset results in a mixed message for the workers who experience the paradox of this belief versus reality.

The bumper car experience offers a dynamism to the journey of an organization's life that has a belief system that is congruent with reality and believable both by the employees and the organization.

Within the bumper car reality, we think of a holistic reality in which there are continuous and simultaneous experiences of agony and ecstasy. We must think in terms of Yin/Yang where we have opposites in shade, but similarity in form. We have fluidity, not rigidity. As one diminishes the other grows. The opposites are simultaneously dynamic in balance and static in tension. Importantly, there is a circle, which binds the two as one. It is both agony and ecstasy at the same time.

This is a key principle in our pleasure seeking never-let-them-see-you-sweat culture. In the pursuit of happiness, we forget that happiness is not found at the end of the journey but along the way. We take it a step further as Campbell did, to say that it is the journey, i.e., the joys and trials together, that are the bliss of life.

As we grow spiritually, we come to recognize that it is the stretching of the emotions that provides the depth. Without great joy, there cannot be great sadness. Without agony, there cannot be ecstasy. This is at the heart of holism and interconnection. It is seeing the relationships that bind them together. It is recognizing that everything is interconnected with everything.

The holistic perspective is the recognition that all life on this planet is interconnected in countless, profound and subtle ways. Holism emphasizes the challenge of creating a sustainable, just and peaceful society in harmony with the Earth and its life. It involves an ecological sensitivity, a deep respect for both indigenous and modern cultures, as well as the diversity of life forms on the planet. Holism recognizes that human beings seek meaning, not just facts or development.

The Mindset of Transformation Education

In the bumper car world, there are guidelines to navigate and operate. They are not absolute rules. They will help us navigate. One of the interesting aspects of the Bumper Car journey is that there are occasions when it works to be linear. The idea is to have the flexibility and wisdom to be able to shift paradigms at will.

What follows is a set of expectations about how to navigate in the bumper car world. It is important that these expectations become a part of the in-service training program. Employees are held accountable for applying these expectations in their work with the children.

Above all, the upper management needs to believe in the system and do whatever is necessary to make the system work. But within the boundaries of that system, they should have a lot of leeway. The principles are flexible. They do not tell managers or employees what to do or not do in any given situation. Instead, they guide decision-making by requiring one to be flexible and contextual in their thinking.

Part of the rationale is reflected in what professor of management, Jim Collins discovered as a key reason why some companies are able to transition from good to great. [Collings: 2001]

Companies that move from good to great are very disciplined and have a culture of discipline. This is essential in group care and educational organizations.

Ordinarily, what tends to happen is that each staff person brings his/her expectations, values and beliefs and assumes they are consistent with those of the organization. If the employee's beliefs, values and expectations are not in sync with those of the child-serving organization, they undermine the impact of the cultural approach. In effect, the out-of-sync employee brings with him/her the lack of meaning and dysfunction the children experienced prior to admission.

Components of the mindset needed to navigate in a dynamic, chaotic environment that is so much a part of work with behavior-disordered and emotionally disturbed children, are described as the *Expectations of Life*. These expectations refer to what an employee or a member of the Board of Trustees will experience in an organization focused on motivating transformation and change.

Norms Not Rules

> *Understand the situation and act in context.*

Any society that is predominantly rule oriented becomes life restricting rather than life enhancing. Our society is changing so rapidly that rules cannot keep up. To properly prepare children for the decisions they will make in the world, we must teach them to focus on the concept behind the rule, rather than the rule itself.

Spinning Plates

> *Often we must manage myriad tasks with insufficient time and resources.*

In day-to-day terms an example of spinning plates is having the expectation for yourself to carry out your job responsibilities, agreeing to stand in for your neighbor at a volunteer function, then getting a call not to forget your son's open house at school tonight only to find out at the last minute that the report that was due in two days is now due tomorrow!

Be a Brinksman

> *We come to know our true potential when we are pushed to the brink of the impossible.*

How many times have you reached the point of NO MORE! "I can't run one more lap, Coach!" "I can't take on another project!" "I can't handle one more problem today!" This is the testing point. Brinksmanship is when you find yourself thinking, "I can't," but you do manage somehow to persevere for that one more lap. Brinksmanship is probably best understood by athletes. They are constantly pushing themselves to total exhaustion in hopes of becoming a little bit faster, stronger or more skillful than the day before. We can only grow by constantly challenging our assumptions and our perceptions about our own potential.

Change Is Constant

Expect change, because we live in a dynamic environment that calls for constant reevaluation of decisions and assumptions.

In the 1990's we witnessed the change in the world order. We realized that there is a shift in the U.S. population makeup by the fact that in 1992 more salsa was produced in this country than ketchup. Public education is on the verge of being privatized. We are truly experiencing a renaissance in politics, business, religion, the professions, sex roles, the workplace and most every other aspect of our culture.

Decide then Re-Decide

Don't stick to old decisions when you have new information.

After calculating all the odds and talking with the jockeys, you've decided to bet on "Lucky Lady" to win the fifth race. You feel confident about your decision. Then during the third race it rains; the track is very muddy. "Lucky Lady" runs well on hard packed track, but you've heard she can't get out of the starting gate in mud. Would you still bet on "Lucky Lady" to win? Unlikely! You'd review the horses again, talk to a few more jockeys and go with a "mudder."

Own It

When you're looking for the problem, start with yourself.

We've all done it. Something goes wrong and we suddenly declare, "Not me!" or "He did it!" Regardless of whom we point the finger at, one thing is consistent: "I'm not responsible!" This is neither a creative nor effective solution to a problem or crisis. What is important, and takes some creativity, is trying to prevent the problem from recurring. What could I have done to prevent that outcome? What did I do, or not do, that may have contributed to the problem? This type of self-analysis leads to effective outcomes, helps prevent problems, and creates an environment in which children can experience the value of introspection. As Walt Kelly's Pogo said: "We have met the enemy, and it is us."

Be True to Your School

Model the values you espouse.

Before one can be "true to one's school" one needs to know what one's school is. In the Transformation Education model, the "school" or philosophy is to provide a growth-producing environment for the children, families and adults served. This can be done only if the organization is child centered rather than staff or board centered. It requires the same thing of the board, management and staff as it does of the children. For example, when a child does not want to share what happened because she is afraid of group retaliation, the staff should respond by saying: "One must have courage and trust the staff to protect you. It is always best to face your fears." When a staff or board member is experiencing problems with colleagues, s/he must also be willing to face fears and trust things will work out in the long run.

A Master Teacher Is a Master Learner

Teach by example and always be open to grow personally and professionally.

The best teachers are always the best learners. They teach what they need to know. They are constantly seeking knowledge and searching for the truth. They convey a sense of wonder about the world and everything in it.

Count on Using Mission Math

Value mission, not recognition.

There are people who are so focused on goals, objectives and doing things right, that they forget to do the right thing. It is not what you do, but rather how you do it, and for what purpose. The three types of gardeners exemplify this. The first gardener prepares the earth, scatters the seeds and sits back to let nature take its course. Let us call this the Johnny Appleseed approach. The second gardener designs straight rows, waters once a week and occasionally picks a stray weed or two. This is the weekend gardener approach. The third gardener is in his garden from morning until night watering, weeding, hoeing, fertilizing, thinning and talking to his plants. He understands all there is to know about the care of plants. If a problem develops, he seeks out the answer so that his garden grows and prospers. This is gardening with a mission and with caring, contribution and commitment.

Say No with Compassion

Develop the courage to deliver a difficult message with respect and compassion and then do it.

It is difficult to be direct and honest with people, when it may mean hurting their feelings or telling them something they don't want to hear. All of us want to be liked. Too often, we try to avoid those situations that might cause conflicts in relationships. However, evasion and avoidance do not make problems go away. Delaying the message usually causes more grief by increasing your stress level. You are left with the feeling of misleading someone. Others appreciate empathy and directness as it leaves them with their self-respect even when they are being told "no."

Don't Sign It Until the Quality Is in It

Do it over until it is right!

The best lesson anyone can teach a child is that one's work reflects oneself, one's family and one's organization. To do something of quality means one has to have the patience for many revisions. Particularly, this is the case when it is not a routine practice. Try to cook a four-course meal when you don't know how to cook. Frustration over revision wanes when one understands that revision is not the exception. It is the rule in producing a quality product. Each revision is a step toward quality and a gain in knowledge.

Work Is Fun

> *Working where our talents lie brings joy and enriches life.*

Wait a minute! What do you mean work is fun? Work is drudgery. "Putting in your time," TGIF, "Another day another dollar" and " Life begins when the dog dies and the kids leave home!" Unfortunately, that's the view too often reinforced in TV programming and commercials. We need to help children recognize their talents and reinforce the use of them so they can find a vocation that interests and stimulates them.

1+1=3

> *In problem solving the sum is greater than the parts.*

Whenever two parties have a disagreement, you can bet there are three sides to the issue: what each party has to say about it through his or her experience, and what emerges after they sit down to share their concern with one another.

There Is No Growth without Pain

> *Accomplishments are attained through struggle and self-discipline.*

Most of us understand there is no such thing as a "free lunch" and that success is made up of hard work and discipline. We constantly need to make choices that result in changes in our lives. That makes life difficult.

Ready, Fire, Aim

> *Assess the risk, begin to act and then make adjustments along the way.*

The social, political and economic environment is so dynamic that one cannot wait to act until we gather every piece of information or viewpoint available on the subject. This is not to imply that we should sacrifice quality for timeliness. But the faster you act the more time is available for correcting or refining the course of action.

Make the Covert, Overt

> *When there are unstated issues among individuals and groups, bring buried thoughts to the surface for discussion.*

When the covert becomes overt, it can be dealt with. Avoidance of issues only delays pain and results in frustration and despair.

Application of Assumptions and Expectations in Organizational Life

The following example highlights the importance of beliefs and expectations, and reflects how organizational life operates within the Transformation Education approach.

When the principal of our school in Chillum, Maryland, departed to take another job, we made three poor hiring decisions that plunged the school into chaos. Each new principal lacked the competence to lead. We hired a firm to conduct a national search. We landed a qualified principal from the West Coast. The principal's husband was not able to move for a year, resulting in a coast-to-coast marriage involving trips back and forth by the principal.

The vice president of programs supervised the principal and confronted her when she exhausted her leave time. She informed her any future leave would be granted without pay. The vice president based the decision on the belief that generic leave was an organizational policy she had a duty to enforce.

The principal worked long hours and many weekends. She felt the organization's generic leave policy had "nickled and dimed" her considering all the hours she worked. The vice president pointed out that everyone in an executive management role works long hours yet adheres to the generic leave limit.

The chief financial officer (CFO) told the principal not to worry; that he would not dock her pay. He noted that since she began, referrals and academic scores were up, staff turnover was down and staff morale was high. The principal had contributed greatly. She should travel to see her husband and not worry about the generic leave policy.

This decision infuriated the vice president, who took the matter to the president. He called a meeting of his four vice presidents to discuss the application of the aforementioned beliefs and expectations of life to the issue.

He reminded them of the assumption that "Crisis is Positive" and "Life is a Journey" and the issue presented an opportunity for clarifying organizational policy and defining expectations of members of the executive management team. He acknowledged, that there is "no growth without pain."

The president revealed that he believed the correct course of action was taken by the CFO for the following reasons: The mindset of executive management should be the mindset of an owner of a company. The owner has a variety of contracts with each individual, but the primary measuring stick is the concept of contribution. How much did the principal contribute to the organization? In this case, a lot! What were the risks to the organization if the principal left the organization over the dispute on generic leave?

If the principal were to leave, we would experience inquiry and distrust from the board of trustees (another management miss-hire?). Risking the principal's departure also risked a decrease in referrals and lower staff morale. This in turn could lead to increased staff turnover, lower student academic performance and an increase in out-of-control student behavior. It might also mean increased student discharges and property destruction by angry students (i.e., revenue loss and increased expenditures).

The president explained that the CFO demonstrated an understanding of the holism assumption. Everything is connected, that is, if the principal was not able to maintain her relationship with her husband we would have a principal who was spending a great deal of her mind time worrying about her marriage rather than her job. Executive management needs to apply the principle of "mission math" to determine how to handle this situation. Her use of leave warranted exception because it served the best interest of the organization.

The vice president of programs felt we needed to hold one another accountable and "Be True to Our School." She said we had to realize the generic leave policy limit applied to all staff. There is no such thing as compensatory time in our organization. Furthermore, what would happen if the principal started to extend the same liberty regarding leave to her staff?

She pointed out that everyone who serves on executive management works until the job is done. The principal had worked no more hours than anyone else and was not acting like an executive manager, yet she wanted to be treated as one. No executive manager could use all the leave provided. Absence beyond their leave time would create a problem for the organization. The principal's misuse of the system was a symptom of her lack of organizational skill and should not be rewarded.

The president pointed out that the principal was accountable because she had contributed in significant ways. The principle of "Norms not Rules" proved the key to resolving the conflict. You can't take more leave than you have, but in the principal's case we have more to lose by holding her to the leave expectation. This is a situation where "Shades of Gray" come into play. We cannot have ultimate truth—given the pursuit of ultimate truth could result in greater harm to the organization, staff and students than bending the rules in this situation. The best we can do in the pursuit of truth is "lean toward the light."

The vice presidents came to agreement that the best course of action in this situation was not to make an issue of leave time and to be supportive of this bicoastal marriage arrangement. The CFO acknowledged it would have been better for him to discuss his concerns with the vice president of programs rather than informing the principal she could take the leave with pay.

Up until now we have limited our discussion to identifying the beliefs, values, assumptions and expectations that express messages of transformation. We will now turn our attention to identifying the conveyers of cultural messages in a child-serving organization, i.e., the operational systems, the people, the physical environment and the program/curriculum.

SECTION III
Implementing the Culture

The next four chapters detail how we deploy the operational systems and design the role of the employees, the physical environment and the program/ curriculum. When this new design is in place, the culture is highly effective in transforming emotionally and behaviorally disordered children into thoughtful children who possess the skills necessary to lead a successful life—one filled with caring, contribution and commitment.

CHAPTER 5
The Operational Systems as Cultural Communicators

Principle: A child-serving organization is more than a host for the professionals. The organization itself serves as the critical component for transmitting values and fostering emotional and intellectual growth.

Value, the leading edge of reality, is no longer an irrelevant offshoot of structure. Value is the predecessor of structure. It's the preintellectual awareness that gives rise to it. Our structured reality is preselected on the basis of value, and really to understand structured reality requires an understanding of the value source from which it's derived. [Pirsig: 1974]

One cannot create a transformational culture without organizational systems that express values and beliefs. We must first recognize that the systems are not simply designed to accomplish the organization's production goals in the most effective and efficient manner. Systems themselves radiate the assumptions and beliefs of the culture.

For the purpose of this discussion we will highlight the culture card system, the staff development system, the meeting system, the problem-solving system and the recognition system.

Reengineering the Systems: Flying the Plane as You Reconstruct It

In reengineering the organization, we found you cannot simply move out of one system into another. It is a process, the very process we discussed earlier in terms of personal or organizational growth. It is through attempting to adopt the principles and values day to day that we design and develop our systems. As we intentionally put our principles and values into play, we gain the wisdom and experience to make the right choices.

Culture must be built while you are living it. It is analogous to trying to build an airplane and flying it at the same time. It would be similar to flying a Wright Brothers special while converting it into a sophisticated Stealth Fighter. This represents the prime environmental condition we experience when we try to change our organizational culture.

Like the Titanic effect we feel that we must begin turning around our organizations immediately and with great haste, or we will be unable to avoid the iceberg of cultural destruction.

Furthermore, it is not enough that we understand all the components and the process for changing our organizational culture. We will make mistakes and errors and will have to make ourselves vulnerable to those who work and volunteer in child-serving institutions. We must have sufficient vision to pick a course and learn on the way. We must formulate an ideology or an ideological structure toward which to move.

In the process of developing our organizational culture, it is not essential that all of the cultural transmitters or systems be brought along at the same time and rate for there to be integrity. Given the scope of organizational change required, this is seldom possible or even desirable. Based on our experience, our employees and the community, our youth struggled to accept the disparity in messages between what we achieved and what we had yet to accomplish. What mattered were our actions and beliefs. Were we acting with integrity and did our intentions appear honest and sincere?

The Communications Systems

More critically, it is essential to understand the nature of communications in the context of culture. With our linear mindsets, we most often think of communication within the organization as written language or speech. We must go beyond our words to communicate messages through the appearance of our physical environment and the quality of the items in our surroundings.

Our clothing, our hair, how and what we eat, how we walk, the dynamics of our meetings and how our organizations solve problems speak volumes! It is important to evaluate all these factors for the messages they send in implementing the cultural approach. These are the vehicles that alter the structure of a child's mindset and are the primary tools of influence.

Nomenclature

Nomenclature has a great impact on both the mindset of the child and the staff. It frames the basis of the problem. Relabeling everything in educational terms conveys that we are educating for life. Clients and patients become students; intake becomes educational admissions; treatment plan becomes personal growth or educational plan; family therapist becomes family life educator; child care workers become youth life educators (not counselors or house parents); and social workers become school councelors. These terms convey that the organization is formulated around the goal of change through education rather than treatment of an illness.

Group care administrators must create educational and journey language throughout their organizations. An important aspect of language in group care is how things are labeled and described. The cultural approach emanates from education not medicine.

The medical approach assumes that if one relieves the problem or cures the condition the normal function of the body will take care of the rest. Using a medical model to cure social or emotional problems is insufficient because we still need to teach the desired thought patterns and behaviors once the problem is eliminated. In essence, the medical model fits medicine and conveys the right message to its practitioners. But it does not fit group care or send the right message to its practitioners. As educators, we communicate an integrated message of change, growth and normalization to the children we serve.

Given that funding sources and accrediting bodies are steeped in a medical model, it becomes essential that organizations, such as group care agencies, are multilingual when talking with funding sources. That is essential to transcend the confusion that may result from converting to educational nomenclature. We must become translators to those who have not made the change.

The change in terminology will likely threaten many of the organization's professional staff. Our family therapists became very upset when they learned that their service was now listed under family life education in our promotional publications. They perceived a difference between family life education and family therapy.

Their expertise, family therapy, required a special type of training. They wanted to be known by their method and validate their professional approach. They saw family life education as something less than family therapy, and certainly different. They had difficulty understanding that they could maintain their identity as family therapists but must view their work as a part of family life education.

Each organization has to take a good look at its name. An organization's name delivers a powerful impact. The Correctional School provides a different image and expectation. St. James' Treatment Center for Emotionally Disturbed Children creates a stereotype in the public mind. You get a different message and image from names: The South Dakota Boys Ranch, the Starr Commonwealth School or Boys Town.

We realize how much consternation is involved in changing the name of an organization. We have had that experience. This again is part of the wisdom principle process where vision, courage, struggle and transformation are the demonstration of organizational commitment to those principles. Name changes can be brought about rapidly as long as you have the courage to deal with the reaction. Or, you can go more slowly by perhaps adding something to the name and eventually eliminating the undesired name. Then again you can consider creating a foundation under the old institutional name to fund the existing service.

Speech and Language

Speech and language have much to do with conveying that one is functional in American society. Many of the children who come to group care convey social failure and dysfunction through speaking poor English. This is one of the major messages they send that conveys they are members of the underclass.

Charles Case [Case: 1977] articulates the relationship between culture, language and communication:

> *Human behavior is totally involved with communication. Speech is one form*
> *of communication that is a special and distinctive tool of man. Speech is not a*

passive tool such as a hammer or a pen, but by its own structure affects the user in important and unsuspected ways. It illustrates the nomemic structure of culture in a way few other aspects of culture can.

The classic tale Pygmalion illustrates the power of language to transform. We use the movie My Fair Lady to assist staff and students to understand this basic concept.

The staff's language and the language the students are permitted to use in group care has a tremendous impact on behavior change. Case points out that if children hear a language style that is social and affective, but low in information content, this is their model. They do not hear analytical or expository language often enough to develop the capacity to understand its meanings.

At each stage of children's linguistic growth, they are dependent upon their environment for the materials that permit that particular growth stage to be fulfilled. Only by special training can they come back later and make up what they may have missed and misunderstood. This is why it is critical to expect staff to use English correctly and to be aware of the children's English. They should evaluate their effectiveness in expression of correct English. In this way, the proper use of English is ingrained in the staff's mindset, and ultimately, the children.

The language children are exposed to affects their mindsets and views of the world. The language and speech patterns tell children how to perceive time, space, matter and other components of their environment. If one wears blue-tinted glasses, the world will look blue. If one reverses a pair of binoculars, the world shrinks; if one is partially deaf, the world's cacophony is muted. What one hears is what he's trying to hear, and what one sees is interpreted from the perspective of the mindset one has adopted.

This was reiterated to us on a trip through a national park in Canada. As the guide led us, he explained to our tour group what we missed: how the shrubs were lower in some areas than in others because moose were eating them; how certain berry bushes grew by the watering hole because bears drank there and deposited berry seeds through their excrement.

According to Case, some Native American Indian languages have few if any time-orienting markers such as past, present and future tense endings. They express time differently. The tense structure of the language is expressed by their constant emphasis on locating events relative to time.

Some languages vary in their use of command or styles. English is replete with forms that are means of imposing one's will over another: "go," "come," "do," "eat," "shut up." But coercive expressions are not universal. In some languages, the usual way of getting someone to do what you want is more circuitous, subtle and polite. To the Native American, one does not have the right to impose one's will on someone else. Their language structure has a paucity of coercive forms. Consequently, this type of language structure affects child rearing. Native American parents tend not to order their children, but guide or assist them, to show the way.

To implement Transformation Education, pay a great deal of attention to the language of the organization, its employees and its children. The attention should focus on language as both thought patterns and content.

Language as Thought Patterns

It is difficult for both staff and children to use words differently from the way they were learned. They identify with the language associated with the images, feelings and beliefs of those who cared for them. We each have imprinted in us the way we were socialized and the rules of interpretation programmed into us by our families and guardians.

We learned our current way of communicating in an integrated way; i.e., experienced emotion, environment, symbols, tone of voice, situational context, etc. that reinforced the language and a way of thought. If we learn not to put endings on words–"You don't mean nothin' to me!"–we come to hear the word as complete. It is strange to hear it said in another way. We come to know who thinks as we do, just by hearing how we pronounce endings. Completeness and detail for these youngsters is not important to strive for, because they think doing it mostly right is good enough.

When language use is challenged by insisting that the child or employee complete the word with the ending "g," it is more than a grammar lesson. The child is being asked to rethink expectations. This will frustrate the child. When the child can no longer use his learned way to express himself, a great conflict will result because the core of the child's thought pattern is being challenged. The staff should endorse this struggle. This is an indicator that the child is changing and progress is being made.

Challenge is not enough. For children to learn language and its usage in a different way, they must be immersed in a culture that uses grammar correctly, and in a way that reflects the wisdom principles. Children only learn a new way of communicating by experiencing the staff and an environment that communicates differently. The children learn what is grammatically correct and what reflects the thought patterns of wisdom.

Language as Content

The content of the language used by children referred for placement in residential care is essentially comprised of violence, sex, drinking, cars, sports and problems. These children reflect a large segment of society. They demonstrate the lack of intelligent conversation and reflect the society's neglect of children.

If one were to analyze the content of the everyday language of many Americans, we would hear sports, the weather, sex, situational comedy, television shows, soap operas and consumerism. The content of adult conversation should not be filled with what one would see on TV. There would be little discourse on the dynamics of human behavior, the environment, new discoveries in science and medicine, analysis of the day's world affairs and literature. This is essentially viewed as "boring stuff" to most people.

Likewise, the content of children's conversation reflects the anguished, diminished viewpoints of a society that has virtually abandoned them. Their conversations are what you hear spoken by many fractured families, substance-abusing parents and victims of sexual, emotional and physical abuse.

To effect the content of language, children must be exposed to discoveries and engage in conversations about how things work. Their natural inquisitiveness must be reinforced. If children spend all their time talking about things that never lead to wisdom, they will never gain wisdom. It is essential that language become a core topic of the in-service training program in a child-serving organization.

Dress as Communication

Child-serving organizations should assist disadvantaged children to access the mainstream and become economically viable. This is essential for empowerment. So many of the children referred to group care are from poverty backgrounds and are culturally impoverished. A priest, Father Jim Sholes, has a parish in one of the poorest sections in Omaha. He asked corporate executives why their companies were not hiring the residents of his neighborhood. The companies admitted they were put off by the residents' lack of work ethic, their manner of speech, how they carried themselves and how they dressed.

Father Jim teamed up with the chief executive of the Union Pacific Railroad to develop a program in his school. They would teach corporate behaviors to children in kindergarten to 8th grade. The children demonstrated that they could learn these skills without being alienated from their neighborhood or families, thus function in both cultures.

Our expectations for dress are consistent with our organizational values. Children are expected to wear clothing that is age appropriate and in good taste in style, design and color. All attire must be in good condition. A child's clothing must be clean, fresh smelling and free of holes, tears, stains, wrinkles and scribbling. Clothes must be freshly pressed, hung on hangers or neatly folded in a drawer. All clothing is to fit properly. Clothing that is too loose or tight is not to be worn.

The Group Care Meetings

The meeting structures we have developed are designed to express an equal focus on education, problem solving, communication and personal growth in our group care program and our school. We use meetings to communicate the values of our organization.

Curriculum Meeting

The curriculum meeting is held for two hours on a weekly basis, on a day separate from the meeting focusing on the children's growth plans. This is important. Too often meetings that focusing on how to resolve the behavior problems of individual students "bleed" over into planning meetings and usurp planning time.

The purpose of the curriculum meeting is varied. One emphasis is to present, review and understand the monthly curriculum calendar. Another is to provide the youth life education supervisors an opportunity to make a presentation and have it reviewed by the organization's experts in group care. The third purpose of the meeting is to review and monitor the implementation of the curriculum and the living unit's systems.

The leader of the curriculum meeting is the program and design specialist; the participants are the youth life education supervisors and the program director. The program director's supervisor serves in an ex-officio capacity. Minutes are a rotated responsibility for everyone but the chair of the meeting. The fourth meeting of the month is dedicated to the presentation of the monthly curriculum calendar and the focus of the theme for the next month. The remaining three meetings operate as follows:

- One youth life education supervisor presents each week on how s/he carried out a portion of the curriculum, an intervention with a student or group, or how the supervisor supervised a youth life educator in the life space. This component of the meeting takes place for 30 to 45 minutes. The presentation is critiqued by the other participants.

- The second part of the meeting is a systematic review of the rationale and procedures associated with the group care manual. Each meeting is dedicated to focusing on sections of the manual. Below is a sampling of the topics discussed:

- Clothing curriculum	- House maintenance and tool kit
- Morning routine	- Weekends
- Meal presentation	- Etiquette and table conversation
- Behavior motivation	- Television and movies
- Welcoming a new student	- Study hour
- Mail	- Snacks
- Volunteering	- Birthdays
- Holidays	- Telephone
- Summer vacation	- Gifts
- Reading material	- Property destruction

Each youth life educator supervisor is assigned the responsibility of selecting the discussion topics for any given meeting. The goal is to discuss each item in the program manual (there are 102 items) at least once during the year.

Once the item is selected the program manual is opened to the corresponding topic under review. Everyone in attendance reads the policy. Is the stated policy consistently executed in the life space? If the policy or procedure relating to the topic needs to be amended —or a new policy or procedure needs to be created, it is revised at this time. This auditing procedure ensures awareness of program design. This allows key staff to reconnect with the rationale and procedure. It ensures that key staff are reflecting on the messages being sent by our operating system. All policy and procedure revisions/creations must be reviewed and approved by the administrative team. Anything less than complete consensus is brought to the vice president of programs for arbitration.

The final step in the review is a life space audit by the program design specialist and the program director. Together they observe the aspects of the program manual in action. If the program is not in working harmony with the procedure or the policy, the policy and procedure are made consistent. The group concentrates on the topic until the policy and procedure are congruent with the way the program is designed to operate and the staff deploy it.

Administrative Meeting

An administrative meeting also takes place for two hours every week. The participants of this meeting are the program director, the youth life education supervisors, the program design specialist and the school counselor, i.e., clinical staff person. The purpose of the administrative meeting is to:

- Coordinate and monitor the tasks of the members of the team and others who have responsibility for the team.
- Establish broad goals for the group care program and define the vehicles through which these goals should be accomplished.
- Monitor the integration of all aspects of the group care program, i.e., curriculum, therapy, school, volunteers, group life, the tone of the milieu and to facilitate integration when breakdowns occur. Some of these issues include: birthdays, holidays and religion, accreditation standards, school attendance, racial tensions, drugs, alcohol, scapegoating, language, physical appearance of students, tone of the group, sexuality, stealing, phone use, safety, upcoming events, rituals and rites of passage.
- Discuss admissions for the program and identify the tasks to prepare for a new student.
- Discuss operational issues such as maintenance of the facility, scheduling and new initiatives.

Growth Plan Meeting

A growth plan meeting is held each week to focus on formulating or reviewing a student's growth plan. Each student's growth plan is reviewed at the meeting on a 12-week cycle. Those in attendance for the formal growth plan review are: the parent or guardian, the student, the program director, the school counselor (clinician), the youth life education supervisor, the psychiatrist, a youth life educator and the referral worker.

The growth plan meeting is chaired by the program director, and the chair's responsibility is to prioritize the meeting agenda and develop a plan of action for dealing with unfinished business in the meeting. The school counselor (clinician) is responsible for taking minutes and updating the growth plan.

The meeting takes place in the following way:

- The program director identifies the business that will be discussed at the meeting.
- The program director asks the school counselor to give a brief history of the student's life prior to the current placement and the issues and/or questions the growth planning team needs to address.
- The program director asks other team members if they have additional issues to consider.
- The program director determines which issues or questions will be discussed. An appropriate subgroup of team members will be assigned to resolve pending issues and questions.
- The program director sums up at the end of the discussion and identifies which team members are delegated tasks to complete.

A sample growth plan is presented in Appendix 7 to provide the reader with an understanding of how the growth plan rubric is aligned with the values and beliefs of the organization.

Symbols and Ceremonial Systems

We discussed earlier the sixth sense that interprets messages and integrates them into a larger context that provides us with meaning. Much of what the sixth sense interprets is the nuance and symbolism of our communications. During the Watergate hearings, the investigating Congressional Committee struggled to obtain the tape recordings of various key discussions. Instead, a transcript of the tapes was released. The committee wanted the taped accounts to hear the tones and nuances of the words used.

When we discuss the transmission and reception of messages, we must ask: What are the symbolic messages we are transmitting? In our culture where "information" is everything, we are not as tuned in to the subtle shades of meaning as are most cultures. This is not surprising given the stress on "facts." In the world of science, if it is not quantifiable, it doesn't exist. We have let the symbolic and ceremonial language of our culture slip. We must begin to reacquaint ourselves with the language of symbols and use of our sixth sense. What are the symbolic messages our decision-making and actions communicate to others about our beliefs and values?

A dramatic and well-known story of the power of symbolism comes from the Bible:

> *Now when Jesus was at Bethany in the house of Simon the leper, a woman came up to him with an alabaster flask of very expensive ointment and she poured it on his head, as he sat at the table. But when the disciples saw it, they were indignant, saying, Why this waste? For this ointment might have been sold for a large sum, and given to the poor." But Jesus, aware of this, said to them, "Why do you trouble the woman? For she has done a beautiful thing to me. For you always have the poor with you, but you will not always have me. . . . Mark 14:3-7*

This erroneous understanding of this chapter is: Why try to alleviate the conditions of the poor? No matter what you do there will always be poor people. This is the exact opposite of what we believe the passage is intended to convey. It suggests to us that the giving of a highly valued object to one who has nothing demonstrates the highest principle of caring. If this principle were accepted and practiced it would alleviate much of our poverty. By demonstrating the principle of true caring, we understand the real key to the successful resolution of the disparity between the disadvantaged and the advantaged. How many hearts have been awakened by this story? With our cultural emphasis on bottom line, we tend to miss or dismiss the symbolism and argue for selling the ointment.

We are using myth here as defined by Joseph Campbell. Campbell committed his life to the study of how ceremonies and myths are used in cultures. He argues that we should see myths not as great lies, but as great truths. [Campell: 1988]

> *Myth is the secret opening through which the inexhaustible energies of the cosmos pour into human cultural manifestation. Religions, philosophies, art, the social forms of primitive and historical man, prime discoveries in science and technology, the very dreams that blister sleep, boil up from the basic magic ring of myth.*

So how does the symbolism and nuance of language affect our organizational environment, personnel, operations and curriculum? We need to recognize that our interactions and relationships are, in essence, ceremonies that communicate messages beyond the obvious. We must construct each component of our systems to speak in strong support of the values and beliefs we want to convey. We will provide the reader with three examples of ceremonies, i.e., the culture card system, the recognition system and the problem-solving system, that express the organizational values addressed in earlier chapters.

The Culture Card System

The culture card system is an effective tool for ensuring there is a clear and consistent message describing our organizational culture. The Children's Guild uses this system to teach how the organization applies the wisdom principles and its foundational beliefs in the workplace. By using this system, the organization's beliefs and the expectations are integrated into the daily thoughts and behaviors of staff.

We borrowed and adapted this concept from the Ritz-Carlton Hotel chain. The Ritz-Carlton has repeatedly demonstrated that this system is an effective management approach to build and maintain consistency throughout its organization. They use what is called "line-up," a daily meeting where an aspect of the card is discussed to ensure consistency of service in every Ritz-Carlton hotel in the world. The Ritz-Carlton is the only company in the world that has received two Baldridge Quality Awards for Excellence.

The tangible symbol of this system is a tri-fold, wallet-sized card known as the "culture card." Printed on the culture card are the foundational beliefs, values and practices of The Children's Guild. We include our mission, vision statement, problem-solving process, definition of Transformation Education, foundational beliefs and our workplace expectations. Employees are expected to carry the culture card with them for ready reference.

A culture card meeting is held daily. It is our version of The Ritz-Carlton's "line-up." A manager discusses a foundational belief, value or workplace expectation. The same principle is reviewed by all Guild programs and departments each day. Every employee in the organization receives the same message on the same day. The manager presenting the message discusses how the principle is manifested in the organization and applied to an employee's particular area of responsibility. (The contents of our culture card can be found in Appendix 1.)

After 28 days the meetings recycle. During the course of a year an employee who works in our school will hear each component of the culture card a minimum of 5 times. A twelve-month employee will hear each component 6 to 7 times per year.

School staff are expected to arrive at 8:00 a.m. Students arrive at 8:30 a.m. By scheduling an all-staff assembly at this time, the principal can easily complete a 15-minute culture card meeting prior to the students' arrival. On the other hand, staff who work in the business office might meet at 9:00 a.m., when all the employees in that department are scheduled to arrive for work. Staff working the group homes hold their culture card meetings during each shift change. Since the group home staff operates a 24-hour-a-day program, they repeat the same culture card meeting two times per day.

Culture Card Meeting Agenda

The agenda for the culture card meeting is established by the department manager or supervisor. It includes:

1. The definition of the organizational principle or workplace expectation to be highlighted and a vignette associated with the principle
2. Data relevant to the work of the employees engaged in the culture card meeting
3. A list of any events or visitors to note for that day

The first component of the agenda is a reminder of one of the foundational beliefs, values and life skills or workplace expectations listed on the culture card.

Review of a Principle

Let us take the wisdom principle of "caring," which is also part of our mission statement, i.e. "Teaching children the values and life skills to lead a successful life; one filled with caring, contribution and commitment." The meeting begins by reviewing with employees what caring means. The manager would read a statement like this:

> *"Caring does call upon us to alleviate suffering. It may call upon us to endure suffering. Caring is not static but dynamic in its meaning. Caring means we care about one's self and we care about others. Perhaps in its most destructive form "caring" has come to mean never hurting anyone or anything. To suggest that life should be free from hurt is the antithesis of caring and is contrary to the basic wisdom stories regarding caring. To care means that we recognize and accept the difficulties in life as assisting us in gaining deeper personal meaning and growth. Caring is not to prevent struggle or pain, but to assist in guiding children and others to understand painful experiences and to draw the meaning from them."*

The second aspect of this component is reading aloud a short vignette* on the meaning of the foundational belief, or an explanation of the workplace expectation. A manager reads a vignette to exemplify the practice of caring as described in the review above:

> *"Mrs. Johnson's team has been experiencing substantial student behavior problems for the last several weeks. At the most recent team meeting, two of the five team members complained that the school is accepting students who are too difficult and that more staff are needed to manage the class. The teacher challenged this idea and said: 'That is not the problem. We do not show up to team meetings on time. Sometimes, team members don't show up to team meetings at all. When we do meet, most of our time is spent on complaining and blaming. We don't plan the day with the students in enough detail. We*

don't coordinate our efforts. We talk behind each other's backs. The students are not too difficult. They are simply picking up on our team dysfunction. We need to get our acts together before we can expect behavior to improve.' The other team members sat there and said nothing."

The leader emphasizes the courageous caring of the outspoken teacher and lack of caring and destructiveness of the silence of the other team members.

* Once the manager or supervisor develops comfort with the culture card meeting, s/he no longer needs a vignette to explain the meaning of the items on the culture card. S/he will use an example that occurred recently that all those who report to them are aware of or can identify with easily. For example:

"If you care, you don't pull into the parking lot right when the shift meeting is supposed to start. You arrive 10 minutes earlier, park, say your hellos and sit at the table, ready to meet. Even if you have to leave for work a half an hour early so you don't get caught in traffic. Caring means you don't come in fifteen minutes late and apologize for not being here on time because the traffic was bad."

Sharing Relevant Data

The second component is the relevant data the leader shares with the group. The data shared reflects the need staff have for readily usable information. Data shared with school-based staff might include:

1. Crisis intervention data
2. Attendance
3. New admissions
4. Discharges
5. Indicators (budget performance, accidents, being on time)
6. Scheduled tours
7. Expected visitors
8. Scheduled meetings
9. Staff call-outs

Sharing relevant data keeps the focus of the staff on the effective operation of the program. When the data shows an increase in crisis intervention services, the leader can remind the staff of what is occurring.

The leader might report: "The increase in crisis intervention services is normal given we have a large number of new students following a large number of discharges. Therefore, the increase in crisis intervention services is not the reflection of a problem but is a part of a normal cycle encountered in serving emotionally disturbed children."

If the increase is a problem, the leader's report might say: "The increase in crisis intervention services is a reflection of poor lesson planning. I'd like all the teams to work harder on lesson plans.

If you need help with planning or ideas, Jack Jones is available to work with you on developing your lessons. All you have to do is contact the school secretary to schedule a meeting with him."

Before the staff meeting concludes, a significant daily event is highlighted. The staff might be told: "Remember we are all about making people feel welcome. I know of two prospective admissions visiting today. If you see people you don't know sitting in the waiting room please find a way to say 'hello' and make them feel welcome."

Events or Visitors

The third component of the culture card meeting is for the manager or supervisor to list events or visitors to take note of for the day.

Deployment of the Culture Card System

The CEO is responsible for ensuring that the culture expresses the beliefs of the organization. Defining those beliefs and workplace expectations are his/her responsibility and that of executive management. The CEO leads an annual workshop that focuses on the beliefs and workplace expectations for management and supervisory staff. The purpose of the workshop is to ensure that managers and supervisors understand the information on the culture card. Each manager or supervisor is assigned to develop four vignettes from the list of wisdom principles and workplace expectations. Once the vignettes are written, copies are distributed to each manager/supervisor. The vignettes are reviewed and discussed by the group. Authors revise and edit their vignettes as needed and resubmit them for the group's approval. In each vignette, there is a basic message that is learned. These messages are listed under each vignette. The vignettes are then assembled and published for use in culture card meetings. The creation of the vignettes by the management group is a good way to ensure that each manager and supervisor understands the meaning of each principle on the culture card. As previously mentioned, when supervisors and managers become comfortable with the process, they no longer need canned vignettes. This is because they become adept at drawing their own vignettes from organizational life.

The CEO has editorial control over the vignettes to ensure that management and supervisory staff understand the organization's philosophy. By having the workshop annually, the CEO ensures the vignettes are current, and includes any new relevant programs developed during the course of the year. The vignette workshop provides an opportunity for newly hired managers/supervisors to learn how to apply the organization's philosophy in everyday management practice. It also serves as a refresher course for senior managers/supervisors.

The Culture Card System and How the Brain Learns

The culture card system is designed to be compatible with how the brain learns. Our brains are not wired to learn on the first try. Rather, the brain is designed to learn through trial and error and repeated application of general concepts to specific events. Also, the brain is best able to store and retrieve information when the information is presented in context with something relevant and familiar. The culture card system provides a minimum of six repetitions in a school year and eleven in a calendar year of the organization's values and beliefs and scores of familiar, relevant examples of the ways these values and beliefs are applied in the workplace.

Culture card meetings are held daily. The values and beliefs of the organization become an ingrained habit through the practice of ritual. A ritual is an activity that is consistently triggered by an event. Our brains love rituals. Rituals are familiar, predictable and provide our minds the repeated stimulus necessary to form powerful neural circuits. The "event" in our ritual is the meeting. The "activity" triggered is learning and applying the fundamental beliefs and principles of the organization. This brain-friendly approach will optimize the organization's ability to teach its beliefs and practices.

As we all know, habits are hard to change. The physiological reason for this, as noted earlier in the chapter on how the brain operates, is that neurons (the brain's communication agents) travel along axons (the brain's highways) and connect to other neurons to form learning "circuits." The more often the impulse travels on the same highway circuit, the wider the highway becomes and the faster the impulses travel. This makes it harder for the impulse to travel a different circuit. In other words, once a learning circuit is formed, it operates very efficiently and is difficult to reroute. Through the culture card system, old circuits are interrupted and the ritual of applying the beliefs and principles of the organization builds new, strong circuits radiating the organization's cultural beliefs. In another word–transformation.

Using the Problem-Solving Model

Defining the problem is the most important component of the problem-solving process. The four steps presented below assist staff in accurately defining the problem.

A key component of Transformation Education is not to ascribe blame to others. When things go wrong, we initiate a process that focuses on learning and improvement. We like to remind management and staff that a problem tends to emanate from our own behavior, poor communication or an ill-defined or malfunctioning system rather than one's coworker.

The problem-solving process is sequential and comprised of the following four components.

Start With Yourself – Problem solving begins with you. Start your solution to any problem by reflecting on the following questions:

1. What have I done to contribute to this problem?

   If a problem has an impact on you, chances are you have contributed to it in some manner. The more you think about it, the more likely you are to identify your contribution to the problem. Once you identify your role, take responsibility. If you honestly cannot identify anything you did, then move on to the second reflective question.

2. What have I failed to do that has contributed to this problem?

Sometimes it's not the things we do that contribute to a problem, it is what we haven't done. If you have identified your contribution, you acknowledge that omission as an invitation to others to join the problem-solving process.

By starting with yourself, you avoid the primary barrier to effective team problem solving: fixing blame on others. We have seen blame work its destructive influence many, many times. When you assign blame to coworkers for a problem, their natural reaction is denial, defensiveness or aggression. By blaming, you extinguish in those team members the very resources needed to solve the problem: creativity, strategic thinking and imagination.

From a neuroscience point of view, this "natural" reaction to being blamed for a problem is a function of the brain's limbic system. The limbic system is the locus of emotion in our brains. The amygdala is the sentry of the limbic system, standing protective guard by screening each and every bit of sensory stimulus coming to the brain. If the amygdala senses an emotional or physical threat in the sensory stimulus, it secretes hormones in the brain designed to heighten physical awareness and protect against the threat. One of the hormones secreted is cortisol, the human stress hormone.

Cortisol causes an increase in blood pressure and heart rate; blood flow is rerouted from the extremities to the major organs. Respiration is speeded up and breaths are shallower. The blood carries less oxygen. This translates into a person biologically stressed, when confronted with "It's your fault!"

With cortisol on the loose, the brain has more difficulty accessing the frontal lobes. The functions of creativity, imagination, planning, strategic thinking and problem solving are dimmed—the resources needed to address a problem are neutralized. Further, the "blame game" can instigate a cortisol reaction that chemically inhibits access to the brain's executive center. The reactions of denial, defensiveness and aggression are the amygdala's way of combating the perceived threat. Until the threat is removed or significantly reduced, it is physiologically impossible to engage your team or coworkers in optimal problem solving.

By leading with your contribution to the problem, you serve as a model for others. Personal responsibility reduces the chances of setting off the neurological alarms that make problem solving problematic at best. By defusing the blame factor, you focus on solving the problem at hand and benefit from everyone's best thinking.

Communication—Once you have engaged others in seeking a solution, evaluate the communication patterns surrounding the problem. As much as 80% of the cause of any one problem can be directly attributed to a breakdown in communication. Communication either was nonexistent, incomplete, unclear or misunderstood.

Sit down face to face and review the following questions:

1. What are the specific expectations for this project or activity?
2. Were those expectations clearly communicated? How and when?
3. Were those expectations received and understood? How do you know?

This query method often exposes communication breakdowns that led to the creation of the problem. Many problems are born of poorly communicated ideas and expectations. By reconstructing communication patterns, you can frequently identify what went wrong and when. Most important, you'll raise awareness of these communication patterns with your team members.

Systems—After analyzing your contribution to the problem and the communication patterns surrounding it, assess whether adequate systems exist to support the project or activity in question. A "system" is a group of elements that interact and function together as a whole to produce a product or result. A well-designed system should produce the results we want.

The two primary elements of our organizational systems are resources and processes. Resources include people, knowledge, money, supplies and equipment. A process is a series of steps designed to produce a predictable result. The resources initiate or support the process, resulting in the outcome.

With inadequate resources, the process will not and cannot produce the desired outcome. The resources must be increased, or the process redesigned to consider the smaller resources in the process design. If adequate resources exist but the result is undesirable, the process is not organized correctly. The process must be redesigned.

People—So let's check our own contributions to the project. We examine the communication patterns. The organizational systems are assessed. If necessary, repairs are made. Despite all of these checks and assessments, the problem persists. We are left with a review of the job performance of the key team members. This is the final step and is conducted only if all the other steps are thoroughly evaluated.

It is our belief that employees in child-serving organizations work hard and are motivated to do a good job. If, however, a job performance review is indicated, it should be done compassionately and with courage. When possible, employees should be coached and supported through the process of change to achieve the desired performance.

Applying the Problem-Solving Model: Kiosks

Kiosks in our schools say a lot about us. The purpose of the kiosks installed outside the classrooms in our schools is to reflect to all who walk the schools' hallways the quality of learning inside the classroom.

One of our senior managers was chronically frustrated with the inconsistent effort in constructing the kiosks at our flagship school. Applying the problem-solving model, he discovered the cause was not what he initially believed. At the beginning, he clearly expected to advance through the entire process. He got no farther than step one. This is a common outcome when the process is conscientiously applied.

Diagnosing the problem: As Walt Kelly, the creator of the cartoon, Pogo said: "We have met the enemy, and it is us."

Faculty use of the kiosks to achieve this purpose has been chronically inconsistent. Kiosk construction has been of widely variable quality. In many instances, executive management intervention is required to motivate faculty to even use the kiosks. Maintenance of the kiosks, once constructed, is consistently poor.

What have I done to contribute to this problem? Once the manager really thought about it, there were two significant things he did to contribute to the current state of the problem. First, he made an assumption that once the kiosk concept was explained to the school leaders during training, they would immediately take ownership of them and implement the organization's expectations for their use. This was both a mistake in judgment and unfair to the leadership because a single lesson or individual experience in kiosk use is not sufficient to support ownership or competence in kiosk use.

Second, he expected the leaders to contact him with questions or requests for assistance regarding the kiosk project. It was unrealistic to hold this (noncommunicated) expectation of school leadership given the leadership changed several times during the year.

What have I failed to do that has contributed to the problem? First, he failed to provide the follow-up communication and support to school leadership about the kiosks. Instead of relying on an isolated training session, he should have provided a continuum of information, given examples and support to ensure the leaders had the knowledge and resources needed to carry out the project.

Second, he failed to carry on a dialogue with the leadership—both formally and informally—about their progress with kiosks. His lack of communication about the project took the issue "off the radar screen" and likely communicated the message that the kiosks were really not a priority.

Next, he quickly gave up providing feedback about the poor condition of a number of the kiosks because of a fear of being "too critical" to staff members who appeared to be under considerable stress already. By failing to provide feedback, he inadvertently "lowered the bar" about kiosk expectations and communicated again the message that kiosks were not a priority.

Significantly, he had not yet developed a manual on the kiosk use, philosophy and processes. Without these key concepts in writing, the only methods the leadership has to learn about and implement kiosk use are to either ask him or guess, neither of which is a constructive choice. Access to the senior manager is extremely limited and knowledge should not be centralized in any one individual if the organization is to effectively deploy its model. Guessing leads to inconsistency, frustration and discouragement.

He failed to insist that school leaders schedule adequate time during orientation to teach kiosk use and accommodate kiosk construction. He mistakenly assumed that school leaders were adequately trained regarding kiosk use and could adequately conduct this training. There was no need to continue the problem-solving process; he was the problem.

The Recognition Systems

The core activity of Transformation Education is to create and maintain an organizational culture that promotes growth and change. The children must consider the organization's culture as authentic. That will happen if the children are drawn to the avowed values and beliefs radiating from the employees. The culture must be designed and operated to motivate children to grow and change.

The development of an organizational culture that generates growth and change is a complex, monumental task. The innumerable components that interact to form a culture must be identified, evaluated, modified, implemented, adjusted and maintained. The work of building culture must also be intentional and precise. Each decision about what is placed in the culture, and tolerated or favored in the culture, must be assessed against the purpose for which the culture is to be used.

Will insertion of this cultural element promote growth and change in the people experiencing the organization?

The implementation of a recognition program that identifies and elevates the thinking and behavior desired in the culture can contribute significantly to its creation and maintenance.

The criteria for recognition communicates the most important behavioral expectations of the organization. Those employees recognized are role models to others. The mindset and behavior of a recognized employee strengthens the presence and frequency of the desired thinking and behavior in the culture. As the recognition program is repeated through the years, the valued behaviors are revisited, reemphasized and ingrained into the fabric of the culture.

The critical question is what kinds of thinking and behavior are most valued by a Transformation Education organization? If the organization can answer this question clearly and precisely and establish a system to identify those who fit the criteria, employee recognition can make a powerful contribution to the organizational culture.

The key to employee recognition is to support those who carry out the mission, values and beliefs of the organization. This relatively simple idea is sometimes overlooked. The most important value in building a culture with the power to transform requires employees to move from selfishness to selflessness. Simply translated, selflessness means:

- Caring
- Contribution and commitment
- Vision
- Courage
- Will
- Willingness to struggle, transform and achieve enlightenment

These values fit the journey metaphor discussed in chapter 2.

The trap you want to avoid is rewarding those staff members who mix metaphors by bringing ideas from other organizations that are adverse to a Transformation Education culture. Those who have worked in for-profit companies bring the market metaphor with them. The market is all about acquisition and promotes competition. The market metaphor separates winners from losers. Primary recognition is given in the form of bonuses, trips to exotic places for being a top salesperson, jewelry, tickets to sporting events, the employee-of-the-month parking spot, etc. The emphasis is on winning, not transforming. Even gifts aim to thank and keep the customer. This type of recognition fits the acquisition or market concept.

Those who worked in a social service agency come with the body metaphor. The body metaphor's goal is unity– to make everything harmonious and equal. This style appreciates everyone. All the teachers get an apple and a luncheon on Teacher Appreciation day. The same concept applies for Secretaries Day and Social Worker's month. You get recognized just for being a member of the profession. It is like Mother's Day. Good mothers, abusive, and neglectful mothers, and outstanding mothers all get recognized.

Keep in mind that there is a difference between appreciation and recognition. Appreciation is the responsibility of the management and supervisory staff. Appreciation is comprised of words of encouragement and acts of support and gratitude for an employee's effort or skill or helpfulness. Recognition is defined as the organization elevating an individual, group or student whose behavior or thinking is consistent with the values, beliefs and culture of the organization. The purpose of recognition is to motivate employees, members of the community, stakeholders and students to model the values of the organization as a means to get others to adopt the thinking and behavior of those who are recognized. One way to do this is to publicly recognize those that exhibit organizational values in their work lives. An example of how to align recognition with an organization's values follows.

The Monarch Award – *Symbol of Leadership*

The Monarch Award represents caring and contribution. It also symbolizes leadership (a Monarch) and a butterfly (that transformed itself through struggle out of its cocoon). This award recognizes staff members willing to endure suffering so that the mission of the organization can advance. This type of leadership initiates and motivates transformation. The award recipients reflect the soul of the organization.

The award presentation occurs during the organization's annual report to the community. Representatives of the community, members of the board of trustees, elected officials, employees and professional colleagues are present. The Monarch Award honorees and their servant leadership stories are then highlighted in the organization's newsletter. Their names are inscribed on the Monarch Awards plaque and they receive a financial gift and a crystal butterfly.

Mastermind Award – *Symbol of Commitment*

Those who are admitted to the fraternity of the masterminds are recognized for their commitment to their craft. They are able to make a significant contribution to those they serve because they have spent the time necessary to become expert in what they do and are committed to doing it right. The award is given at an all-staff event. The award recipients receive a chess piece (the Queen) mounted on a block of walnut and are featured in the organization's newsletter. A site-based mastermind display features a plaque with each recipient's name. There is no limit to the winners of the award each year.

The Eagle Eye Award – *Symbol of Vision*

An eagle flies higher than any other bird and is never found in a flock. The height at which the eagle flies provides it a vantage point to see ahead and anticipate its next move. At the opposite extreme is the mouse that is so low to the ground that it can only react to what is immediately in its path. Employees who have the vision to anticipate what will happen before it happens in their jobs are recognized with this award. Like eagles, those with vision are unique. The award is a framed image of an eagle given yearly at a day of organizational celebration. The recipient's name is inscribed on a registry associated with the organization's "vision" display.

Brave Heart Award – *The Symbol of Courage*

Struggle and will are inherent in the concept of courage. This award goes to staff members who are willing to be vulnerable yet steadfast enough to face opposition, hardship or danger over time. They are the ones who are driven to do what it takes to foster and motivate transformation in a child, a fellow employee, an organizational culture or a social condition. Courage is demonstrated through effort and overcoming doubt. The medallion award displays the organization's logo and the words "dare to risk." The award is presented during a day of organizational celebration. The names of the award recipients are inscribed on the Brave Heart scroll and the reason for their selection is entered into the Book of Courage.

The Sadie Award – *Symbol of Transformation*

The Sadie Award takes its name from the organization's founder, Sadie Dashew Ginsberg. A transformational leader, Sadie made the seemingly impossible, possible. This award represents the capacity within each of us to grow, change and pursue one's vision in the face of adversity. It is the spirit of the child within each of us that says: "I can do that!" This is the spirit that understands that the true goal in life is serving others.

The Sadie Award is a bronze sculpture entitled Wings. This bronze of a child dressed in coveralls, running and holding aloft a glider, is a powerful image. In the words of the sculptor: "The hand-me-down coveralls represent the toil and the labor of the world, and the mail-order glider and outstretched arms have to do with dreams and aspirations." This award captures the spirit of transformation.

Logo Pins

Staff members receive their first logo pin when they complete the Pre-Service Training Program. This indicates they are aware of the organization's values. They also receive different colored logo pins recognizing recommitment to those values at the one-, five-, seven- and ten-year service anniversaries.

Using the Problem-Solving Model

Another way to foster growth and change in the culture is to align the faculty's recognition of the students with the mission and values of the organization. This is done by having faculty recognize students four times during the year for exhibiting citizenship and courage, and for developing their talents and skills.

The Citizenship Award (Medal of Honor on a red, white and blue ribbon) is given to recognize students who consistently attend school, participate in school activities, generally follow school rules, exhibit good hygiene, respect property, are courteous to other students and take pride in their appearance. The Courage Award (framed certificate) is bestowed on those who demonstrate resiliency in the face of adversity and perseverance in the pursuit of self-improvement. The Talent Award (blue ribbon) recognizes the motivation, sustained effort and achievement required for success in life. This can be in any area of endeavor: athletics, art, performing arts, leadership, academics or a personal achievement. Student awardees are displayed in an organizational display.

Staff Development and Training in Transformation Education

As the Transformation Education model evolved, the development of a training program to meet the need for staff schooled in our approach became critical. The staff development program in any organization transmits to employees the attitudes and norms about how the organization views children and families and how it works with them to produce growth and change, a critical mindset in Transformation Education. We soon realized that our existing training program needed a completely different structure if we were to transform our organizational culture.

A New Model for Staff Development

In most child-serving organizations, supervisors are commonly the people responsible for the orientation of new staff, the job-specific training for new employees and the ongoing educational and skill-building opportunities all employees need. However, placing on the shoulders of supervisors the enormous responsibility of staff development was contraindicated for several reasons.

First, adding Transformation Education training to the supervisors' existing responsibilities would place significant stress on them. Second, the supervisors' availability to learn the Transformation Education concepts was severely limited by heavy workloads. Third, we were aware that the supervisors might not share the philosophical or practice orientation of Transformation Education, at least until they had had adequate opportunity to learn and implement the model. Consequently, we were not comfortable with a staff development and training structure in which the supervisors are the primary conduit because of the high risk that the supervisors may not be communicating the messages desired in the transforming culture.

We then considered using outside trainers as an option, but rejected it. Training staff primarily through outside sources is often not cost effective and may not be philosophically consistent with the agency's desired new culture. Every outside trainer or consultant has a unique philosophy and focus. If this focus and/or philosophy are not consistent with the intended culture, the organization is literally spending money to sabotage itself. Why pay for training that offers conflicting cultural messages about what the agency believes and how it practices?

In the end, we realized that the staff development program must be led and operated by senior management. At least until the supervisors and other mid-level managers could develop expertise and competence in the model, senior managers were the right people to drive the training in Transformation Education.

Once we decided on senior management involvement, we still faced multiple challenges in developing our training program. Like all child-serving organizations, we needed to respond to the latest research findings applicable to our work with children and confront the critical crisis in finding qualified staff.

When it comes to serving children in specialized settings, research in neuroscience, sociology, psychology and social work all point in the same direction. We must expand individualization of educational, mental health and social services to children who had previously received common services under the "at-risk" or "in-need-of-assistance" umbrella labels. But individualization requires very high levels of skill and sophistication in employees. Most child-serving organizations are now faced with training new, inexperienced and often uneducated staff in complex, sophisticated treatment models that require theoretical understanding, conceptual ability, intuition, independent judgment and split-second evaluation in response to behavioral events. How were we to create programs to train staff, many of whom have not attained college degrees, in complex, innovative methods of healing troubled children?

In addition to the problem of complexity, simply finding enough qualified staff was a significant issue. The availability and employability of well-educated, experienced child-serving professionals is at an all-time low. Child-serving organizations struggle to find the financial resources to pay the salaries and benefits necessary to attract and retain seasoned professionals. Turnover of staff in most child-serving organizations exceeds 50%. How could we attract the best of the limited number of staff entering the field?

Our answer was to create our own university system: The College of Transformation Education. We recognized that no school or prior employment experience could prepare staff for our unique approach to serving children. We further recognized that a high-quality, internal "university" would be experienced by many employees as an attractive benefit. Finally, an organization-based college powerfully communicated the importance of continual learning as a primary value of the organization. The knowledge and skill characteristics we required from our employees for success could not be taught and maintained only through supervisor-led training or outside resource training. Instead, they required the creation of a university-like system within the organization itself. In short, we turned inward to deliver the education, resources and ongoing support necessary to deliver the sophisticated and individualized services our children need and deserve.

The Purpose of the Staff Development Program in Transformation Education

At its core, the staff development function in Transformation Education is to minimize the time between an employee's initial introduction to the intended culture of the organization and the employee's positive contribution to that culture. This culture is created through an integration of the physical environment, the mindset of the employees, the design of the program curriculum and the operational systems. The staff creates, models and maintains the cultural messages in each of these areas.

In response to the culture, children model what they experience the staff demonstrating. If staff model to children growth and change, growth and change will be, in fact, generated in the children. Alternatively, if staff respond to the intended culture with inflexibility, hostility and aggression, the children's adoption of the culture will be inconsistent, stilted and nonintegrated. Thus, the role of staff development is to move the employee as efficiently as possible from exposure to the culture to understanding of the culture to maintenance and improvement of the culture.

Much like the children new to the program, new employees spend a period of time reading and reacting to the culture. Ultimately, employees either adapt to the culture, resist the culture or escape from the culture (resistance is examined in more detail in chapter 9). If staff members adapt to the culture, they begin to understand the cultural milieu. They become more skilled at perceiving the multiple cultural cues placed in the environment. As staff members continue to progress, they actively learn to monitor the culture and correct dissonant messages. They begin to contribute positively to the culture and become an integral part of its maintenance. With continued development, staff members gain the ability to "fine-tune" the culture, recreate the culture in a foreign setting and teach others the cultural model.

We designed the staff development program to provide modeling, support and resources to usher staff members along this journey as efficiently and meaningfully as possible so that the culture's messages radiating growth and change always remain strong and consistent.

The Design of the Staff Development Program in Transformation Education

So, how can we offer highly sophisticated training with limited resources yet still meet the increased accountability demands and competition for employees? In Transformation Education, we've done this by creating a three-tiered staff development program including an internal college. The first tier is known as the Pre-Service Training Program (PSTP). The second tier is the College of Transformation Education. The third tier is called Community Supports.

The PSTP is a two-week, 56-hour series of courses to prepare new staff for their role in the Transformation Education model and for the employees' prospective jobs. PSTP is competency based, delivered in an intense, higher education type of environment. It is taught primarily by senior management, with particular emphasis on teaching by the agency leader and any identified "masters" in a particular topic area. The instructors emphasize the values, beliefs and expectations of the organization. A copy of a typical two-week PSTP syllabus is found in Appendix 2. Screening new employees for an organizational fit is a primary function of the PSTP. The organization has identified the employee characteristics that lead to success in the Transformation Education approach. The employee is evaluated during PSTP for this character match. Since senior managers teach most courses, management can interact significantly with new employees. This competence and personal evaluation is important in assessing the employee's thinking and experiences as they relate to caring for children. By the time employees have completed the 56 hours, management has an informed perspective on the employee's likelihood of success in the organization.

At times, employees may be counseled out of continued employment. Some employees do not complete the program or pass the competencies. Other employees decide themselves that Transformation Education is not a good fit and opt to leave the organization.

First and foremost, senior management's instruction in PSTP introduces employees to an enthusiastic and united presentation about the organization's philosophy and its importance. The screening function of the PSTP experience reduces time, money and energy spent on "non-fits." The competency-based nature of the curriculum establishes a standardized level of employee task and conceptual ability before an employee interacts with children in the organization's service environment. The PSTP also promotes a level of professionalism that motivates growth, attracts talent and sets the expectation for continued learning and development by the employee.

The College of Transformation Education

The second tier of the staff development program is structured like a "mini community college" within the organization. It provides employees at every level of sophistication ongoing training in subjects critical to the continued growth and improvement of the organization.

The College of Transformation Education requires that each employee maintain continuing education units (CEUs) as part of his/her job. Staff members are required to complete an established number of hours in the College as a condition of continued employment. The specific number of required hours is determined by the staff member's job classification and length of employment. This ensures that learning is continuous and that employees are committed to ongoing growth and professional development.

The CEU process requires supervisors at all levels to become professional guidance counselors. Supervisors advise on which courses to take as well as the timing and order of the courses. The selection of courses will, in part, be determined by the supervisor's perception of the various strengths and weaknesses of the employee and his or her potential for development. Consequently, the mentoring relationship deepens between managers and employees. CEU completion is a significant component of the staff member's annual performance evaluation. We want an employee who values continuing education and is committed to growth and change.

Staff members failing to complete the required CEUs are generally not eligible for promotion, bonus (if offered) or transfer. To insure fairness and compliance with employment laws, we have designed a course schedule that provides access to classes compatible to each job classification's work hours.

The tracking of CEU credits is the function of the staff development director, program administrator or human resources. See the examples provided in Appendix 2. Maintenance of individual tracking sheets is the responsibility of the employee.

The curriculum design and course offerings vary greatly depending on the organization and the job classifications identified to deliver its services. The basic curriculum design matrix for an agency with both a group home and a school for children with emotional disturbance is provided in Appendix 2c.

Each job classification has four course levels:

1. PSTP
2. Required courses
3. Intermediate courses
4. Advanced courses

PSTP is offered monthly throughout the year. Required courses are offered in October, December, February and April. Intermediate and advanced courses are scheduled according to identified need, teacher availability and logistics.

The College of Transformation Education integrates well with outcome measures and quality improvement demands. The College model provides a smorgasbord of measurement options. Staff view the training as an employment benefit, thereby increasing staff retention.

We came to believe that specific staff training customized to job tasks translates into better student outcomes (e.g., teacher training participation in reading instructional techniques will improve student reading performance.) Financially, we expect that the "school within a school" will produce overall cost savings. There is reduced turnover, lower outside training cost and higher quality service delivery. The College inspires staff to actualize the Transformation Education philosophy and perform to the full extent of their talents and capabilities.

Community Supports

The third tier of our staff development program enables staff members to access community-based programs for education, certification or enrichment purposes. These training opportunities are often in conjunction with courses taken in the College of Transformation Education. This Community Supports tier allows staff access to higher education resources required by regulatory or licensing agencies to obtain or maintain credentials or licenses. Training sessions for Community Supports are categorized according to the following definitions:

1. Community-Based Training Courses (CBT)

   Community-based training courses are provided within a 50-mile radius of one of the program sites. The training sessions are typically developed and presented by professionals and/or professional organizations serving the same client population. CBTs usually require a fee for participation. CBTs may or may not qualify for professional continuing education unit requirements, and may involve local travel expenses.

2. Professional Conferences

   Professional Conferences (PC) are held at a wide array of geographic locations. PCs are typically developed and presented by professional organizations, industry groups, private companies/corporations or government agencies. PCs require a fee for participation. They may or may not qualify for professional continuing education unit requirements and will generally involve significant out-of-town travel expense.

3. Higher Education Courses

   Higher Education Courses (HEC) are provided by community colleges, colleges and universities in or near one of the program sites. These courses may be taken individually or as part of a degree program. HECs require tuition, books and materials costs and generally qualify for professional continuing education unit requirements. HECs may involve local travel expense and/or may qualify for tuition assistance.

4. Self-Study Courses

Self-study courses (SSC) may be provided through a variety of sources including professional organizations, government agencies or higher education institutions. These courses are characterized by the use of print or online study materials followed by a competency exam. A fee may or may not be required and professional continuing education unit requirements may or may not apply.

Outcome Goals

The staff development program has 10 outcome goals:

1. Ensure integration of Transformation Education throughout every aspect of the organization.
2. Establish continual learning as a required condition of employment.
3. Provide and promote mentoring relationships and opportunities.
4. Develop high expectations for skill attainment and job performance.
5. Identify and highlight career advancement processes.
6. Encourage research and collaboration.
7. Provide clear expectations of performance both in task and attitude.
8. Showcase master teachers in the organization.
9. Obtain maximum efficiency from staff development dollars.
10. Improve the organization's ability to promote growth and change in children

By offering intensive pre-service training, an internal College of Transformation Education, and community resources for certification and enrichment, child-serving organizations can provide staff sophisticated training that greatly enhances the application of the Transformation Education philosophy.

Additional Thoughts on Training

Remember the primary goal of a child-serving organization for socially and emotionally disadvantaged children is to bring about change in dysfunctional behavior and to promote normal growth and development. This is accomplished by establishing a culture that teaches the values and life skills essential for a successful life through systems, people, physical environment and the program curriculum. When this is done effectively, a child becomes aware of events and everyday situations that occur in life (the child's mindset) by broadening the child's rules of interpretation.

The best vehicle for staff to become aware of the messages inherent in the culture and their own actions is through situational reviews. A situational review is essentially a postmortem to check the assumption that underlies the decision that was made or that motivates the behavior. Essentially the assumption is checked for context and the outcome of the decision is evaluated for the wisdom gained and the greater good achieved.

This technique was used to analyze how safe the Children's Emergency Shelter was for a ten-year-old boy. The boy had received three stitches in his head when spun around in an overstuffed living room chair that had a swivel base. When the boy stood up, he lost his balance and hit his head on the corner of a coffee table, which resulted in the need for stitches. A safety committee comprised of a nurse, a supervisor, two key administrators and a representative from the Juvenile Court and the Department of Human Services reviewed the incident. They concluded that swivel chairs were dangerous and must be replaced with stationary chairs. When the conclusion of the safety committee reached us, we had the reviewing committee check its assumptions. The committee viewed the chair as dangerous, not that the supervision was inadequate, or that the staff member did not intervene soon enough to stop the use of the chair as a merry-go-round.

After much discussion, the committee came to the recognition that the goal was to teach children how to use furniture properly. The goal was not to control children by depriving them of the opportunity to experience variety in their environment. It was pointed out how important it was for children to experience complexity, particularly children who only experience life in very concrete and unrefined terms. The staff struggled with the situation, but agreed it made sense to keep the swivel chair. The situational review proved to be an effective tool in changing mindset.

Probably the most critical mindset to address through staff development is how staff perceive children in a child-serving organization. The likely first introduction to "on-the-job child care work" in most agencies is physical restraint training. This helps create an initial mindset, although it is unintended, of the role of the childcare worker as a controller of unmanageable behavior.

We are not implying physical restraint training is not necessary but rather that an intensive understanding of how culture works should precede physical restraint training. In fact, by teaching about how culture works before teaching physical restraint, the direct care worker possesses the proper context from which to view the use of physical restraint. In the cultural approach, physical restraint is not viewed as a technique simply to manage out-of-control behavior. It is a technique to manage a physical reaction to the normal part of the change process a child will go through in adapting to a new mindset, i.e., struggle leading to changed behavior.

Another objective of the training component is to instill in staff the importance of having an integrated culture. An integrated culture is one in which the systems, staff, physical environment and program all espouse the same message. Under a Transformation Education model, the furniture, the language, the posture of the staff, the policies, the problem-solving process, the presentation of the food and the way staff dress send a consistent message. When integration and cohesion of message is emphasized, staff and children come to understand what is asked of them.

Thinking in Context

Teaching the staff to think and make contextual decisions in a change-and growth-oriented culture is considered a high value. Too often, we think of training as that which is provided to us through guided instruction. In the context of culture, training is any experience where the learner is exposed to cultural principles. This suggests that the meetings we hold to make operational decisions are also training exercises. This remains true of virtually any interaction, especially those that are experienced as real. The value in considering all such experiences as training cannot be overemphasized. It is the primary mode of transmitting actual beliefs and practices.

Discernment is the compass in a changing and growing culture. Discernment is emphasized in Transformation Education. The greater the staff's ability to discern (variations in shades of gray, nuances of symbolic communications, etc.), the more the children are likely to develop their sixth sense and their appreciation for quality. Furthermore, the greater the discernment by the staff, the greater the opportunity for students to grow morally and spiritually and to ensure that the organization is a caring place for children and staff. The emphasis on context and discernment is captured in what Harvard professsor of psychology, Dr. Ellen Langer, calls "mindfulness." This concept is the foundation for understanding at a more perceptive level.

As we have previously stated, we have been educated since kindergarten to be outcome oriented. Our goal-oriented, rather than process-oriented approach, is what creates the problem. This single- minded, context-free approach to viewing the world creates a mindset of stability and certainty. However, when the knowledge is applied out of context, there is a high price to pay.

We have presented numerous examples of out-of-context thinking found in group care organizations. Eliminate the swivel chair rather than deal with the lack of supervision of the children. Langer [Langer: 1989] states:

> *We whisper in hospitals, become anxious in police stations, sad in cemeteries, docile in schools and jovial at parties. Context controls our behavior, and our mindsets determine how we interpret each context. These emotional contexts are generally learned in a single-minded way. Children are not taught that the way they feel in a particular context could be either fear or delight. Instead, children are taught that snakes are frightening, sunsets are peaceful, mothers (and mother-like people) are loving. Emotions rest upon premature cognitive commitments. We experience them without awareness that they could be otherwise, without awareness that this is the way we constructed the experience. Without looking closely and noticing that the same stimulus in a different context is a different stimulus, we become victims of the associations we ourselves constructed. When we are tormented by unwanted emotion we assume it could be no other way.*

Framing training with an emphasis on discernment supports moral development of children and the goal of change. Once staff recognize this they understand the importance of what Dr. Langer called making decisions with creative uncertainty, i.e., confident that the decision may be made but without being certain of the reason. The children experience this creative uncertainty and benefit from judgments made within the contextual framework.

Dr. Langer goes on to say:

> *Some may argue that to teach children about the world conditionally is to make them insecure. This belief may result from a faulty comparison. If the world were stable and we taught stability that might indeed be better than teaching conditionally. The inappropriate comparison, however, would seem to be between teaching with absolutes when the "facts" are conditional*

versus teaching conditionally when the "facts" are conditional. Will children taught, "It depends" grow up to be insecure adults? Or will they be more confident in a world of change than those of us brought up with absolutes?

Creating organizational models with a new paradigm is not without risk. We learned that when we tried to change the culture at a child-serving organization that served delinquent youth. We were continuously frustrated by bureaucratic rigidity. The bureaucrats could not think anew or disenthrall themselves from the established ways. Let us share that experience with you.

The shelter had previously been used as a juvenile prison. We rehabilitated the building to make the bare block walls and high ceilings warm and inviting. The rehabilitation included everything from new, larger windows and sheet rock walls with wallpaper, to new lighting and furnishings.

The property, with high, chain-link fences surrounding it, giving it a prison yard feeling, was converted into a beautiful park complete with waterfalls and a playground capped with a red tension structure flying overhead to keep off the rain and the summer heat. This was designed to enhance the children's well-being, stimulate their imaginations and assist them to engage in an exploration of ideas and values.

Our innovation, the creation of a positive, value-laden organizational culture and corresponding environment for children and youth, were the envy of our colleagues. It also raised red flags for the licensing reviewer who viewed our attempts at creating a discovery environment as placing children in danger of being injured.

After a comprehensive review, the Department of Human Services refused to acknowledge in any way the positive impact this was having on the children. Instead, they rigidly adhered to their archaic interpretation of safety. They equated safety to keeping children in cement box rooms in walled-off, sterile environments. A walk in the park, where you could dangle your feet in a shallow stream emerging from a carefully constructed waterfall, was placing youth at risk!

The Job Is Never Done

We have focused on some of the key operational systems that radiate our cultural messages. Virtually every operating system needs to be reviewed for alignment with both beliefs and values. We need to ask if the culture we create is sufficiently developed and articulated in a way that it actually directs staff behavior to achieve its desired end. Hopefully, the foregoing examples have provided the reader with an understanding of the level of detail needed to establish an effective operating system.

Articulating operating systems so the staff can actually execute them in a child-serving organization is a mammoth job that takes years. Realistically, it is ongoing and can never be completed. This is due to the underdeveloped nature of child-serving organizational systems. Many of these systems have largely relied on expertise and oral tradition to do their work with children. Ongoing systems development is necessary to carry out effective and consistent service. We will now turn our attention in Chapter 6 to the roles of key staff in the Transformation Education model.

CHAPTER 6

People as Transmitters of Culture

Principle: The focus of management efforts is on transforming the disparate individual beliefs and values into alignment with the beliefs and values of the organization.

> *I refuse to accept the idea that the "isness" of man's present nature makes him morally incapable of reaching up for the "oughtness" that forever confronts him.*
> *– Martin Luther King Jr.*

Transformation Vs. Transaction

There is a difference between transforming leadership and transactional leadership. Transforming leadership focuses on changes of attitudes, beliefs, values and needs, whereas transactional leadership concentrates on substituting one thing for another.

Given that this book is all about transforming mindsets it is essential to distinguish change from transformation. James McGregor Burns does an excellent job of this in his book *Transforming Leadership* [Burns: 2003]. McGregor defines change as substituting one thing for another, to give and take. This is what he attributes to leaders who are involved in transactional leadership. He views transformation as causing a metamorphosis in form or structure, a change in the very condition or nature of a thing, a change into another substance, a radical change in outward form or inner character, like the horse and carriage turning into an automobile.

> *In broad social and political terms, transformation means basic alterations in entire systems-revolutions that replace one structure of power with another, or the constitutional changes America achieved in the late eighteenth century. Bernard Bass of the Binghamton group has distinguished between the "first order of change," or changes of degree, and a "higher order of change," constituting alterations in "attitudes, beliefs, values and needs." Quantitative changes are not enough; they must be qualitative too. All this does not mean total change, which is impossible in human life. It does mean alterations so comprehensive and pervasive, and perhaps accelerated, that new cultures and value systems take the places of the old.*

Is transforming leadership measured simply by the number of alternations achieved? The more transactions, in short, the more transformational change? No, the issue is the nature of change and not merely the degree, as when the temperature in a pot of water is gradually raised to produce a transformation: boiling. Time and timing can be crucial. Continual transactions over a long period can produce transformation. If such incremental changes take lifetimes, how long should people wait? [Burns: 2003]

The leader of a child-serving organization initially must create or recreate the organization. In so doing, leadership reshapes the organizational mindset. A good leader wants a revamped organization that consistently generates intelligence, meaning and life skills, and builds a child's character. Once this occurs, the focus of the organization shifts to a transactional leadership. For this reason, most of this chapter concerns the role of the Chief Executive Officer. We acknowledge, though, that the CEO cannot create a culture that motivates transformation in employees and children without the help and support of key management and supervisory staff.

Role of the CEO

Visionary Leader

In a change-oriented culture, leadership matters, not management. Leadership implies change to a different state. Management implies maintaining existing situations. [Bennis and Nanus: 1985] Leadership is critical in creating organizational change.

Change requires the staff to enter into unfamiliar territory. The chief executive officer must be willing to model this expectation. S/he must adopt a mindset of operating from a visionary sense of the future. S/he exhibits or conveys a futuristic mindset through the planning and problem-solving process.

It is not possible to use the rational planning model to envision the future. A rational planning model only works if the information it collects is correct. The future is vision and change. Visionary leadership projects a picture of how an organization will look at some point in the future. In short, it is necessary to project the culture you wish to establish.

The transformational leader must have a kung fu approach to organizational development. Foresight is required to judge how the vision fits into the way the organization's environment might evolve. On the other hand, hindsight insures that the vision does not violate the organization's traditions and culture.

A world view is needed to interpret the impact of possible new developments and trends; perception allows one to see appropriate detail and perspective; peripheral vision is essential to comprehend possible responses by other stakeholders to the new direction; and a process of visioning is used for continuous synthesis of other "visions" as the environment or the organization changes. [Bennis & Nanus: 1985]

Another aspect of the leader's visionary role is articulating the strategic vision. This involves connecting present circumstances to the possibilities of the future. Strategic vision enables leaders to make on-the-spot decisions that are consistent, so that their actions support the message in their words. It requires the ability to recognize that particular decisions or events can become focal points, or new ways of thinking and acting. Strategic vision requires the patience to endure over a long period of time. [Manasse: 1989]

Often, strategic vision by the leader is viewed as hopping all over the place. The creative process has its necessary zigzags and detours. Visionary leadership takes the undefined path. It makes no sense to judge a visionary leader based on a rational planning perspective. Achieving something for the first time is truly a learning process, a continuous activity. What one has already learned strongly influences what one will learn next. Each experience shapes the next choice of direction.

Chief Cultural Monitor

A colleague, Dan McGinley, who directed the Gibault School for Boys in Terre Haute, Indiana, in 1989, wrote an editorial stating that the most important leadership task for a chief executive in a group care agency is to instill moral leadership. [Caring: 1989] He said that if the chief executive wishes the staff to be moral and to encourage children to be moral, the organization must be designed to recognize, encourage and support moral action.

The chief executive does this by recognizing the organizational culture as the primary determinant of social behavior. A chief executive is the one who establishes or maintains the culture in the organization. We have come to the realization that it is the chief executive who models and develops an employee mindset consistent with the system's values and beliefs.

Servant Leader

Children cannot grow and develop emotionally, socially or spiritually unless they are able to serve something larger than themselves. Be it one's family, a cause or an idea. In sum, the culture builds character. A transforming culture needs a servant leader with a mission to serve. Mission is defined as the extent that a person has communicable, altruistic purpose for what s/he is doing, especially for his/her vocation or profession. The servant leader is directed by a purpose larger than him/herself and a belief system that the path of life has a meaningful, worthwhile direction.

The role of servant leader requires one to believe the best is not good enough. Idealism is a key attribute of servant leadership. The servant leader understands how important it is to share the power inherent in his position as leader. This is critical as management expert, Stanley Greenleaf points out [Greenleaf: 1977]:

> *The servant leader, knowing that an organization designed for change cannot be effective without sharing power, establishes a management group with optional balance between operators and conceptualizers. This will create the needed tension amongst the group and provide the servant leader with the opportunity to demonstrate struggle, the embracing of it and the management of it. The operating talent (i.e., craftsman, secretaries, therapists, maintenance, etc.,) will move the institution toward its objectives, in a given situation, from day to day, and resolve the issues that arise as this movement takes place. This will call for interpersonal skills, sensitivity to the environment, tenacity, experience, judgment, ethical soundness, and related attributes that the day-to-day movement requires.*

Conceptualizer

A CEO needs to be a good conceptual manager. If a CEO lacks this talent, it is important to ensure that the conceptualizers on the management team play the key role in the organization. The conceptual managers have both organizational hindsight and look-around-the-corner insight. They see the organization as a whole entity and can adjust goals, analyze and evaluate operating performance, and foresee contingencies before operators do. [Greenleaf: 1977]

The talents of both conceptualizers and operators are necessary for a high level of organizational performance. The optimal balance is when both operators and conceptualizers understand one another, respect one another and depend on one another. The conceptualizers need to remain dominant. They generally recognize the need for operators, but the reverse is often not the case. This is why it is critical for a leader to ensure that conceptualizers play the key role in the organization. Doing this will create great strife until a sense of community is achieved. A sense of community surfaces in the life of the organization when individual differences and talents are celebrated as gifts. [Peck 1992] It is not about competition, but recognition of who has what talents.

Operators can get a great deal done and move an organization toward its short-term goals, but without conceptual talent, an organization can only do well within an established pattern. It cannot reform or reorganize itself when it needs to do so. The following example makes the point.

Our day care center employed a knowledgeable director and operated a well respected day care program for 16 years. Despite its public reputation and attractive building with a large traditional playground, the center had not increased its enrollment in years; enrollment was low and it was incurring significant deficits each year. The executive vice president saw an opportunity to build a new center with a unique playground and curriculum, and thereby increase enrollment, consolidate the campus and better educate pre-schoolers.

The director was threatened by the changes and used her influence to subvert innovations. When she could not enlist the support of the chief executive, she took it upon herself to covertly inform the board of directors, expressing the havoc she felt this was creating for her staff and parents. She eventually resigned, as did many of her staff. The resignations frightened the parents and threw the center into chaos. This resulted in the board questioning the viability of the program. The management team counseled us to close the center. Instead, we fought to keep it open. Two years following the director's resignation, the day care center, with its new focus, enjoyed a statewide reputation for quality and innovation, doubled in size, became profitable for the first time, and built a second center.

Integrator

In a cultural approach, all the elements within the organization interact. The integration of the organization is essential to its effectiveness. The primary, but not the sole, integrator of the organization is the chief executive. To carry out this role, s/he must possess an understanding of how the culture is put together and how the various messages are used to express the culture. By possessing this knowledge, the chief executive can assess how action in one area of the organization may or may not affect the organization in a seemingly unrelated area. The various actions also should be consistent with the organization's values and beliefs.

There are two concepts of integration: coordination and cohesion. Both are essential to providing a culture that has the power to change behavior. Coordination is the integration concept that gets the primary attention in today's management approaches. We refer to organizational psychologists, Lawrence and Lorsch's definition of integration: "A process of linking together and coordinating the work of inter-dependent sub-units in an organization." [Gannon: 1979]

Here integration refers to coordinating departments. We want to make sure that when the salesman says he will deliver the carpet on Tuesday, the factory will have had the carpet made, the retailer will have had the carpet delivered and the carpet installer will be available on Tuesday to install it.

The more differentiated an organization, or the more departments or services it has, the more integration (coordination) it demands. In business, the concept of integration, as coordination, works well if the organization produces a well-defined, commonly understood product. This is also why corporations establish their research and development departments separate from ongoing company operations. Change is something separate from a commonly understood product.

In Transformation Education, the principal product is change. Given this product, the integration means cohesiveness, not just coordination. Cohesiveness translates into the continuity of message throughout the organization. Cohesiveness is central to a mentoring culture. It is the consistency with which the wisdom principles are conveyed throughout the culture, through the environment, beliefs, systems and people. The importance of cohesiveness is readily apparent when we stop to think about it in the context of mission or unity of purpose. If the team "fell apart" or the army "crumbled" under attack, we are saying the central spiritual glue, the raison d'être, evaporated, and with that, the organization.

Chief executives in the Transformation Education culture strive for cohesiveness throughout the organization, given the natural tensions inherent in running a human services organization, as well as the nature of a change-oriented culture. [Thompson: 1967]

The inherent tensions within child-serving organizations emanate from several factors: the organization's founding principles, the professionalization of its services, the nature of its board and the impact of changing government policies.

The founders of these organizations wanted to alleviate a social problem of their own time, whether it was exploitation of children, homelessness, mental illness, etc. In essence, this is when these organizations had a culture of change and growth. When these organizations professionalized, this changed their cultures.

The professionals brought with them a belief about the etiology of the problem. They emerged from a profession that was organized to remedy it. Whether the problem was psychological imbalance, unsocialized behavior or spiritual impoverishment, specialists were hired who possessed the expertise to alleviate the problem. The key managers of these organizations were recruited from the professional staff. As a result, the daily operations of these organizations are managed in a way that is consistent with the beliefs and values of their particular profession.

The boards of these organizations became populated with members of the business, corporate and professional communities. Part of their contribution to the organization is to share with the chief executive their way of thinking and expertise. The unintended result is that the thinking and values that were consistent with the business and/or professional communities compete with the philosophical and spiritual values of the founders, or worse, supersede them.

Government funding and regulation has the unintended consequence of infusing a mode of legalistic thinking into the organization. This legalistic mindset crushes the spirit of the founding message. It creates a situation in which many staff and boards believe if they are to err, it should be on the side of protecting themselves – even at the expense of the organization or the children it serves.

The cohesiveness is a critical ingredient in determining the positive impact that the organization's culture will have on children. This is one of the greatest challenges the chief executive faces in attempting to execute Transformation Education.

Given the prospect that current organizations do not recognize the power of culture to educate, neither the board nor the staff recognize cohesion as the chief executive's responsibility. The chief executive is often considered the senior manager, whose primary job is to ensure that the organization runs smoothly. In practice, whether in higher education, public schools or human services, it is up to the individual departments or professionals to determine their own culture, as long as they are able to coordinate their actions to deliver a consistent product.

Professional conflict will arise once the chief executive takes the responsibility for communicating cohesive organizational messages reflecting the organizational culture. The chief executive is likely to be viewed as a micromanager or control freak. The chief executive is bucking the established way of doing things. Yet in the Transformation Education model, the buck stops at the chief executive's desk. S/he must ensure a cohesive system of values, beliefs, environments and systems within the organization. Without this leadership, a fragmentation of the culture results from the inconsistency of messages between the organizational culture and the subculture of each profession.

When the messages conflict, a struggle is likely to occur between the organizational culture and the subculture. The subculture feels its perspective has been overlooked. It will most often, however, boil down to a power struggle over which values will dominate the culture. The chief executive will most likely be regarded as being dictatorial for challenging the professional culture.

The chief executive usually tries to manage the departmentalization and specialization with a team approach. These teams are to ensure each individual, department and profession that their point of view will be known. This is an opportunity to defend their department's or profession's position. They're essentially equivalent to parallel play rather than a cohesive group. The chief executive can only manage departmentalization by eliminating it. The organization is the living unit. It is the organization that is the common group around which to organize and identify.

The fractionalization created by the mixed mindsets governing the organization creates inefficiency. To resolve the conflict requires the chief executive, staff, management and board to come to a common understanding. The fractionalization counteracts the concept of the therapeutic milieu, as it results in sending double and triple messages throughout the organization. This has the same effect on children as a dysfunctional family.

Developing an organizational thought process and value system consistent with the concept of change and wisdom is a key responsibility of the chief executive and the members of the management team. A conflict between Martha, the director of administrative services, and Janet, the principal, highlights the issue.

> *Janet purchased a pen and pencil set for her desk and submitted it on her expense account. It was approved by her supervisor, the chief executive, who sent it to bookkeeping for reimbursement. Janet was free to manage her own budget.*

> *Martha's responsibilitiy as director of administrative services is to review expense accounts. She ensures duplicate ordering isn't occurring, that the items are coded properly and system abuses aren't occurring. Martha worked in an underfunded social agency for twenty years before assuming her current position. When Martha saw the cost, it set off her frugal alarm. She called Janet to ask why she can't use Bic pens and number 2 pencils. Martha feels ownership for the total organization and believes it should conserve money whenever possible.*

> *Janet was angered by the call. She viewed a pen and pencil set as an unquestionable expense for three reasons: 1) Principals should establish a tone of professionalism by the look of their office. 2) All school expenses are reimbursed by the State Department of Education. The cost of a pen and pencil set was not an issue that took money from the agency budget or with which Martha had to concern herself. 3) Martha is not Janet's supervisor and had no right to question her expense account.*

> *The conflict does not just emanate from their respective backgrounds and roles. It also stems from Janet's preference for clarity. She believes only her supervisor, not her coadministrator, has a right to question her purchasing decisions. Janet is comfortable in a bureaucracy. She interprets Martha's actions as inconsistent with good management.*

> *To Janet the mere fact that Martha questions the expense account challenges her professional identify, integrity and assumptions about how an organization should operate. Martha views her question as a moral imperative of her position, an action consistent with an organization that values debate and questions assumptions. In her eyes, she is a good manager. She believes a good manager resolves the issues at the lowest level of the organization.*

Weiner points out that these tensions are prevalent in human services. These conflicts cause the chief executive to spend a great deal of time managing the tensions that exist. How does the chief executive convert these administrative tensions toward growth and change? These tensions, and the resistances they create, are both predictable and necessary. They provide the opportunity to demonstrate and interpret the wisdom principles in everyday work life. The staff conflict also provides the opportunity for the children to witness the character growth of the chief executive, staff and organization. Weiner states [Weiner: 1982]:

> *"In management, one must deal with the issues of value since everything we do, every decision we make and course of action we take, is based on our consciously or unconsciously held beliefs, attitudes and values. This being the case, the starting point of human service management is reflected upon in examination of the values of the management theory or approach that underlies the organization. It is important for the chief executive to recognize that the values that underpin the management approach to human service organizations emanate from the chief executive's own perception of human existence and reality.*

The values of the organization are the values of the chief executive. Therefore, the key task of the chief executive is to understand and make clear his/her value stance. This will automatically create a tension in the organization. Other managers and other employees may have different value stances. They might want to control decision making from their value stance, as opposed to the one expressed by the chief executive.

Innoculator

We began this book with a review of the *Hardwired to Connect* study sponsored by Dartmouth Medical School, the YMCA and the Institute for American Values. The study emphasized that children lack most is a sense of meaning and connection. The CEO's focus concentrates on the importance of meaning in the organization. That is essential. The organization must be infused with meaning, for that is what is sorely lacking in the lives of emotionally disturbed and behaviorally disturbed children.

There are two primary ways the people in the organization infuse meaning into it. One is through the employees' understanding of the beliefs and culture of the organization and

working hard to practice and maintain them. The other is through the management and supervisory staff's success as integrators. The more integrated the values and beliefs are in all aspects of the program/curriculum, the physical environment, the systems and life space interventions, the more effective they are in challenging the dysfunctional mindsets these children possess.

Role of Executive Management

The role of executive management is to:

- Capture the assumptions underlying each component of the organization's culture
- Limit the staff development program to training consistent with Transformation Education
- Hold staff accountable for the mindset of Transformation Education through the performance review system
- Control the look of the physical plant
- Ensure the organization's ceremonies and recognition systems are aligned with Transformation Education's principles, beliefs and values
- Infuse the mindset of Transformation Education in policies and program curriculum

- Design systems that are aligned with a change- and growth-oriented approach

We have continuously maintained that the primary responsibility of the leader is to design and maintain an organization that expresses wisdom, while fostering growth and change. The leader is not a lone ranger. This task requires the support and involvement of the executive management team. Capturing the messages of an organization is difficult. Simply tampering with the organizational chart or redefining the authority and responsibility of the management staff cannot accomplish it.

Change will only be effective if it permeates every aspect of the organization. A common understanding of the rules of interpretation must be shared by all staff members. For this to occur, the CEO and the top management staff need to get their hands around each component of the organizational culture: the staff development program, the performance review system, the look of the physical plant, the organization's ceremonies and recognition systems and how its policies are written and implemented. All aspects of the organization must be infused and designed with messages that are consistent with a change- and growth- oriented approach.

Role of Middle Management

The concept of manager that best fits with the Transformation Education approach is described by Marcus Buckingham and Curt Coffman in their book *First Break All The Rules.* Buckingham and Coffman did a massive study of great managers across a wide variety of organizations and reported on it in their book.

The role of supervisory staff, like the role of all management staff, is to look inward into the everyday operations of the organization. They are responsible for ensuring that the messages being sent by the people, policies, operational systems, physical environment and program/curriculum are consistent with the avowed mission, values and beliefs of the organization. Furthermore, managers are expected to grasp the work style, goals, needs and motivations of those they supervise to use these attributes to guide them in a way that will ensure the use of their talents to achieve high performance. [Buckingham & Coffman: 1999]

Role of Employees in Transformation Education

The employees in a change- and growth-oriented culture all have one role in common: maintaining the culture. This responsibility can only be actualized (1) if each employee understands the beliefs, values, expectations and assumptions that uphold the way the organization operates, (2) if each employee works diligently to ensure these values, beliefs, expectations and assumptions are expressed in the culture, and (3) if each employee contributes to the process by integrating and aligning these beliefs with all the processes and vehicles for expression throughout the organization.

This is easier said than done. What makes it difficult is how managers and employees view their jobs. It is pretty typical for the chief financial officer to see results as the most important part of what gets accomplished. The CFO will most likely comment: "If you don't make your budget goals you won't be around to share your philosophy!" The director of your educational component or your clinical staff will approach it from a different perspective. "We don't have time for all this philosophy stuff! What counts is instruction. Do the kids learn? I'm focused on the needs of the kids, not philosophy!"

	Student Prior to Admission	Enrolled Student or Student in Placement	Discharged Student
Filter on the world	HO_ _ _ _ _	ST_ _ _ _ _ _	CHO_ _ _
Adults			
School			
Future			
My Conclusions about culture:			
_____			
_____			
_____			
_____			
_____			
_____			

What is not recognized is that we can't just focus on results. Remember, our product is the change and growth of emotionally disturbed children so they can lead successful lives. One will easily understand the importance of the value messages we send to a child by the exercise we do with new hires to point out the role of each staff member in the Transformation Education approach. We begin the exercise by passing out a worksheet to each participant.

After passing out the form, we ask the staff person to write about the student's perception of adults, school and the future prior to admission into our residential program or school.

The usual response is that the student views adults as "untrustworthy," "unreliable," "inconsistent," "hostile," "insensitive." When asked how these children view the school they reply: "a place to fail," "boring," "unfriendly," "not relevant to everyday life." Their response to how the children view the future is met by replies such as, "bleak and nonexistent," "don't think about it much." We are reminded that African-American youth who come from impoverished, violent neighborhoods don't expect to live to age 30.

When these employees are asked how we expect the child will view the world following discharge from our organization, we get the opposites: "adults are seen as reliable," "consistent," "trustworthy," "caring," "sensitive." When asked how the discharged students view school they again reply with opposites such as, "fun," "friendly," "relevant," and "a place to demonstrate achievement." They believe the discharged students will see their future as hopeful and promising.

We then ask them what the children will need to change about their perceptions of adults, school and the future. The participants will point out that students will have to go through a struggle to give up their preadmission perceptions. We point out that there will be no struggle if the staff members we employ are inconsistent and insensitive, if the academics are presented in a boring and noncontextual way and if we cannot inspire them with a vision of what they can be and do.

We ask the participants to fill in the blanks: Most figure out that the words are hostile, struggle, and choice. We conclude the exercise by asking them to fill out their conclusions about culture. We take their responses and underscore the power of culture.

The only way we can truly change children's worldview is by presenting them with an alternative culture that will generate struggle. If we don't create such a culture, we actually harm the children. We reinforce their negative perception of adults and take away their opportunity to experience a different way of life. In effect, we minimize or even eliminate children's choices in life. This is truly an ethical concern. After all, the government funds we have been provided are supposed to promote change and growth, not reinforce dysfunctional or antisocial behavior.

Building Trades – the Analogy for Organizational Structure

The way the building trade is organized is analogous to the organizational concept of Transformation Education. The chief designer of the building is the architect. To be a good architect, one has to possess a vision of what is possible. The CEO plays a role akin to the principal architect. The executive management staff's roles are similar to that of the general contractor. They ensure integration of the various departments. The public relations coordinator, accountant, quality improvement coordinator and support staff play the roles reminiscent of the skilled tradespeople and the labor pool.

This same organizational structure is replicated throughout the programmatic component of the organization. The vice president of programs plays the role of general contractor and integrator of the program services. The middle management staff members have the responsibility for integrating and coordinating the work at the treatment team level. They also serve as quality control experts and construction site supervisors to help manage the everyday problems that arise. The professional staff serve as representatives of the various trades and the aides and support staff serve as the labor pool, who are responsible for carrying out assignments given to them by the tradespeople and the work site supervisors.

What follows is a more detailed discussion of the management, supervisory, professional and direct care staff in a group care setting. By providing this example, we believe the reader will gain a true understanding of the level of detail and specificity needed to operate the Transformation Education approach effectively.

Application to Group Care

Before we can discuss any of the roles in group care, it is important to share a basic assumption. Most group care programs are less effective than they could be. We believe the reason is that the responsibilities of the positions are too broad and basically unachievable along with a lack of expertise of the direct care staff.

The role descriptions outlined below were designed to minimize turnover of the direct care staff, program supervisors and clinical staff assigned to residential units. By minimizing turnover, each could focus on their primary job responsibilities. With excessive turnover, they are constantly reacting to crisis situations that staff shortages leave in their wake. Unfilled vacancies in the direct care ranks and problem behaviors are provoked by poor management practices and budget shortfalls. With this in mind, let us begin our discussion with the role of the director of the group care program.

Director of Group Care

By director of group care we are referring to the department head for a residential or group home program. This individual's role should be limited to managing the day-to-day operations of the program. This includes staff recruitment, training and supervision, monitoring the fiscal budget of the program, ensuring a safe and secure residence and meeting regulatory compliance mandates.

The director of group care also is responsible for managing admission and discharge of residents and leading two of the four weekly meetings—the administrative team meeting and the weekly staff meeting. The purpose and content of these meetings will be discussed under the chapter on systems. His/her supervisory role extends to overseeing the work of the site supervisors for each group home or living unit, the clinical staff, the secretarial staff and consultants such as dieticians, nurses, psychiatrists, etc.

It is important to note that the program director is not responsible for supervising the programmatic component of the group care program. This component is the responsibility of the program and design specialist, who reports to the vice president of programs (chief programming officer).

Nonetheless, the everyday responsibilities of the program director are immense, as are the responsibilities of the program design specialist. It is important not to mix or add on to their designated responsibilities. That will result in diluting the focus of program operations.

Under the Transformation Education model, the director of group care limits his/her focus to ensuring that the direct care staff and supervisory staff are cooperating with and supporting the efforts of the program design specialist; that the education, health, clinical and safety needs of the children are being met; and the physical plant is in good shape. The director of group care's budget responsibility does not extend to the programmatic component of the program. This is the responsibility of the program design specialist.

Program and Design Specialist

The program and design specialist reports to the vice president of programs. S/he ensures the implementation and execution of the Transformation Education curriculum in the group care program (see the chapter 8). The program and design specialist is responsible for the program budget, the design detailing the daily structure and routine and aesthetics. The specialist stimulates the learning of knowledge and skills by the direct care and supervisory staff. S/he teaches them by demonstrating the activity and then auditing them as they carry out the activity.

The weekly program meeting is led by the program and design specialist. This is where the execution of the program, structure and routines are discussed and reviewed on a weekly basis. The development of systems, purchase of materials, planning of special events, and preparation and management of budgets to carry out the group care program come under the purview of this position.

This position calls for a person with a creative vision to visualize and design projects that promote learning and enhance physical environment. This is akin to a window designer in a department store or a "Martha Stewart." They perform the makeover of the group care environment, which traditionally has an institutional look and lacks sophistication.

Their displays have a sense of "hominess" that excites the senses, stimulates the intellect and touches the emotions. This person is in charge of purchasing, transporting, fabricating and installing all the elements needed to achieve the desired effect of the project. Under this guidance, the transformations of the physical environment are photographed and retained in a photographic library. The decorative photos will support public relations initiatives, marketing materials and special events.

In their role, they skillfully present a contextual framework for understanding the relationships of their designs to the curriculum/thematic plan and the logistics needed to ensure successful implementation of the activities by the youth life educators and supervisory staff.

Student Coordinator (Case Manager)

The student coordinator works closely with the school counselor (clinician) and has the main responsibility for tracking appointments, maintaining contact with the school and managing paperwork associated with each placement. The student coordinator coordinates and schedules medical, dental and vision appointments, as well as all services with community agencies, schools, therapists and psychiatrists. S/he communicates all essential information to staff and family members and makes certain important information in each student resident's case record is filed and up to date.

School Counselor (Clinician)

The school counselor meets the mental health needs of the student residents. That means s/he counsels and supports their families and oversees the development of the growth plan goals for each student. The student records are also monitored by the school counselor. It is also his/her responsibility to lead the student's quarterly growth-plan meeting. (The structure of the meeting and its operation is discussed in chapter 5.)

Youth Life Educator Supervisor

The youth life education supervisor is the player-coach. The supervisor works side by side with direct care practitioners. S/he is directly involved in caring for the students and directing the milieu program. Online supervision is deployed, meaning the skills and practice of youth life education work are best taught by demonstration. One of the techniques the supervisor uses in online supervision is *modeling*. Modeling in this instance refers to practicing youth life education and problem solving-skills. Whenever time permits, the supervisor solicits from the worker the particulars (timing, tone of voice, wording, etc.) of what was observed.

Hopefully, the youth life educator learns by an *evaluation process* the concepts behind what intervention has or should have taken place. The discussion occurs at the time of the intervention, or later as part of a formal supervisory session.

Underlying the learning process is the concept of *anticipation*. This refers to the youth life education supervisor helping the worker think through the consequences of an intervention, program or plan prior to its inception.

Directing is demonstrating an intervention or a way to execute the job, for example, co-leading a group meeting or a confrontation with a student. The last component of online supervision is providing *a tone for learning*. In this scenario, the supervisor invites the worker to criticize the supervisor's intentions with students and solicits the youth life educator's suggestions of how the situation could have been handled more effectively.

Youth Life Educator

Most organizations refer to this staff position as child care worker. In Transformation Education, we emphasize education, hence the change in job title. Before we can discuss this role in a change-oriented culture we need to address issues of job turnover of direct care practitioners and the necessity to professionalize the role.

The Burnout Myth

Burnout of youth life education workers happens most often when the job is poorly designed and ill conceived and the organizational supports are not adequately in place. We believe the burnout does not have much to do with stress, poor hiring and lack of training. We agree with Rodrich Durkin's analysis. He writes [Durkin: 1983]:

> *For too many years this group has worked in programs that are wasteful, inefficient, and unresponsive to the needs of children. In these ill conceived and inappropriately structured programs, child care workers are chronically over stressed and forced to work at cross purposes, they lack authority and pay commensurate with their responsibility, and they are vastly underutilized.*
>
> *The effects of these stresses were driven home to me by a youngster in a residential treatment program while I worked as a child care worker. He pointed out that the child care workers came in happy and enthusiastic, enjoying the long hours and the excitement of working with the kids; the kids came in messed up, depressed, out of jail and foster homes, etc. Upon leaving, however, the kids were happier, had a few good years, and life seemed not so bleak, while the child care workers left drinking heavily, flunking out of school, getting divorces, wrecking their cars, etc.*
>
> *With few exceptions, we have yet to achieve the therapeutic milieu which Pinet described in his moral management therapy some two hundred years ago. This suggests that our treatment programs continue to be ill conceived and dysfunctionally organized, and that the resulting stresses are most felt by child care workers.*

Focus on Pathology – The Best You Can Get to Is Zero

Durkin puts forth the hypothesis that Al Trieshman, in his classic book, *The Other 23 Hours*, set back the development of the child-care work profession. Durkin believes that prior to

Trieshman writing his book there was only one hour devoted to pathology (therapy) and the other twenty-three were used as a holding tank. Trieshman drew child-care work into the therapeutic endeavor with Life Space Interviewing and manipulating the milieu so twenty-three more hours could be devoted to pathology. Durkin states [Durkin: 1983]:

> *Such a continual focus on pathology raises many problems in terms of self-fulfilling prophecies and iatrogenic illness. If normal, fully socialized adults were subject for just a year to a chronic schizophrenic milieu in the back wards of almost any state hospital, many would develop an iatrogenic and choric schizophrenic syndrome. Children acculturated insidiously as it might be, to the patient role, are at far greater risk. ... The richness and opportunities of everyday life can be better utilized to promote competence in school, work, relation to others, job skills, etc. The skills of raising and treating children are very different. Those good at therapy are not necessarily good at childcare work, and vice versa.*

Durkin goes on to say that the highest priority of group care is to raise children by promoting their competence and normal growth and development. Therapy should be used only to treat pathology that gets in the way of the child's pursuit of competence, or be limited to a regularly scheduled office visit.

Furthermore, competence and pathology may not be opposite ends of a continuum but may be independent personality dimensions. Curing pathology does not mean normal growth; development can and will resume unimpeded. In any event, competence and normal growth and development need to be vigorously promoted, if growth is to occur in this population of children. As a result, the role of the youth life educator is to normalize the child's environment and emphasize the teaching of skills over the treatment of pathology.

The first step in developing competent youth life education staff is to limit their role to carrying out the activities of daily curriculum as defined in the residential program manual and planned by the program design specialist. Limiting the role does not make it any less complex. The mindset one needs is tied to an educational model, having as its intent to teach life skills and values. This model focuses on health and growth and reinforces the strength of each student while recognizing their limitations.

The youth life educator creatively uses available resources to integrate the components of daily living in an educational manner. The specific competencies of this job are listed in Appendix 3.

People and Change

Our discussion to date has focused on everything that is needed to deploy Transformation Education in an organization: its philosophy, the values, the environment, the program/curriculum and the systems. However, we must never forget that people are people. All the in-house training will not be sufficient to attain mastery of these concepts. Adult learners do not give up old habits easily. Chapter 9 will discuss the issue of staff resistance and what can be done to overcome it.

CHAPTER 7
Physical Environment as a Cultural Communicator

Principle: All life on this planet is connected in profound and countless subtle ways.

First we shape our buildings and thereafter they shape us! –Sir Winston Churchill

Prisons do an excellent job of matching their physical environment to their program philosophy. A prison says: You have lost your freedom and independence. We will control you. The physical aspects of the environment are consistent with the purpose of the facility. The design of the prison structure is so effective it even controls the staff. The guards are constantly reminded about the importance of security and control.

All environments have a message designed in them. Schools were designed to prepare workers for the Industrial Revolution. Subjects and curricula were designed to be taught in a sequence in a compartmentalized way. Desks were bolted to the floor in rows in an assembly line fashion. To standardize the classrooms, procedures dictated how many lumens would light the desktops. This was an assembly line design for education. It prepared the population to work in an industrial age.

We are now in a global age, where the social, political, scientific, economic and business institutions are in a turbulent environment. Knowledge is exploding at an exponential rate. This requires organizations such as schools and other child-serving organizations to redesign the messages in their physical environments. The building design now must be in sync with the world our children live in.

The message of the future is "connectedness." This message is the other end of the spectrum from assembly line, reductionist thinking. Connectedness translates into visible connections between purposes and everyday learning experiences. The fit between organizational design and the needs of the workforce and society was the reason we were so successful at industrializing our nation in the past. As has already been stated, schools were designed in a way that prepared the student for a competitive, effective product-making economy.

If we achieved this fit between the design of child-serving institutions and society's needs in the industrial age, we can achieve it again with a new model. We would want today's schools equipped to foster integrated thinking, to enhance critical thinking and problem solving, to demonstrate the connectedness between lifelong learning and its application to everyday living and to emphasize respect for nature and the importance of caring for the environment.

Schools are not the only child-serving organizations ignoring the impact of the design message on the child. Many child-serving organizations continue to "dress" and design their organizations to send messages of a control- and rule-oriented approach to life. Instead of having isolation or quiet rooms, many organizations now have nice carpeting on the walls rather than bare cement block walls. In these instances, we have not engaged in new thinking, but have dressed up the old.

We say re-create the physical environments within schools and child-caring organizations. Foster transformation. Do so in such a way that the physical environment is compatible with the science of learning. How can we continue to justify the dysfunctional, impoverished and toxic environment many children experience daily? We will present some examples that demonstrate how this can be done in a group care and school setting.

The Multi-Sensory De-escalation Room: A New Approach to Isolation

In Transformation Education, our purpose is to promote growth and change in the students we serve. We firmly believe that children with severe emotional and behavioral disabilities have the capacity to change their maladaptive patterns of thinking and behaving. These patterns have developed in response to neglect, abuse, violence and deprivation. While genuine change always happens within an individual child, committed, well-trained professionals can aid children immensely in learning and internalizing new behaviors.

Many children entering child-serving organizations have very little internal control of their thinking and behavior. Consequently, they rely on external forces to control their behavior for them. They require specialized environments in which behavioral control resources are available. Since the average home and public schools do not have these behavioral resources, a child in our programs must transform from an externally controlled child and student to an internally controlled child and student. When that happens, they find success and can return home and/or reenter public school.

A child-serving organization's physical environment, curriculum, behavior management approach and human resources must all assist the student in moving along the growth continuum. The challenge for a child is to move from extreme external behavioral control to age-appropriate internal behavioral control. In other words, the organization must be prepared to handle the student whose behavior requires maximum external control while simultaneously maintaining an environment in which internal behavioral control is valued, taught and rewarded. The Multi-Sensory De-escalation room (MSD) is a useful tool in helping students navigate this continuum.

The Isolation Room Alternative

The purpose of "quiet rooms" or "isolation rooms" is to ensure the safety of staff, other children and the acting-out child by "isolating" the child in a secure (locked) room until the child has "quieted" and no longer poses a threat to others. These rooms are typically Spartan in décor to minimize stimulation to the child. Often, shoes, belts and other items of clothing are removed from the student to preclude the risk of self-injurious behavior (see page 125).

This use of a secured isolation room represents the extreme in external behavioral control. It amounts to incarceration. The child is locked up, isolated and in some cases, "punished" for his/her behavior. Once a child quiets, staff may process and discuss the behavioral outburst with the child until compliance, as defined by the staff, is achieved. In part, the child is conditioned through negative reinforcement to suppress maladaptive behavior. If the child complies with the demands of the staff, the child is allowed to get out of isolation. While this teaches the child to adjust behavior to achieve the specific outcome of getting out of the isolation room, it likely does not teach the child how to avoid getting placed in the room in the first place.

It is true that isolating an acting-out child can be effective in de-escalating him or her. However, there are limits to the positive, applicable life skills a child learns from the experience of being locked in isolation. The child is conditioned to rely on a person and a place outside him/herself to suppress the maladaptive behavior.

Transformation Education believes an out-of-control child may construe the use of isolation/locked door seclusion in ways that are unintended. Its impact may inhibit growth by sending negative messages. The child may perceive that s/he is "bad" or "uncontrollable" and that is why he or she is punished by being locked in isolation. Or, that his/her feelings are as frightening to others as they are to him/her, and nobody knows how to help. So s/he is locked in isolation. The cultural messages sent by use of locked isolation are hard to sugarcoat. They are harsh and severe and frightening. It is difficult to learn new skills when you are locked away alone.

Transformation Education has created an alternative to the locked isolation room. We call it the multi-sensory de-escalation (MSD) room. Combining concepts from several disciplines, MSD rooms are designed to provide children meaningful learning experiences before, during and after a crisis to help them progress toward effective internal regulation of their behavior.

The MSD Room: A Blending of Approaches

Transformation Education embraces the concept that a time of crisis can be an opportunity for learning. That has prompted the design of the space traditionally called the "quiet" or "seclusion" room as a *specialized behavioral classroom* (see page 125). These secure, attractive, functional spaces are named "Multi-Sensory De-escalation Rooms." Envision the scene: soft music, wall murals and indestructible foam tunnels encourage the out-of-control child to interact with the environment as a way of calming down. The ability to use the resources in the environment to calm one's emotions is a critical step in the process of behavioral self-regulation. The MSD room can be experienced positively by the child as a resource and not negatively as punishment.

The murals, manipulatives and music promote engagement and interaction between the child and staff in a nonadversarial manner. Though some children may have to be therapeutically held for safety reasons, many children not ready for staff interaction learn to hide from staff in the tunnel until they are ready to talk. Or, they take a time-out by looking out the window or by listening to the music. Staff are trained to be sensitive both to the child's need for space, and to the child's need to talk and be heard when ready. Though the child's space needs are respected, the child is never left alone or isolated in the MSD room. When used effectively, the MSD room's décor, comfort and nonthreatening environment are experienced by the child as a personal space, more meaningful and ultimately more useful than an isolation room. The concept of the MSD room arose from a blending of three related but distinct disciplines: applied brain research, occupational therapy principles and child development theory.

Applied Brain Research

Brain-based research instructs us that children in aroused emotional states are optimally primed for learning. It has also demonstrated that the strongest learning occurs when multiple senses of the child are involved. As a result, two important pillars of the MSD room approach have been established.

First, children should be engaged in interaction while still in an emotionally aroused state. Contrary to the isolation room approach, children do not need to be completely calmed down and compliant for learning to occur. In fact, if too calm, learning is not as effective. Rather, staff should begin teachable interactions while students' emotional states are still aroused to achieve the most effective learning.

Second, the space used for de-escalation of aggressive behavior should engage and soothe the senses—not dull the senses. The space should be soothing to multiple senses—sight, sound, touch and smell. The space used for de-escalation should offer students and staff a laboratory to experiment with sensations that result in a child exercising some control over emotions.

Occupational Therapy Principles

Occupational therapy teaches that the sensory qualities of certain activities have a modulating influence on a child's behavior. These activities help students organize sensory input, resulting in an "integration" of sensory stimuli. Sensory integration is the ability to take information in through the senses and combine it with previous information, memories and knowledge stored in the brain, and to make a meaningful response. All of us depend on adequate sensory integration functions to carry out daily living tasks. Improved sensory integration in children can lead to better self-regulation and more effective internal control.

Acting out by some children reflects their inability to meet their sensory needs in a socially appropriate way. These children need help in reintegrating their sensory input through the use of specific activities, stimuli and structures. This sensory reintegration training teaches children how to soothe themselves and develops an increased awareness of their body, senses, emotions and behaviors.

These occupational therapy principles encourage us to use the space for de-escalation. Staff members learn to teach children specific activities to help reintegrate their sensory experience and calm themselves when angry, frustrated or threatened. Staff and children effectively use manipulatives in the room to help with the reintegration process, the expression of emotion and the development of self-control.

Most important, occupational therapy demonstrates the power of proactively using the MSD rooms to help students develop internal control instead of using the rooms solely as a reaction to extreme behavior. The rooms are used on a planned, routine basis to deliver "sensory diets." Sensory diets are a series of customized sensory integration activities for each student. They result in the prevention of acting-out episodes as students are taught to self-regulate their senses, emotions and behaviors prior to an extreme behavioral incident. Even though many of the sensory activities are used for children with sensory integration dysfunction, children don't need to have a sensory dysfunction to benefit from the activities.

This proactive, problem-solving method minimizes and virtually eliminates the punitive aspects of a locked isolation environment. This happens even when the MSD room is utilized in response to a behavioral incident.

The Basic MSD Room Manipulatives

The manipulatives available to assist the child in developing self-regulation are briefly described below. These tools can be used proactively (used in a scheduled way as a child's sensory diet) or reactively (given to a child to assist self-regulation or "calming" him/herself in the MSD room).

Six standard items used to outfit an MSD room with sensory manipulatives are divided into two categories: tools used during behavior episodes to calm the child and tools to assist the child during the processing of behavior and preparation to leave the MSD room.

The tools used to calm during a crisis include a large, padded therapy tunnel; weighted blankets; and rounded, brightly padded cushions referred to as "bolsters." The basic idea behind the use of the blankets and the tunnel is that pressure on the body (like a big hug) is very calming. Deep pressure is often very calming to children and can be experienced by lying on our joints (when we lie down and curl up); sitting or lying under something heavy; and by active movement with resistance-lifting, pushing, pulling and carrying heavy things. The tunnel is a snug place that puts pressure on the body. The tunnel can also block out light and the sight of other people for the child that needs safe space. The weighted blanket works the same way, providing the child a controlled hug that the child completely directs. The bolsters provide a safe object on which to act out aggression and are used as a comfortable place to sit or lie down.

The tools used to help children wind down and prepare to leave the MSD room include: Thera Putty; Bendeez plastic fidgets and vibrating pens. Thera Putty is hard to pull and twist, as it does not tear like clay. The pressure and resistance to the fingers, hands and arms are calming and relaxing. Bendeez are another kind of resistive manipulative that children can bend into shapes and twist. Bendeez are particularly useful when children seem "antsy" or need ongoing help calming down. Vibrating pens provide strong pressure and are effective with children who prefer to draw or write while processing rather than verbalizing.

There are scores of additional manipulatives that can be added to this list. As children develop regular sensory diets, tools will emerge that are unique to the child or a particular group of children. These staples will provide a solid start to the use of sensory integration activities in the MSD room. These activities are discussed later in the chapter.

The Greenspan Development Model

The third approach having an impact on how the MSD room is used is Dr. Stanley Greenspan's developmental containment theory. [Greenspan: 1995] Greenspan's theory of how children develop emotionally serves as a roadmap for staff in structuring MSD room interactions to help children grow and develop from their experience. Like the guidance provided through occupational therapy principles, Greenspan's model gives the staff specific intervention techniques for students needing the specialized environment of the MSD room.

Greenspan's developmental growth process plots children along six separate stages of emotional development. An individual student may have a number of coexistent developmental levels, depending upon the skills or stresses that are challenging the child. In the aggregate, each child can be identified at a specific developmental level for the purpose of evaluation, planning and MSD room intervention. Greenspan teaches that adults should engage children in interactions in a particular conversation or situation that helps children move from their present developmental level to the next highest level.

Consequently, staff should assess and identify the developmental stage of each student in the MSD room. Staff should involve the students in interactions that build emotional skills and move students toward regulation of their sensory nervous systems. In the context of the MSD room, the staff members use the tools provided by the occupational therapy staff and/or techniques suggested in the Greenspan theory that move children through the four nonverbal developmental stages toward self-regulating behavior. A brief description of Greenspan's developmental stages and techniques for assisting children through these stages is listed below.

Regulation Stage – When children's behavior is nondirected and not responsive to their environment, they are functioning at the regulation stage of development. At this stage, children's individual sensory needs must be met. For example, turn the switch on for soft music, dim the lights, use tools designed to apply deep muscle pressure, and/or create rhythmic motion.

Engagement Stage – When children can connect and begin relating on an emotional level via non-verbal communication, they are at the engagement stage. Helpful responses by adults that foster engagement at this stage of communication are: mirroring behavior; responding to the children's need for physical distance or closeness by positioning themselves in the opposite corner of the room or closer to the children; use of simple distraction such as tapping, wondering out loud or offering a sensory diet manipulative.

Simple and Boundary-Defining Gestures – When children use and respond to gestures, staff members should use such gestures as shrugging their shoulders, and using exaggerated facial expressions, hand gestures and touch.

Complex and Problem-Solving Gestures – When children have an ability to communicate by connecting gestures and problem-solving then staff should try to extend the gestural exchange. At this stage, the adult's verbalizations should focus on the meaning of the interaction.

Functional Emotional Levels – Verbal: Adults move the children from nonverbal communication by speaking to them in short phrases. This helps children label the emotions they are experiencing. This also helps children separate their emotions from their actions. This is the time to explore alternatives to the way they were acting. For example, "What else could you have done to tell me you are angry other than throw the chair?" If children cannot or will not give you alternatives, then you suggest alternatives that are more socially acceptable.

Complex Symbolic Language and Ideas Stage – This is the stage when a give-and-take conversation occurs. If the child tells you he threw his books because he hates math, you say, "Why didn't you raise your hand and ask for my help rather than throw the book?" He replies, "You are always talking to someone else when I need your help!" You now have a real conversation going and can work out the problem.

Applied brain research, occupational therapy principles and the Greenspan model allow us to devise an alternative approach to working with extreme emotions and behavior in children. This blended methodology results in the following basic principles for the use of the MSD rooms:

1. The primary purpose of the MSD room is to teach children to soothe themselves and regulate their senses, emotions and behaviors.
2. Staff should be trained in and prepared to apply sensory diet activities that utilize the visual, tactile, auditory and olfactory stimulation available in the MSD room to help children organize their senses and gain control of their bodies.
3. Staff should be trained in and prepared to apply Greenspan's engagement activities that use heightened emotional states to move children toward increased regulation of their emotions.
4. Staff should be trained to use MSD rooms both proactively and reactively.
5. MSD rooms are never to be used in a manner that communicates punishment or negativity to the child.
6. Children are never to be isolated or left alone in MSD rooms.
7. There are no locks in or on the MSD room.

Planned Use of the MSD Room

The planned use of the MSD room prior to a child's physically out-of-control behavior can help reduce both the frequency and severity of aggression. Like all behavior, physical aggression has a function intended to help a child meet a particular need. By proactively using the MSD rooms, staff can help children avoid physical aggression by providing both emotional and physical alternatives to meet these needs.

Begin with an Individual Regulation Plan for managing children with aggressive, violent behavior. Typically, the Individual Regulation Plan for children that present violent behavior should be developed within 30 days of their enrollment and will serve as the guiding document for management of their self-regulatory behavior.

The Individual Regulation Plan has three components: (1) Sensory Evaluation and Sensory Diet Plan (2) Social/Emotional Interventions and (3) De-escalation Interventions. Coordination of the Individual Regulation Plan is the responsibility of the clinical services director and the clinical staff. (See Appendix 5 for Individual Regulation Plans for Aggressive Child, Defiant Child, Inattentive Child and Highly Sensitive Child.)

Sensory Evaluation and Sensory Diet Plan

The first step in self-regulatory growth planning is the evaluation of the child's sensory status. Conducted by the occupational therapy (OT) staff, this evaluation results in a measure of the child's current level of sensory integration awareness and skills. From this measure, the OT staff develops a "sensory diet," a menu of activity therapies customized to meet the child's sensory development needs. The sensory diet is categorized into activities that the OT staff carries out with the child. These are activities that other staff may use with the child.

The sensory diet activities are provided to children in the MSD rooms rather than being limited to the OT room. The visual, tactile and auditory resources are available for staff use in the MSD room to help children develop their self-regulation skills. The OT staff trains the non-OT staff in the proper facilitation of the sensory diet activities. Periodically, they supervise the staff to make sure it is being done properly. In addition, OT staff conduct follow-up evaluations to measure the progress children are making in sensory integration function and adjust the sensory diet as necessary. There are sensory diet activities that cannot be facilitated/delivered except by a qualified OT therapist.

It is anticipated that high-profile children (i.e., those who most frequently act out in a physical manner) will be using the MSD room for proactive sensory diet activities daily. The use of the MSD room in this manner will have a dramatic impact. Children will identify the MSD room as a place of comfort, pleasant stimuli and exploration–and not as a place of stress, struggle, judgment and restriction. Staff will demonstrate to themselves the calming, growth-focused experiences by the children. They do not see the MSD rooms as convenient depositories for the most out-of-control children. The disciplined use of the MSD room in this proactive fashion results in a decrease in assault-like behavior. The children using the rooms develop a greater awareness of their senses and increased skill at regulating their senses under stress. Specifically, children will identify and effectively utilize sensory stimuli that calm and regulate their emotions during times of threat, anger, fear or frustration.

Social/Emotional Intervention

Clinical and psychiatric staff provide an initial assessment of an individual child's developmental level using Greenspan's model of child development. Based on the assessment, clinical staff will design activities that promote developmental growth for children whose developmental age lags behind their chronological level. Enhanced developmental skills are designed for children at age-appropriate levels.

Many of these activities can be found in Greenspan's work *The Challenging Child.* These activities can be provided by nonclinical staff with proper training and supervision. Combined with sensory diet activities, these developmentally focused activities provide a powerful therapeutic experience during the proactive sessions in the MSD rooms. Clinical and psychiatric staff periodically review the child's developmental status and adjust the social/emotional interventions as necessary. Evaluation of a child's progress should show a direct correlation between a child's advancement and stabilization at the age-appropriate developmental level along with a decrease in the frequency of assault incidents.

The Individual Regulation Plan form lists the social/emotional interventions commonly used for the defiant child, the aggressive child, the inattentive child and the highly sensitive child.

Individual Regulation Plan

Children newly admitted to a child-serving organization are likely to have behavioral histories of assault. The staff can anticipate the behavior continuing. The above-mentioned interventions likely will have to be applied over time to have an impact on that behavior. Consequently, the proactive use of the MSD rooms will become the primary focus of the staff's efforts. The MSD room will also serve as safe spaces for children whose behavior escalates to violence or imminent threat of violence. The key to the effective use of the MSD lies in the preplanning of such use with staff. Consequently, children likely to use the MSD room frequently to regulate their behavior should have an Individual Regulation Plan. This plan describes the specific interventions to be utilized if and when the child engages in out-of-control physical behavior.

These plans, at a minimum, contain information on the child's pattern of aggressive behavior, the triggers for the behavior, recommended de-escalation techniques, safety practices and examples of alternative behaviors to be taught to the child. Activities from the sensory diet and the social/emotional interventions to minimize the reactive use of the MSD rooms also should be included. The aim of the Individual Regulation Plan is to assist the child through self-regulation should the MSD room need to be used in a reactive way.

We cannot underestimate the importance of planning for an individual child's use of violent behavior. Typically, use of an isolation room or safe space is reactive to a child's outburst. By developing an Individual Regulation Plan that predetermines staff response to a particular child's violence, the organization can maximize the therapeutic impact of each response by customizing the response to the emotional and physical needs of an acting-out child. As a result, the child should respond more favorably to intervention, staff should be less stressed and the needs of the child more quickly met.

We are advocating a substantial change in the approach to treating physical aggression. The MSD room provides the child-serving organization with a unique physical environment to complement a new strategy. Careful evaluation of children's needs and pre-planned interventions to address those needs are the hallmarks of the MSD room approach. By combining sensory diets and social/emotional interventions, the staff can proactively use the MSD room daily. The goal is to foster internal controls by decreasing the frequency, duration and intensity of aggressive behavior.

The MSD room approach is a sophisticated model that will require great cooperation by all levels of staff. The implementation of such an approach through a strength-based therapeutic focus will require:

1. An adaptation of job roles
2. A significant emphasis on evaluation during the child's first several months in the program
3. Careful data collection on children's progress
4. Substantial emphasis on staff training
5. Cross-supervision by various disciplines for successful execution

The benefit to children is that they gain greater self-control over a shorter time. It is well worth the effort.

Interiors and Furnishings Consistent with a Transformation Education Approach

Just as our language, behaviors and practices radiate a powerful message, so does the physical environment. Transformation Education expresses caring and promotes struggle. The physical environment promotes struggle when it sends a message that challenges, overwhelms or creates culture shock to the mindset of the child. This heightens awareness and interest. A challenging experience motivates learning and fosters retention of the learning. Imagine being faced with all that silverware and all those dishes at a formal dinner and not knowing what to do. In a situation like this, the environment grabs your attention. You scan the table setting. You are motivated to learn and expand your level of sophistication.

The majority of children referred to child-serving organizations come from poverty backgrounds and live in a "black and white" world. Those more advantaged have the experience to see shades of gray. Problem-solving ability and the capacity to see alternatives and gradients offers an advantage in today's world. The ability to see more shades of gray, i.e., increased sensibility, is developed through everyday experiences with sophisticated environments. The more sophisticated, varied and challenging the environment, the greater the opportunity for learning.

When dealing with emotionally disturbed children from low-income backgrounds, the organization needs to send messages to the child.

- "We have high expectations for you."
- "You are a valued person."
- "There are so many beautiful things in the environment that require you to exert control over your behavior."
- "You can succeed and will be successful."
- "We foster creative problem solving here."

A more aesthetically appealing, challenging and interesting physical environment helps to make children act in a less primitive way. The brain craves diversity and stimulation. Brain research confirms that physical environments have powerful effects on children's cognitive and emotional functioning. Environments with quality facilities and equipment, inviting atmospheres, high learner expectations and small-group interaction strengthen neural connections and aid in long-term memory, planning and motivation.

Researchers have found that a building's conditions have an effect on delinquent behavior, academic performance and absenteeism. [Cash: 1997] Both the interior and exterior of a child-serving organization have an impact on learning and behavior. Children exposed to adequate green space (trees, shrubbery, gardens and lawns) have better attention spans, cognition and mental reflection. [Kuo: 2001] The access to a beautiful garden or babbling brook can facilitate children's recovery from mental fatigue and make them more receptive to concentration and mental focus. The quality of facilities, coupled with strong academic programs, appear to be conditions essential to learning.

Conversely, schools and group homes with shattered windows, broken-down restrooms, leaky roofs, insufficient lighting and cramped space have a significant negative impact on cognition. Deteriorating facilities also have adverse impacts on the emotional health and performance of students, teachers and administrators. Overcrowding and poor lighting have been shown to distract the brain from deep learning. [Heschong: 1999]

Environmental impact is achieved through creating a well-dressed facility. By that, we mean a facility, like a well-dressed individual, has harmony and balance, and projects a certain character. It is a physical environment that is positive, upbeat, enjoyable and emotionally warm in mood and tone. It emphasizes aesthetic appeal, stimulates curiosity, develops sensibilities and establishes high expectations. It projects a character that is sophisticated in appearance; warm in tone; rich in colors; harmonious in balance; dynamic in character; individualized by facility, unit and room; appealing, open and comfortable. This is achieved through the furnishings and the interior decorating. The pictures of the group homes we operate at The Children's Guild are contrasted with those of a typical group home. The photos beginning on p. 118 portray the power of the environment.

Many times child-serving organizations ignore the principle of individuality and furnish living units the same way. All the furniture is grouped around the television. The room has a stark appearance. They lock things out of the reach of the children. The uniformity sends a message of social control and a rule-oriented way of thinking.

To emphasize individuality, each bedroom should be painted a different shade or wallpapered differently with window treatments that complement the décor. Some rooms should be carpeted; others should have bare wood floors or area rugs. Bedrooms can be carpeted with different colors or textures. Even hardwood floors can have various shades of wood, i.e., some rich tones while others are bleached, some painted. Each room can have a different look, and the desks and beds do not all have to look the same.

Rooms can be comfortable within a sophisticated context. We are not implying expensive, but we do mean sophisticated. Sophistication is important when dealing with youth from socially and economically deprived backgrounds. It heightens their sensibilities to nuance and better prepares them for sharpening their outlook so they eventually can access higher income jobs and relate to middle-class employers. The environment is also designed to be powerful as opposed to muted.

In reality it costs no more to achieve the environment described above than what is currently spent by group care facilities on uninspiring furnishings and buildings. But it does require more attention to design and detail.

We know of a detention facility built to house 10 youths for the cost of $400,000 in the 1980's. It had cement block wall and all types of security systems with chairs so heavy no one could lift them to throw. During the same period we built a well-designed and furnished living unit for 10 children for $400,000 the year following the construction of the detention facility. The big difference was that the detention home looked like a new jail. Our living unit was furnished like it could be showcased in *Better Homes and Gardens*.

Alignment of Environments with Program/Curriculum

Interior design should reinforce the essential messages. The surroundings should reflect our connection to nature and spirituality. By having silk and real plants arranged throughout living units, a warm tone is established. Small animals, such as birds, hamsters, cats, fish and rabbits are also placed in the environment. Fresh and salt water fish aquariums help to create an aesthetic tone, stimulate questions about the natural world and develop an appreciation for God's creations. The plants and creatures provide an opportunity to teach caring and issues related to death and loss.

Having a physical fitness room in the living unit sends the message of the importance of wellness. Artwork of nutritious vegetables and foods could hang in the kitchen. Furniture should be arranged to allow for easy conversation between two or three individuals.

The importance of learning is communicated by the ready access to books, a computer, newspapers and magazines. The magazines purchased should reflect diversity and difference. This is accomplished by purchasing African-American, Asian and Hispanic periodicals for children to browse or read. Picture books, magazines (*Ebony, National Geographic, Popular Science, Boys Life, Seventeen*) and newspapers add to the decor and send a strong message of the organization's value on literacy. A sound system, musical instruments, pottery, sculpture and puppets displayed around the living unit create an appealing, fun atmosphere that underscores the importance of the arts and self-expression. The outdoors and the opportunity to care for animals and plants can be integrated with indoor living through the addition of pets and plants. In this rich environment, children thrive because of the variety of visual, tactile and sensory experiences.

Staff's Role and the Physical Environment

It is critical that the organization design the physical environment so that the design and aesthetics are integrated to coincide with the organizational beliefs, values and curriculum. The staff assist each child in adjusting to the new physical environment.

It is the job of educators to help students become more sensitive to the environment. We assist with the display and personalization of students' possessions. It is critical to understand that this is not an attempt to stifle individuality. We intend to challenge and assist students in changing their overall mindsets and approaches. By immersing students in a contrasting, pleasing physical environment, we set their expectations. The staff facilitates students reactions to the standards set by the environment.

Infusion of Meaning into the Physical Environment

The physical environment can be one of the strongest vehicles for expressing meaning in an organization. There are several reasons for this. There is no better way to understand and experience the diversity and commonality of humanity than through art. For art is the one language that seems to touch children when words do not. Rudolf Steiner, founder of the Waldorf School movement, helps us understand why. "Color is not just seen with the eyes, it is experienced." The design and visual appearance of the classroom, school, living units and grounds truly touch children. They express how we feel about them and what we value. The physical appearance of the facilities children inhabit is more than an extra. It is a constant subliminal message of our connectedness to humanity and our spiritual nature.

Transformation Education School Environments vs. Traditional School Environments

Transformation Education Exterior School Entrance

Conventional School Exterior Entrance

Transformation Education Interior School Entrance

Conventional Interior School Entrance

Transformation Education Cafeteria

Conventional School Cafeteria

Transformation Education Hallway

Conventional School Hallway

Transformation Education Gymnasium

Conventional School Gymnasium

Transformation Education Music Room

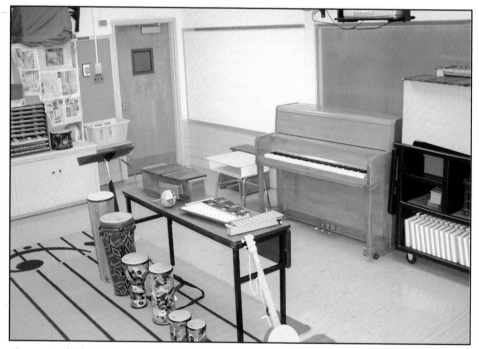

Conventional School Music Room

CREATING THE UPSIDE DOWN ORGANIZATION

Transformation Education School Library

Conventional School Library

Transformation Education MSD Room

Conventional Isolation Room

Transformation Education School Courtyard

Conventional School Courtyard

Transformation Education Group Home Living Room

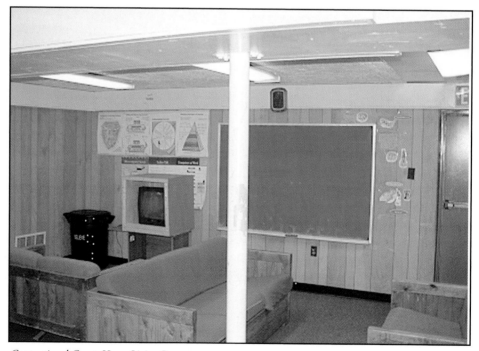

Conventional Group Home Living Room

Transformation Education Group Home Dining Room

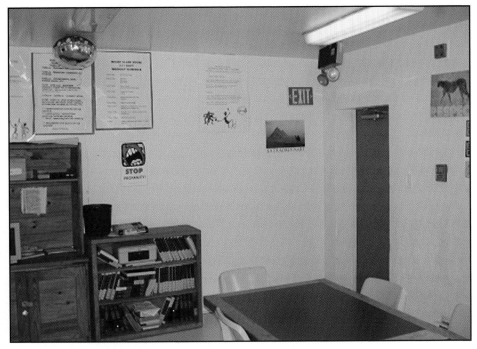

Conventional Group Home Dining Room

Transformation Education Group Home Bedroom

Conventional Group Home Bedroom

Transformation Education Group Home Meeting Room

Transformation Education Group Home Conservatory

CHAPTER 8
Curriculum/Program Themes

Principle: Culture is the most powerful force available to child-serving organizations for transmitting prosocial values and transforming one's mindset.

Knowledge is power. —Sir Francis Bacon

We believe we must challenge and confront students' established mindsets. We want to stimulate growth and direct change by presenting novel experiences for them to process. This is achieved through the use of a master curriculum comprised of eight focus areas. We use the words curriculum and program interchangeably to convey the activities, the values and beliefs of a change- and growth-oriented culture.

The concepts we present are extensively practiced in our group care program and special education schools. The time and emphasis we give any particular theme varies, depending on the setting and the needs of the students at any given time. This chapter will share the themes emphasized in the group care program. Their application to the school is similar, if not identical. We demonstrate in our teaching that life is connected, and we are convinced children learn best and most through experience.

Emphasis on a Normalized Experience

Our group care facility resembles a private boarding school. Our children frame their experience as students; staff are faculty; child-care workers are educators; clinical staff are school counselors and supervisors are educational coordinators. This is the normalized student experience at our group care facility. Consequently, the living units are viewed as dormitories, the activities as classes and students have requirements and electives.

It is assumed that children learn through play, socialization and work experiences. Activities are considered as equivalent to math, science, history or language classes in an academic school. We never withhold activities in the curriculum from a student. We find that the intensity of the cultural expectations creates enormous pressure on each student to develop a new mindset or worldview. This level of heightened interest derives from the activities, our boarding school environment and mentoring by an education-directed staff. As the pressure on students increases, they will quite naturally react strongly, angrily and aggressively. This is a key indicator that they are struggling to understand and ultimately adopt a different mindset. After all, that is our purpose–growth and change.

If a youth acts out within the context of a particular activity, we do not discontinue or eliminate the student's participation in this or any other activity. The activity is never the primary goal; it is always the effect of the activity on the student that is the goal. A negative reaction to the activity is therefore neither good nor bad. The child's behavior is simply reactive and should be seen within the context of personal growth.

Emphasis on Connectedness

Another major tenet of the curriculum is that life reflects the connectedness of the Universe. The staff offers the curriculum in an integrated way. Every activity has a social, spiritual, emotional, physical, aesthetic, vocational, intellectual or cultural dimension. When we plant a garden, there is a spiritual perspective, that is, the harvest and the life force that makes plants grow. The vocational aspect deals with a small-scale agribusiness, the need for transportation, the types of jobs needed and the commodities to be marketed. As we work the garden, there is an aesthetic perspective for our students to consider, organizing the rows and weeding around the vegetables. The cultural and emotional components have to do with the size content of the garden and the approach to pesticide use, and the emotional component is reflected in pride, sharing its contents and eating the vegetables.

Emphasis on Experience

The curriculum is experientially based. It adheres to the principle that the art of learning is the result of experience. A rich learning experience contains the following attributes. [King: 1988]

1. The action is direct, personal, recent and done by the learner. It is not watched or listened to by the learner.

2. The experience involves the use of most of the five senses.

3. The consequences of any decisions or actions are immediate and personally involve comfort, feelings or other people.

4. In the mind of the learner there is ownership of the experience. Ownership implies two things: responsibility and the desire to learn. Responsibility is the willingness to hold oneself accountable for one's actions and reactions. The learner does not behave as if someone else is accountable. Nor is the learner expecting someone else to hold him/her accountable. S/he is accountable. Secondly, in the mind of the learner, there needs to be the desire to learn. This is not to be limited or restricted to the reasons the learner or teacher has in mind.

5. The learner perceives a risk. This risk most commonly shows itself as an emotion. In reality it is adrenaline.

6. There is a concerted attempt to have the learner visualize, relate to, internalize, reflect upon and/or draw conclusions from these reactions, feelings and emotions.

7. The experience happens in an environment in which the doer is not comfortable. In this condition the learner has to rely upon how he feels. Society has yet to teach the learner to respond "properly" in that environment.

8. Experiential learning is the use of both halves of the brain in concert. Most traditional activities used in schools are restricted to the left brain. That can be attributed to the many university professors who are left brained.

9. Safety is the only situation in which the leader or teacher has the right to say "Stop!" or to dictate a particular procedure. There are many kinds of unsafe situations: emotional, social, physical and even spiritual. It is the responsibility of the leader or teacher to create an environment in which the acts are safe.

10. A student's reactions to some stimuli may be an inappropriate reaction. Some would call that a mistake, but an inappropriate reaction is an excellent source of information. If you learn something from an inappropriate act, how can it be considered a mistake? It is a mistake only if you learned nothing.

11. It is the teacher's job to create safe experiences. The teacher creates an environment in which the student can react, either well or poorly, as many times as necessary to learn whatever it is that s/he is going to learn. "Going to learn" as opposed to "should learn" is another important concept. In truth, the teacher is not always sure what will be learned.

Curriculum Components

There are eight curriculum areas that overlap with one another. These areas are: spirituality, wellness, enrichment, careers, culture, citizenship, life skills and academics. The goal of each curriculum area and its content are summarized below.

The Spiritual Life Component

Meaning is missing in the lives of the students who are referred to group care placements. It also tends to be missing in the organizations and schools designed to serve them. The meaning of the Transformation Education approach is expressed through the nine core principles we refer to as the "Wisdom Principles." We will briefly review our discussion in Chapter 2 of these principles to assist the reader's understanding of how they are aligned with the curriculum.

The Wisdom Principles are an interpretation and a restatement of the collective cultural wisdom developed over thousands of years. These principles are found in the classic stories and religions that depict the common human struggle to understand and experience a meaningful life.

The first three principles address the central moral question: "Toward what goal is all personal growth directed?" It focuses our values and it asks what we hope to achieve in life, and what we want our children to become. From heroic stories across cultures and time comes the response: The central goal of growth is to move toward selflessness and away from selfishness. The principles of caring, making a contribution and showing commitment address this goal.

Caring – Caring calls upon us to alleviate suffering and to endure it. It is dynamic in its meaning: to care about one's self and care about others. To care exclusively about one's self and be "totally selfish" at six months old is good. It is precisely what is required for both the young child's survival and that of our society. To live in this manner when one is 50 years old is not good. Being self-centered is the opposite of caring. Selfishness is destructive to self and society. At its most mature level, caring is the concept of giving up one's self for the greater good of the larger community.

Contribution – Contribution is the demonstration of caring. It is the acting out of one's belief, the giving and the enduring. It is the act of giving of one's self for a higher purpose or for the life of others.

Commitment – Commitment is contribution over time. It is the continuous dedication to grow in our ability to care and contribute. It is to live mindfully with the constant awareness that every decision is personal and every choice is moral.

The second set of principles addresses the question: "What is the process through which growth occurs?" The response emerges by recognizing that growth is the continuous process of life. We reach new levels of understanding in processing the challenge of living moment by moment. The process of growth is expressed by the principles of struggle, transformation and enlightenment.

Struggle – Struggle is the prerequisite to growth. It is life enhancing, not life defeating. Struggle results from the continuous state of tension that exists between that which is familiar and that which is new. This crisis brings with it the opportunity to change.

Transformation – Transformation is the act of becoming. It requires the dying of one's former mindset and the emergence as a new self with greater understandings. It is letting go that empowers us to move on.

Enlightenment – Enlightenment is a new state of awareness, a higher level of consciousness, a greater acceptance of one's responsibility and moral obligation. The state of enlightenment, however, is transitory. Like the horizon, it is always before you. After experiencing enlightenment, struggle reoccurs as the next phase. The cycle continuously repeats itself. The drama of struggle and enlightenment continues as we transcend into greater awareness of self and community.

The last set of three principles addresses the question: "What are the skills needed to achieve growth?" We need to understand what the goal is, and to engage in the process of achieving growth. These skills are expressed through the principles of vision, courage and will.

Vision – Vision is the ability to see beyond to what one can become. It is opening one's mind to a new picture of reality, new levels of caring, contribution and commitment. It is also seeing the process one must experience for growth to occur. It is seeing with the mind that which is invisible to the eye. It is the ability to discern the greater good.

Courage – Courage is demonstrated by attempting to achieve one's vision. It is the act of placing one's self in a position of risk: becoming vulnerable enough to face the unknown and to be open to struggle. Courage is to risk even making bad judgments. To use an old adage: Good decisions come from experience. Experience comes from what bad decisions have hopefully taught us.

Will – Will is courage over time. It is the ability to risk continuously for growth and be ready to give your all for life. It is perseverance, against all odds, to believe in and strive toward living out the wisdom principles.

The spiritual/moral development curriculum allows the student an opportunity to examine one's self and one's value system. It also sends the message that one's goal in life is to move from selfishness to selflessness.

In the school setting, the message of selflessness is integrated in the curriculum. We incorporate character themes such as respect, honor, honesty, etc., in lesson planning. Then the theme is infused in lesson planning and emphasized. If honesty is emphasized, teachers raise the issue of truthfulness in science, such as the ethics of not exaggerating the outcome of experiments. In English, stories with the theme of honesty are read and discussed. In social studies, the teachers ask if it was okay for our U.S. ancestors to lie, when questioned in the 1860's about the whereabouts of a slave or when queried about who might be involved with the Underground Railroad.

In the group care setting, the curriculum consists of the following content:

Service Learning – Here the focus is on volunteering. Students undertake community improvement projects and assist individuals or organizations in need. They participate in the Adopt-A-Highway program, assist in nursing homes and churches, and develop sites and trails in state and community parks. Volunteering requires more than lending a hand. We attempt to infuse meaning in service learning. Our educator staff assisted a group of physically challenged elementary school children when they swam once a week at the YMCA. The staff shared the process of how it was done, infusing meaning in a service learning activity.

Several of the residents from our older boy's group home volunteer along with two of the staff to assist the YMCA swim leader. They assist wheelchair-bound children in and out of the water. The boys also stand by the children to support them as needed. The staff prepare the boys on how to respond to the physically challenged children by sensitizing them to the situation, e.g., not to stare, to respond to the children as they would to any child, providing them with an understanding of the diseases that crippled their muscles, answering their questions and emphasizing the importance of following the directions of the swim leader.

Following the activity, our students process what happened and how they felt. They discuss such issues as: how hard the physically challenged children were trying; how they felt when the children did not thank them for helping; and how helpless they felt when the children would not listen or respond to their directions. The boys also discuss how they react in the same way at the group home and how this must make the staff feel.

The constant involvement in service learning projects builds commitment to volunteering. It also transmits the message that the boys have a responsibility to contribute to the life of the community, i.e., they are not to see themselves as victims. They need to come to love their fate. The problems they have faced allow them the opportunity to experience and learn new things. They meet caring adults who can serve as role models. The message is: We are all interdependent. We all need help at certain times of our lives and are able to provide help at other times during our lives. This is the way society works.

Pets and Plants – Students learn through hands-on experience of the life cycle in caring for plants and animals. Examples are: gardening, caring for birds, caring for house plants, tropical fish, turtles, lizards and small mammals. The following incident exemplifies the connection between the spiritual life program and animals.

> *The students in the older boys group home found a stray kitten and asked if they could care for it. One day the oldest boy in the group home, who had a long history of child abuse, convinced some of the younger boys to throw the cat out of the window to see if it would land on its feet. After several drops from the third floor onto the driveway below, the cat died. Instead of punishing the boys, the faculty held a two-day mandatory conference. A film on the history of child abuse was shown. The boys learned about the cycle of abuse. Throughout history the way man treated animals determined how children and women were treated. The conference explored the feelings of being helpless and powerless to prevent a parent or guardian's abuse to their siblings and how they had to deal with the fear of reprisal if they tried to prevent it.*

> *With the help and involvement of the youth life educators, the boys signed up to volunteer at the local animal shelter. The program and design specialist understood their need to develop a sense of awe and appreciation in animals. He took them to dog shows where they saw Pugs and Great Danes. These boys were used to dogs living outside the house. They witnessed people pampering dogs. Next they were introduced to a woman who ran a shelter for abandoned reptiles. They were fascinated by huge*

snakes and lizards and became involved in the rescue effort. They learned to care for the smaller, malnourished reptiles at the group home and restore their health. The boys began raising turtles and learning about them. During the course of the year, animal experts were brought in to teach how animals think and feel. A stray cat ended up in the yard one day. The boys asked if they could care for it. The staff agreed but only if the cat would be a community pet. Initially, the cat would live in the tool shed in the backyard. After a short time the cat was moved to the utility room. After school, the cat was permitted supervised movement in the houses. The boys took the cat to the veterinarian to get it immunized. For the past year, they have been caring for the cat with no problem. The intervention took place over two and a half years. Our point is that there are no quick fixes to changing behavior. But pets and plants are an important part of Transformation Education and infusing meaning into a group care experience.

Worship Experience – Students in our group care program are encouraged to attend the worship services of their choice with staff or volunteers. We encourage students to become actively involved in religious education consistent with their religious traditions. Students are also exposed to worship services and beliefs other than their traditions. This fosters respect and understanding of religious views different than their own. The approach below makes worship a challenging and engaging activity.

The Summer Club program is designed as a structured, sequential, experiential learning opportunity for each student. Each faculty member selects an area of interest s/he would like to explore and markets the course to see how many students sign up. Each course is a fun activity that requires the development of skills, knowledge and etiquette. One of the courses was "How do you spell GOD?" It explored the major religions in the world. The students who signed up for the club visited a variety of churches, mosques, synagogues and temples to witness different types of religious services. They met with religious leaders to learn about their traditions, history and beliefs. By the end of the summer each boy's worldview had grown along with his tolerance and respect for difference.

Values Clarification – The students are exposed to moral dilemmas encountered in life through the purposeful use of movies, TV and theater. In this way the students explore his/her values system and have the opportunity to compare values with peers and adults. Popular culture bombards youth with a plethora of value messages. Some of these messages are life affirming and respectful; others are destructive, violent and exploitive. Transformation Education views culture and the messages it radiates as a very powerful force. Realizing there will be a popular culture for every generation, it is an important program goal to develop students as critical thinkers and listeners. It is impossible to protect children from the realities of everyday living. The goal is to fill each student's mind with messages that build character, nurture a student's moral and spiritual growth and extend sensitivity to others.

The minds of adolescents interpret differently what they see on television and in the movies and hear in lyrics than adults in their 20's and 30's. The direct care staff need to realize this. Adolescents lack the living experience, emotional maturity and brain development that adults possess. Nudity in a movie that is natural to a scene, a sexual act demonstrating affection, a lack of humanity of a character or making a social statement is not viewed that way by a child or an emotionally troubled adolescent. It is the responsibility of child-serving organizations to expose youth they serve to literature, music, film, programming and theater that promotes growth of the spirit, and inspires caring about others, sacrifice for one's family and loved ones, and a commitment to a purpose larger than one's self.

Television in the Transformation Education model is treated as a controlled substance. Watching it is a passive activity. It is important that the staff take charge of the TV. The intent is to turn television viewing into a mindful activity. A tool we have found useful is a guide to critical viewing of television. It is called *Taking Charge of Your TV*. You can obtain a copy from the National Cable Television Association. The guide has been produced in partnership with the National Parent and Teacher Association.

Television programming is controlled by the program and design specialist in consultation with the program director and youth life education supervisors. The program and design specialist is equivalent to the head football coach who calls the plays. The TV programming, movies, theater, video/DVD rental, concerts and the radio station in the living unit are the responsibility of this team. By consolidating this responsibility the value messages established by the organization become clear to the faculty and students.

Casual viewing of TV is not permitted. Students' understanding of the television-watching policy is explained in a mini media course. Other media are discussed in the course as well. Students attend a training program before they are permitted to watch TV. They learn that all TV programs are deliberately constructed, piece by piece, to generate a desired effect in the viewer. We want our students and staff to understand that we do not interpret a television program in the same way. That is due to our personal identity, level of brain development, facility for conceptual thinking and life experience. The mini media course discussion addresses violence and sex on TV and the economic purpose of TV.

When our faculty members watch TV with the students, the programs are used to stimulate conversation about the topics the program addresses, be it sex, violence, poverty, corruption or loyalty. During the commercial breaks, our faculty engage the students and challenge them to think critically. We ask what they anticipate will happen next. The goal is to improve their verbal expression as well as thinking. TV shows are used as a springboard to reading and other activities. It creates the interest to go to the museum to learn more about the Incas or to visit the aquarium.

Watching the Super Bowl provides a good example of how it works. The program and design specialist works with the faculty to help them understand the popular culture surrounding the Super Bowl. Following the training session, the faculty goes shopping with the boys to create a festive atmosphere. The two teams' colors serve as the party's display in the selection of tablecloths, plates, napkins, etc. The *TV Guide* is consulted, and the faculty use the information to help build anticipation for the game by promoting the TV programming before the game. The boys have a great interest in the cheerleaders, dancers and singers that perform, and the Super Bowl commercials.

The pre-game show includes spot coverage of how players have overcome adversity, and the United Way commercials show the players volunteering in the community. The players acknowledge their mistakes of missing curfew or getting involved with drugs, and how they were able to put their lives back together. The faculty will use these opportunities to discuss these issues during commercial breaks. The lessons learned by the rehabilitated players help the boys see how they apply to their own lives. Once the game begins, the boys who are interested will watch, while the others leave the room for another activity. While drinking a soda, eating chicken wings and watching football, it is a good time to explore the values of the game and evaluate the commercial messages.

Journeying – Spiritual and moral development can result from participation in adventure-based programming, such as camping, challenge courses, repelling, travel and trips. Journeying tests a student's mettle. Faced with a challenge, the student requires the use of most of the five senses, trust in others, an appreciation for God's creation and awareness of the force of nature. Journeying encourages the student to reflect on the experience. We will present two journey experiences to share how this is done.

Most of the residents in our group care program are African-American boys from inner-city neighborhoods who are not familiar with the beach. A week's vacation to Rehoboth Beach, Maryland, was planned. To prepare them, the students were provided a course on how to enjoy the beach. We picked Rehoboth because the boys had made a lot of comments about gay men, and members of the gay community regularly visit it. However, we did not inform the boys about the gay population beforehand because we knew they would not agree to go.

The boys wanted to go on the trip in their Timberland boots and long pants. We took them shopping, explaining they needed swim trunks, hats, suntan lotion, a blanket, a cooler and other beach accessories. We talked about showering after they left the beach and that many people sometimes ate seafood after "chilling out" all day. They took swimming lessons to prepare for the adventure. A day after we arrived we walked the town of Rehoboth, just to window shop and eat ice cream. The boys noticed some of the men holding hands and commented on the practice. When we explained they were gay, the boys immediately wanted to leave.

On the way back to the house we rented, we had a discussion about tolerance. The boys were able to go to town several more times that week without making comments or staring. Later in the summer, the boys noticed a few gay men walking hand in hand at a festival in downtown Baltimore. They were able to handle the situation in a socially acceptable way.

An environmental science project also served as a journeying application. We took a class trip to a creek across the road from our school. One of the social workers developed an environmental science lesson to underscore the importance of clean water, and had them test the creek water to gain an understanding of its purity. The testing revealed sewage leaking into the water supply. After notifying the city government, the city tested the water and confirmed that sewage was indeed leaking into the creek. The class discussed the issue of runoff and learned that they could help the problem by planting trees. In a two-month period the class planted 200 trees to help filter the runoff water, and the city repaired the sewage problem.

Each example emphasizes a different aspect of journeying. The beach trip provided a multisensory experience. It placed the students in a personally challenging situation with the gay population, and provided an opportunity to gain an appreciation of God's creation, be it differences in human beings, intense heat, power of the ocean waves or the beauty and vastness of the sea. The trip to the creek emphasized the force of nature and the fragility of our environment. The students came to understand the importance and power of trees in filtering, maintaining and protecting the water supply. It also provided the opportunity to reflect on the importance of God's creation and humanity's role in protecting it.

The Wellness Curriculum

The wellness curriculum demonstrates the integration of mind and body. Using traditional therapies, youth can work out their inner feelings. Wellness encourages, through example, the prevention of illness. Through stress management, friendship development, physical fitness, nutrition and understanding of the normal growth and development process in individuals and families, wellness can be an ingrained habit. This area of the curriculum mostly is directed and taught by the clinical staff. The intent is to help students understand the stresses they have in their lives. The instruction illustrates how to deal with stress and how to manage anger. Engaging children in traditional psychotherapeutic treatment occurs when appropriate. Issues of trauma and grief are also part of the instruction.

Educating the students about normal human growth and development in children and families is emphasized. Understanding healthy, nonsexual friendship with members of both the same and opposite sex is explored. This is achieved by creating simple courses presented in an experiential way. The content of these courses cover human sexuality and family life as experienced in two-parent, single-parent, blended and adoptive families.

Physical and dental checks are the direct responsibility of the student coordinator. The program director is directly responsible for nutritious meals and snacks. The program and design specialist in the group care program and the physical education teacher in the school are responsible for developing a positive attitude toward exercise. They offer a Fitness for Life program that includes exposure to activities that condition the whole body.

There are a plethora of therapeutic approaches to address the pathological behavior these children exhibit. In the Transformation Education model, a good clinical intervention is just as important as basic instruction on what we consider normal behavior. Only by having a clear understanding or vision of what is normal, can a child judge what is socially inappropriate or bad parenting. Hopefully, this is learned from their daily interaction with the faculty. They need to have this directly taught to them as well. We truly have nothing to add to the conversation in this respect. Therefore, we will limit the how-to component of curriculum to physical fitness as it relates to Transformation Education.

Our economically deprived students need to expand their interest in physical fitness. They have little experience with golf, bicycle riding, swimming, skiing, tennis, racquetball, hiking and rock climbing. There are two benefits to exposure to these activities. These activities are associated with higher social economic status, radiating a message that with skills the students will be successful in life. What they learn is that these activities take place in unfamiliar settings and require social behavior and etiquette quite different from what they know.

A lack of physical fitness is a national issue that is leaving its effects across the physical health, mental health and education fields. Poor nutrition and a lack of physical activity are the norm with a majority of our students. The national data suggests young people are eating less healthy and more often, spend less time exercising and have an overall lack of understanding about their individual physical health. Poor eating habits and inadequate exercise have skyrocketed the rates of obesity, heart disease, high cholesterol and diabetes. The nutritional health and fitness of emotionally disturbed and behavior-disordered students most likely are poorer than the national averages.

We try to foster the adoption of a mindset of wellness in our students. In our group care program, we use the YMCA for physical fitness. For day students, we carry out this program as part of the weekly regimen of the school.

To improve the physical health of the children, we approached it in the following way. We accepted the fact that our students suffer from myriad mental health and social disorders that limit their abilities to participate productively in team activities. Our students will spend a majority of the time struggling with the social aspects of a team game like basketball. We knew if we were to truly make a difference in the students fitness we would have to concentrate on an individual physical fitness program. We were able to find a vehicle that allowed them to achieve their optimal fitness level on equipment they can access throughout their life.

We learned that we could create an individual fitness program—equivalent to providing a personal trainer for each student—by using equipment that our local YMCA had in place. We received a grant and purchased the equipment, but many YMCAs and gyms have this equipment available for public use.

The physical fitness equipment is called Cybex. This series of machines is simple to use and easily adjusts to fit any body type. The equipment allows for a correct warm-up and cooldown for an individualized workout. The students are able to set their own goals and create an individual workout plan. The physical education teacher ensures that the components are developmentally appropriate and personally challenging. The students can work the upper body muscles on seven of the machines; they can concentrate on their lower body on four others.

The equipment is fitted with Fitlinxx, a state-of-the-art computer software program that designs an individual's exercise workout. It is like having a personal trainer. There are small display screens on each piece of equipment and a database kiosk, where students enter their individual personal identification number. This number, after the initial set-up by the physical education teacher, brings up the individual's developmentally appropriate and personally challenging fitness program.

Fitlinxx incorporates the cardiovascular equipment into its program as well. The duration of their cardiovascular workout is recorded and entered into the Fitlinxx database. Fitlinxx tracks the students' efforts and rewards them with points. The Physical Education teacher can use these points to create displays to motivate the students.

The personal coaching and guidance that Fitlinxx provides means that "non-P.E." staff do not have to worry about the protocol or the content. Children will be performing their workouts safely and effectively. The prescription and tracking software delivers an effective wellness curriculum with personalized programs. Providing one-on-one coaching and guidance to a high level would be very challenging without the support of Fitlinxx. The computerized workout equipment has a proven track record in attracting and retaining more "at-risk" individuals to a regular program.

In the same ways that exercise shapes our muscles, heart, lungs and bones, it also strengthens the key areas of the brain. Exercise fuels the brain with oxygen as well as triggers the release of neurotrophins, which enhance growth, impact mood, cement memory and enhance connections between neurons. [Jensen: 2000]

The nutritional aspect is as important as the exercise component of wellness. Many of our students have eating habits that lead to unhealthy lifestyles. Junk food, skipping meals and snacking are common eating habits of our students. The interrelationship of eating well, exercising and getting enough rest are presented as one integrated curriculum. Instruction on the risk of drugs, alcohol and the effect of stress on the body is included in this whole body approach.

The developmentally appropriate curriculum delivers effective messages for children served by a child-serving organization. There are several video resources to help students learn fitness as a lifestyle. Go to www.sunburstvm.com to locate the video resources on the following page.

- *Managing Your Health* – This in-depth series examines a range of topics including weight control, digestion, headaches, depression and addiction. It teaches students to take care of their bodies and avoid unhealthy habits. (130 minutes)

- *Healthy Habits for Life: Teen Hygiene* – This tape helps students develop and maintain good personal hygiene into their teenage years and beyond. Students will learn the advantages of maintaining proper hygiene at school and home. This is written to the national health standards. (20 minutes)

- *Nutrition and Exercise* – One of the great myths is that people can lose weight just by exercising. The truth is that diet and exercise must work together for the best results. This video teaches students to eat well and exercise efficiently. (25 minutes)

- *Fat or Fit Health Quiz* – This intriguing program encourages students to think about their food choices and the resulting health consequences. (30 minutes)

- *Human Body: Major Systems* – The human body is a wondrously complex machine made of flesh, bones, muscles, organs, blood vessels and highly specialized systems that function together to sustain life. This fascinating program examines this incredible machine, from simple cells to DNA. Students will love this inside look at the human body. (50 minutes)

- *Human Body: Musculoskeletal System* – Students are amazed at how the skeleton, muscles and joints work together to create motion. With commentary from medical experts in sports medicine, this program offers a unique perspective on the body system, which allows them to move through daily life. (50 minutes)

- *Weight Training Video* – Students learn everything they need to know to start a well-balanced weight training program. This video uses slow motion, freeze frames and detailed graphics to demonstrate the proper positioning for optimal muscle gain. (57 minutes)

- *Stress* – Learn the difference between negative stress that creates anxiety and positive stress that creates winners. Enlightening research and compelling examples show how untreated stress causes mental and physical damage. NBC News teaches relaxation techniques for keeping tension in check. (30 minutes)

- *Build a Winning Attitude* – This entertaining, informative video will motivate students to believe in themselves and pursue excellence in all activities. From getting the proper amount of sleep to facing daily challenges, the program explains a variety of powerful, effective life strategies. (30 minutes)

By demonstrating in an exciting and innovative way, new healthier ways of living, students will gain the skills necessary to lead more healthy lives. This translates into regular exercise, eating healthier and eliminating the use of alcohol, tobacco and other drugs. A wellness curriculum improves our student's chances of living a successful life.

The Enrichment Component

The home enrichment curriculum is very much a Martha Stewart approach to life. The underlying premise is that an appealing living environment matters. We expose our students to the principles of good housekeeping, interior design, presentation and preparation of food and ideas for decorating and preparing for the holidays, seasons and special occasions. An attractive home environment sends a strong message of caring as it stimulates the brain.

The home enrichment begins by hiring an interior decorator to select wallpaper, paint, carpets, furniture and decor to create an environment that is sophisticated, rich in color, harmonious and dynamic in character. Rooms are individualized in decor, open and comfortable. Attractive surroundings are another way to establish high expectations for the students and the faculty.

Each year, students tour the home and garden show to garner ideas and visions of how to decorate. They are exposed to feng shui. They are taught how to hang pictures, and a great deal of effort is expended in developing decorating plans for the living unit. They shop, make, display and arrange items to motivate enthusiasm for the season, holiday or event. Students learn that people "eat with their eyes." We instruct the students how to prepare food and present it in an appealing way. Setting the table properly, cake decorating, holiday displays and using table etiquette are stressed.

The Career Component

A regular opportunity to explore the world of work is integral to Transformation Education programming. Students gain an understanding of the educational requirements and economic potential of various careers. Career instruction values a good work ethic and sharpens attitudes about quality work skills. These are the activities in this curriculum:

Career Awareness – This acquaints students with a wide variety of career options. Speakers from various fields and professions share their experiences and describe their fields. Trips are scheduled to businesses and organizations to give students a first-hand look at work settings and product(s) produced.

Career Exploration – Students (14 and older) explore careers through professional testing to measure their interest in various clusters of occupations. Once the clusters are identified, students learn about the related occupations along with the skills, education, working conditions and salary associated with various careers. Work shadowing–going on the job with an employee–helps students get a feel for that job from a realistic perspective.

Students are encouraged to take on volunteer and paid jobs around the campus to develop their work ethic, learn how to take direction and learn good work habits. The basic idea is to foster students' interest in their future. Students connect interests, hobbies and what they learn in school to what is possible in the world of work.

The key is discerning a student's interest. The story of Hank makes the point. Hank is a very bright boy who was dealing with intense feelings of rejection by his family. He was placed in foster care at age 15, did not attend school often and dropped out at age 16. He had an intense interest in flying and airplanes.

He lied about his age and landed a job driving a tow truck for an independent auto repair shop. After driving for several years, he purchased a tow truck and started his own business. Hank was not successful in operating his own towing business.

He moved on as a long-distance trucker, operating an 18-wheeler. He then learned to retrieve and tow 18-wheelers that had gone off the road into deep ditches or gullies. He next established his own trucking business, owned a tour bus and went into the truck repossession business. This permitted him to fly, at company expense, all over the U.S. to retrieve trucks from individuals who were delinquent in making payments on their bank loans.

Today at age 45, he owns his own trucking business. Hank had an intense interest in transportation all of his life that began with airplanes. By understanding a student's interest and doing what we can to support it, we can turn failure into opportunity.

The Cultural Component

We expose our students to the arts, dance, music and cultural traditions that comprise American society. Exposure is necessary, but not sufficient. A great deal of time and planning precedes involvement. The experts in the arts and/or the program and design specialist prepare the faculty and the students for what they will observe and the questions to ask. This prepares the faculty to engage the students and not limit their involvement to just walking through the museum. The example below details how the students were prepped for a day trip to the Museum of Art and to the stage production *Phantom of the Opera* in New York City.

For eight weeks the students learned about different artists and forms of art such as impressionism, modern art, cubism, etc. They did their best to create art in the different styles they were learning about. They were familiarized with the story behind *Phantom of the Opera* and were told that when people go on trips, they usually bring back a souvenir. The boys each were provided with an opportunity to earn $25 to take with them on the trip. They were impressed that they were able to identify artists and understand the art in the museum. They thoroughly understood and enjoyed the *Phantom at the Opera*, and all came back with keepsakes for their rooms.

The Citizenship Component

The vehicle for encouraging positive leadership, self-empowerment, skills in public speaking and generating an attitude of peace and nonviolence is citizenship. Citizenship is a responsibility. We should know national and international issues and the impact these events have on Americans. The three activities used to encourage citizenship are student government, advocacy and peer mediation.

Each week a Town Meeting is held, offering students an opportunity to contribute as members of their community. The goal of the Town Meeting is process oriented. It serves as a forum to practice meeting skills, present ideas, research issues, make decisions and demonstrate their responsibility in carrying out tasks given to them at the previous meeting. They learn to prepare, develop and present proposals. They learn the various roles community members assume and figure out who has influence in the group. At the Town Meeting the students learn to abide by rules, norms and decisions agreed upon by the community members.

Each student takes a turn as the Town Meeting moderator, working closely with the youth life education supervisor. The moderator presides over the meeting, maintaining parliamentary procedure, facilitating the meeting, controlling the agenda and achieving an outcome for each topic.

Staff members work with the students to prepare them in carrying out their roles in the retain meeting. The students are taught parliamentary procedure and how to create an agenda. The youth life educator supervisor has the responsibility of preparing the moderator before the meeting. The moderator learns to anticipate what will happen in the meeting. The youth educator also readies the moderator to present issues in a way that will retain the members' attention. To support the success of the Town Meeting, faculty are requested to keep their schedules open to help students by offering positive recommendations. The early success of these meetings is heavily dependent on how students and faculty can relate to each other during the meeting. The guidelines for the moderator are presented below:

- Create a well-planned agenda and follow it closely.
- Get everyone involved in the meeting.
- Avoid power plays by suggesting members research their ideas and report back at the next meeting.
- Remain an impartial leader and have a goal in mind to achieve.
- Be aware that the main purpose of the meeting is the process itself.
- Periodically summarize the content of the discussion during the meeting.
- Help members clarify their positions. Work to achieve harmony by using humor or being conciliatory if it is necessary to keep order.

The agenda is simple so it is easy for the students to follow.

- Call to order
- Adoption or revision of the agenda with member's help before proceeding with discussion
- Approval of minutes
- Old business
- New business
- Student and faculty concerns
- Adjournment

Students gain a voice by learning how to lobby state and national representatives on behalf of their interests. To foster interest and awareness in civics, the youth life education supervisor provides the staff with a daily newspaper article. The program and design specialist consults with the youth life education supervisor on the weekly content of these articles, as well as provides structured questions. The news articles are discussed during dinner, and issues are noted. Students are engaged so they understand the complexities of the issues.

Sometimes issues are taken from the legislative agenda of the child-serving organization's state association. If they relate to children living in out-of-home care, we encourage their involvement. They are encouraged to write a letter to the local legislator representing their living unit. On occasion, they have testified before a legislative committee. This gives the educator staff an opportunity to demonstrate how the legislative process works and what a citizen can do to advocate on his/her behalf. The following example demonstrates how students can be involved in a local issue.

People were using a clearing adjacent to a road near our group home to dump old furniture, refrigerators, tires and assorted trash. One of the faculty members observed an older woman standing by the clearing shaking her head. He approached her and learned that every time the city removed the trash at her request, someone else came along to dump more. The faculty member said he worked with boys who live in a group home on the other side of the clearing and offered to engage the boys in helping to solve the dumping problem.

He suggested the woman and her husband meet with the boys and the group home faculty to work together on the project. He learned the woman's husband is politically connected to the city government and that the couple were members of the Orthodox Jewish community. A meeting was arranged with the group home students, their faculty and the couple, who were reluctant to meet at the group home because the boys frightened them. Their desire for help with the dumping problem overcame their fear.

The couple and the boys joined forces to attack the problem. The students decided to use a video camera to record dumping activity. The couple obtained the assistance of a city truck and cleaned up the dump site with the boys. During a brain storming session, the boys came up with the idea to develop the clearing into a little park with benches and flowers to alter the look of the site. They also staked out the site to catch someone in the act which proved ineffective since they could not mount a twenty-four-hour seven-day-a-week effort.

The couple arranged a meeting with their city council representative and the boys to discuss the problem. The city councilman arranged for more police surveillance but the dumping continued. The boys continued videotaping and contacted a local television station. A neighborhood watch, including the adjacent neighbors, was formed. Through this shared experience, a group of African-American teenagers and an Orthodox Jewish couple came to know, respect and understand one another. Tolerance grew in the neighborhood from this experience. The word "citizenship" took on real meaning. Thanks to the combined neighborhood effort, the dumping ceased.

Helping emotionally disturbed and behavior-disordered students learn how to resolve conflicts in a nonviolent way is an important aspect of citizenship programming. It is even more important for professionals who work with inner-city youth. In these children, violence is a prevalent occurrence in their neighborhoods. They have seen people they know lying dead in the street. They have heard repeated sounds of gunfire. Police sirens are a common sound. Advantaged children have been spared this street violence. Most of us in America will never experience, in a lifetime, what these children experience in a month.

A tried and true way to assist adolescents with conflicts is to use one of the peer mediation programs available today. The goal of mediation is to work out differences constructively. Students in the peer mediation process, as either mediators or disputants, learn a new way of handling conflict. Trained students help their classmates identify the problems behind the conflicts and to find solutions. Peer mediation is not about finding out who is right or wrong. Instead, students are encouraged to move beyond the immediate conflict and learn how to get along with each other—an important skill in today's world. Peer mediators ask the disputing students to tell their stories and ask questions for clarification. The mediators help the students identify ways to solve the conflict.

A key element of any mediation process is letting each student tell his/her own story so someone understands his/her perspective. Not every kind of problem is suitable for peer mediation. The adults in charge can best handle assault or criminal activities. However, name-calling, rumor mongering, bumping into students in the hallways and bullying are handled quite well through peer mediation.

The basic process for peer mediation begins with agreement on the ground rules. This means the participants should be willing to solve the problem, tell the truth, listen without interrupting, be respectful, take responsibility for carrying out the agreement and keep the situation confidential. If this is agreed, each student tells his or her story. The peer mediator verifies their story with the participants. The peer mediator helps the disputants generate possible solutions. Potential solutions are discussed and evaluated. The peer mediator comes up with a solution both parties can live with. A contract is then signed and the issue is considered closed.

The Life Skills Component

The skills needed to maintain the students' health, achieve social acceptance, manage leisure time and live independently are essential life skills students need. While there are a host of life skills to be taught, what follows is an example of one skill implemented in the Transformation Education approach to alter a student's mindset.

Wardrobe and Dress – Remember the goal of Transformation Education is about radiating messages. Two of the major message senders are personal hygiene and the manner in which we dress.

As we all know, clothing is an extremely important factor in the lives of children, particularly adolescents. It represents much more than warmth and protection; it often represents status (or the lack of it) and identification with one type of group or another. How one dresses greatly affects how a student feels about himself. Learning to purchase affordable clothing that makes a good appearance and is appropriate for a particular event is generally outside the realm of students when they enter group care. A good program for clothing purchase and maintenance features lessons on budgeting, color selection, styles and owning a wardrobe suitable for a variety of occasions.

Our instruction offers a competing message to the clothing styles of inner-city street life. The wardrobe and dress curriculum requires students to dress and look in a way that increases their chances to succeed economically and socially in middle-class society. The trick is to permit only clothing purchases that help students conform to broad societal standards and yet still represent a unique sense of personal style. Emphasis is placed on neatness, appropriateness for the occassion, comfort and clothing with a classic look.

Lessons in color analysis, proper fit, fashion sense and seasonal variations ensure a student's pride in how s/he presents him/herself. Clothing must meet those standards. From a community perspective, clothing other than a standard JC Penney or L.L. Bean type of look is not permitted. Disallowed is a sense of dress that fosters a disenfranchised look that identifies with street life or an exciting, rebel lifestyle.

The clothing policy is explained to the students as part of the procedures for welcoming them to placement. The welcoming procedures represent the value messages of the program. Our welcoming procedures provide the context for how the wardrobe and dress procedure is implemented.

The program director or youth life education supervisor welcomes the new student and gives him the Welcome Manual. The program and design specialist presents the student with a welcome gift for his room (poster, stuffed animal, plant) tailored to the interest and age of the student. Within 24 hours, a welcome party is held for the student, planned and arranged jointly by the members of the house. The party includes the new student's favorite food for dinner and an activity s/he might enjoy. During the first 72 hours, the student is presented with:

- A portfolio to keep track of the memories of his/her stay
- A tour of the community
- A color analysis and haircut
- A clothing shopping trip
- A hygiene kit

A youth life educator inventories the student's clothes at admission to determine needs and appropriateness. Clothes that do not meet the organization's standards are boxed up and stored until discharge. Personal luggage to tote new clothes replaces the box or garbage bag most of these children bring. An appearance and color analysis expert assists each student analyze his/her skin tone and the type of clothing that compliments his/her body type. Prior to the shopping trip, the student is shown the *Look Book*. Developed by the program and design specialist, this book shows catalog and magazine photos that represent acceptable clothing.

The criteria for selecting the wardrobe is outlined below:

- Clothing should represent a reasonable variety of colors and patterns, and at least two items must be consistent with the student's color analysis.
- A student must purchase sleep attire.
- There is a $50 limit on a sneaker purchase with the organization's clothing purchase funds.
- Designer brand name clothes are not encouraged.
- Trendy fashion clothing is not permitted with the organization's clothing purchase funds. A student may purchase trendy fashions with his/her own money, but the educator staff determines when and where it is appropriate to wear them.
- Emphasis is placed on purchases that reflect good economic value and can be machine washed.

The Academic Component

Holistic education is aligned with Transformation Education. The emotionally disturbed and behavior-disordered children referred to our program tend to fragment reality. They isolate events and information. Often, they do not make the connection between their behavior and the outcomes they experience. This mindset of fragmentation and disconnection is reinforced by the piecemeal educational programming offered these children in most public schools and even in many nonpublic schools specializing in special education services.

Holistic Education is predicated on the assumption that nothing can be truly understood apart from its larger context. What makes Holistic Education effective is that it rearranges the mindset, i.e., the child's cognitive map, from a fragmented perspective to an integrated one. It changes the way the child looks at the world and processes information. This is consistent with socialization and therapeutic aspects of Transformation Education. It reinforces connections between what happened in the past and how the past has an effect on the present and future. It also helps the child gain the thinking skills and insight into the connection between feelings, behavior and consequences and to understand family dynamics.

Since students spend 33–45% of their awake time in school or involved with school, educational institutions must send the same message of connectedness. A Holistic Education approach does this by emphasizing context, concepts over facts, questions over answers, process over content and meaning over knowledge.

Should the reader desire a more complete understanding of Holistic Education, we suggest contacting Holistic Education Review, P. O. Box 1476, Greenfield, MA 01302 and request a reprint of "What Is Holistic Education?" (Vol. 1. No. 1, Spring, 1988).

One aspect of Holistic Education is integrated lesson planning. This approach assists students in understanding the interconnectedness between concepts. It also utilizes a life problem-oriented or project approach. The focus is on conceptualization and not memorization. When students experience learning, they remember it and can apply it to future lessons. Just as with music, until you "feel" the music, it isn't real. Research on brain functions supports the importance of "feeling" the learning experience.

Let's take a history lesson dealing with music. First the teacher uses a story, about Louis Armstrong, the jazz musician, for example. The story would be accompanied by a graphic organizer (see appendix 6). It serves as a unifying theme among curricular concepts. The story line provides a central theme, or main idea, upon which the curriculum is integrated. Each graphic organizer outlines concept connections for the subjects: reading, social skills, math, social studies, language arts, music, art, physical education, science and health. The story below is read to the students.

> *When Louis Armstrong was a little boy in New Orleans, he heard an old man on the street corner singing a song about a sick woman who was rushed to the hospital. When her husband arrived at the hospital, he found her lying on a long, white table and cried, "There'll never be another like her! Lord, there'll never be another for me!" Louis Armstrong never forgot that song, and in 1948, he recorded it, under the title, "St. James Infirmary Blues," playing trumpet and singing the song. It was the only sad song Louis Armstrong ever recorded, and it became one of his biggest-selling recordings.*

> *Louis was a cheerful boy. What his childhood friends remembered about him was that it was so easy to get him to laugh and that, more times than not, he had a smile on his face. He also loved to make other people laugh. All his life, Louis loved the food he'd eaten as a child in New Orleans. Instead of signing his letters "Sincerely Yours," he'd often sign them "Red Beans and Ricely Yours."*

> *In 1913, when Louis was twelve years old, he celebrated New Year's Eve by*

firing a pistol into the air at midnight. The neighbors called the police. Louis was arrested and after his trial was sent to the Colored Waif's Home where the music teacher, Peter Davis, taught him to play the trumpet. Over the next few years, Louis became one of the best trumpet players in New Orleans. Louis himself said that by the time he was 17, "I could read music very well...I could blow harder and longer without getting tired." A musician who knew Louis said, "High C is a hard note for any trumpet player to hit, but when Louis was at his peak, he would hit high C's like they were tennis balls."

At 17, Louis was playing lead trumpet with The Fate Marable Band on the paddlewheelr excursion boat called the Dixie Belle. The boat would travel the Mississippi River from New Orleans, Louisiana, to St. Louis, Missouri and back again. Soon people from other parts of the country were talking about the great young trumpet player Louis Armstrong. In those days, Louis was very generous with his money. He would treat his friends to tickets and silent movie shows. He sometimes paid to get his fellow musicians' instruments out of pawn shops so they could keep their jobs on the riverboat. As a result, Louis was usually broke. That changed later. By the late 1930's , Louis Armstrong would become on of the highest paid musicians in the world.

As Louis' fame grew, he moved to Chicago where he played in night clubs. From Chicago, Louis moved to New York City where he formed his own band and recorded his music. In February, 1934, the readers and staff of Esquire Magazine *voted Louis Armstrong the greatest jazz trumpet player in America and called him the "King of Jazz."*

Louis was a little embarrassed by all this adulation. He just kept on playing and singing and recording best-selling songs like "On the Sunny Side of the Street," "Mack the Knife" and "Hello Dolly." He recorded "St. James Infirmary Blues" with the great jazz pianist Earl "Fatha" Hines forty years after he'd first heard it on the streets of New Orleans. Today, that city boasts an eight-foot-high bronze statue of Louis Armstrong. New York, the city Louis moved to, dedicated a museum to his reign as the "King of Jazz."

It has been our experience that emotionally disturbed and/or behavior-disordered children are often bored by the ways daily living skills are taught. The same lack of interest carries over to how activity and lesson plans are delivered. Oftentimes the planning is insufficient. Or, it might be presented out of context and not be sophisticated enough to hold the child's interest on a consistent basis. The result is that a great deal of class time is dedicated to the teacher reacting to out-of-control behavior. Challenging, well-thought-out activities and lesson plans are a core component of the Transformation Education program. The activities and academic lessons should be presented in a brain-compatible way. For a detailed discussion on this technique, we recommend reading Mariale M. Hardiman's *Connecting Brain Research with Effective Teaching: The Brain-Targeted Teaching Model,* (Scarecrow Press, Inc., Lanham, Maryland, 2003).

SECTION IV
Monitoring and Adapting Culture

This section will give the reader an understanding of employee resistance to transformation. We will present ways to manage it through the use of the performance review and the continuous quality improvement system. The section concludes with an anecdotal report on the impact of Transformation Education on organizational growth and its vision for the future.

CHAPTER 9

Resistance to the Use of Culture as a Tool to Promote Transformation and Growth in Children

Principle: The focus of management efforts is on transforming the disparate individual beliefs and values into alignment with the foundational beliefs and values of the organization.

The truth is always simple. Finding the truth is difficult! –Andrew Johnson

With change, comes resistance. Transformation Education is no exception. Transformation Education does not translate into making minor changes in an organization. The assumptions and beliefs of Transformation Education will challenge the beliefs that the majority of the employees accept as the way an organization serving children should operate.

In our experience, staff resistance begins to build against the methodology of acculturation even before the assumptions and beliefs are understood or evaluated. As we began to discuss using culture as a methodology to create a new organizational mindset, alarm bells sounded. By considering the organization as a culture, we were striking a deeply rooted fear. We were exposing the unwelcome truth about our role in society, as agents of social control, not heroes of downtrodden children.

There was a dark suspicion that we were not supposed to discuss such things. We were professionals engaged in treatment. However, the existing service model was off the mark. We were not looking behind the inappropriate behaviors of emotionally troubled children to understand the meaning for the outbursts. Instead, child-serving professionals responded to inappropriate behavior by attaching consequences. We were more congruent with corrections and training rather than treatment and education.

Therefore, management and supervisory staff, who are trying to foster a transformation of the organizational values and beliefs, require a foundational basis for believing they are performing an ethical, transformational service to children. What follows is an explanation of the ethical basis of Transformation Education and recommendations on how to manage the change process.

Culture and Control

The first level of resistance is the accusation that what management is proposing is wrong. It is wrong because efforts aligning a culture with the values of an organization get misconstrued by employees as "cultism," "group think" and even "religion."

A fundamental understanding in Transformation Education is that culture as a force is neither good nor evil. That it can be used for either is also apparent; it can achieve "excellence" in either direction. Perhaps the most familiar culture of evil was that created by Hitler's Germany. It can be argued on many levels, especially in the area of organizational management, that it achieved excellence and that as a chief executive, Hitler was an extraordinary leader. The central problem, however, is that he was evil.

Supposing that "good" is easily determined, however, is to deny the reality of life experience. What then are we left with, when we seek to develop a culture that promotes growth and meaning in the lives of troubled children? It is our proposition that by continuously searching for what is good, we become more alive and sensitive to what is truly good. Searching, especially in our current culture where we honor certainty, may be an extremely uncomfortable position for many employees. If there is to be cultural change, however, we must learn to be open, searching, evaluating and discerning about it.

We should not be overly dismayed as we face the future. We have guides. There are basic "truisms" that have emerged across cultures and time. These truisms we hope to capture in the wisdom principles elucidated in chapter 3. The search for these truisms within the context of daily life is how we discover what is good and brings meaning to our lives.

The novel *1984* is a powerful depiction of a culture designed to control the mindsets of people. It would be erroneous to say cultures do not influence mindset. We see the power of multiple cultural influences on values and assumptions throughout the world. Perhaps more germane is to understand how such cultures are allowed to evolve. While we most often think of it being imposed militaristically, this method is perhaps the least effective. Far more powerful is the innocuous. When the culture becomes bound by its own self-imposed notions of absolute truth it rigidifies. It then no longer is capable of seeing new truths even when faced with the breakdown of its culture. It desperately continues to cling to the past even when faced with a future that is no longer viable.

> *Error never shows itself in its naked reality in order not to be discovered. On the contrary, it dresses elegantly so that the unwary may be led to believe that it is more truthful than truth.* —*Iraneous of Lyons*

If the deliberate designing of a culture sounds Orwellian, it is only because we assume that we are already free of a cultural mindset. This denies the reality of the social, economic and educational systems through which we have learned our values and our thought process.

Now, the control of human behavior has always been unpopular. Any undisguised effort to control usually arouses emotional reactions. We hesitate to admit, even to ourselves, that we are engaged in control, and we may refuse to control, even when this would be helpful, for fear of criticism. This should not dissuade us from understanding and employing the power of culture to influence mindset. If the existing organizational culture is outmoded, ineffective and reactionary, let's change it for the better. To do less denies the reality of the social, economic and educational systems through which we have learned both our values and our thought processes.

Despite living in a "free society," we live in an American culture and many subcultures that control our behavior and thinking whether we choose to acknowledge it or not. We are like fish in water, no more free of cultural influences than individuals from any other culture. After all we are immersed in a culture. What we have to be concerned about in child-serving organizations is this central question: Are we serving children in the best ways? Or, are we trapped by the rigidity of our own cultural beliefs and prevented from doing so?

It is interesting and perhaps quixotic to note that the conscious creation of culture and manipulation of messages is historically regarded with deep suspicion precisely because it smacks of militaristic brainwashing. Yet, many of the techniques used to change "wrong thinking" children in group care today are akin to those we see in authoritarian regimes.

Behavior-modifying drugs, isolation cells, intensive counseling, the deprivation of normal life experiences and other highly structured behavior modification techniques are employed to change a troubled child's behavior. Our culture has done an excellent job of applauding the self-delusion of those who work with emotionally disturbed, delinquent or socially and economically disadvantaged children. The general belief is that they are society's last bastion of help for these children. It can be argued that purveyors of child-serving organizations are their cultural jailers.

We have spent over 20 years working on the implementation of the philosophy and operating systems of Transformation Education, and can easily predict the process an organization uses to adopt this approach. What follows is not for the faint of heart, but hopefully our experiences and eventual success will help child-serving organizations better manage the predictable stages of the adoption process.

The First Experience

Our work with Transformation Education began in 1981 at an organization that was a cross between a child welfare and juvenile justice organization that was approaching its 100th anniversary. It had lost its mission because there was no longer a need to serve orphans and re-invented itself as a provider of services to delinquent youth. It did a great job of this and upgraded its staff with professionals from social work and criminal justice. However, the professionalization of its staff and the change in clientele created a mindset of treatment and social control and the creation of the systems to enforce it. When state funding formulas and laws pertaining to delinquent youth changed, the agency needed to reinterpret its mission to remain financially viable.

The organization made a decision to focus its efforts on serving emotionally disturbed children and adopting Transformation Education as its operating philosophy. However, to do this would require a total transformation of the organization from a place to punish youth for being "bad" to one that prepared them to be successful in life. However, these changes were resisted vehemently by both the professional staff and the referral sources.

Over the course of the first two years of our administration, both groups did everything they could to block change. The referral sources, no matter how much the new approach was explained to them, felt it was not right to grant to children of welfare mothers, drug addicts, mentally ill and the incarcerated, opportunities to learn how to ski, ballroom dance, eat a lobster, ride a horse, explore the heavens with a telescope and more.

In order to gain more independence from reluctant referral sources and gain incremental revenue, the organization began to serve children from other states. Since the organization was the first, and only, agency receiving out-of-state referrals in the state, it created some ill feelings with county government officials. "It's not right for other states to send their garbage here. We don't send our garbage to them!" one local commissioner commented.

Many of the staff resolved their lack of fit with the more value-centered approach by leaving to take other jobs. Along with some of the others who replaced them over the next eight years, they started an active effort to discredit the organization whenever they had the opportunity. The organizational changes that threatened their professional mindsets angered and hurt them.

It took 11 years but eventually the disgruntled former staff members and the local referral sources used their influence to damage the agency's reputation and hurt it financially. These actions forced the organization to focus on survival rather than innovation and change.

"Rocky" Country

The next stop for Transformation Education was at the Family Service Agency of Philadelphia, another century-old organization. This agency was experiencing major financial problems due to the social work staff's unwillingness to offer anything but nine to five office-based individual and group counseling.

United Way was the primary funder of the organization. The United Way representative explained that they would withdraw their funding if the organization continued to limit its services to office-based counseling. There were tremendous unmet needs to serve families in housing projects and problem children in the school system. The previous CEO had been forced out of the agency by the staff when he attempted to alter the program and their work schedule. The staff belonged to a city-wide union.

The board of trustees was interested in Transformation Education as a means of renewing the organization and bringing its services up to date. We were successful in gaining the confidence of United Way. We expanded services to a housing project and received a contract to establish a special school for children who were expelled, suspended or having great difficulty being managed in a public school.

As you might deduce, the social work staff resisted the precepts of Transformation Education. They did everything they could to undermine attempts that would cause longer office hours or make them serve the community. Their union fought the changes. They went on strike and managed to get the contract in the housing project revoked and offered to another bidder.

They even managed to prevent the establishment of the special school.

In time, we were able to win the battle by defeating the strike and implementing the changes necessary to move the organization forward. But we lost the war. The board chair could not tolerate the contentiousness resulting from the changes. When the counseling staff said they lost confidence in our leadership and could not work for us, the board chair sided with them and we were on our way to Baltimore. Not long after, the Philadelphia agency, which had been one of the first casework agencies in the United States and a leader in the field of social work for many years, ended up closing its doors.

Transformation Education Travels to Maryland

The Children's Guild in Baltimore, an established child-serving organization that serves emotionally disturbed children, was the next site to implement Transformation Education. We encountered an organization with a great reputation that was using the combination of a behavior-modification and medical model to operate its nonpublic school and its group home program. The model worked for the most part in the group home, but the staff had great difficulty managing the children and educating them in the school. The organization had definitely lost a sense of meaning, for the staff had structured the organization so their needs took precedence over the needs of the children. When Transformation Education was introduced, 90% of the staff and 50% of the management resigned or was terminated.

The clinical staff members were the most threatened by the assumptions inherent in Transformation Education. Citing the mass exodus and firing of the staff, they contacted the Maryland State Department of Education and managed to investigate the organization. They called the *Baltimore Sun* to complain. An investigative reporter visited the agency to report on the discontent. We were able to get past this as well as overcome several staff members who brought concerns to the board of trustees about how the agency operated. The journey and struggle to establish and give Transformation Education the support that it needed to flourish was not easy.

The Typical Implementation Process

We learned from these experiences how to implement Transformation Education more efficiently. We know now the natural occurrences and reactions a leader must be prepared to manage. Let's outline the normal course of events one is likely to encounter when trying to implement Transformation Education. These events have occurred even after every attempt has been made to educate and involve management and staff in the process, incorporating their ideas, answering their questions and offering them support.

Remember, there is a difference between transformation and change. As was stated in chapter 6, transformation has to do with replacing the power structure with something different. It is a complete metamorphosis in form or structure. Change is keeping the same concept but substituting one thing for another. In essence, change is moving from the English saddle to the western saddle. Transformation is exchanging the horse for the car. Resistance is inevitable and techniques to manage change are not identical to those needed to manage transformation. All the phases one encounters to bring about transformation are outlined below. These phases are progressive and predictable, but not linear.

Honeymoon Phase

The ideas of Transformation Education are always embraced and understood by the lay community and the board of trustees. The board and the lay community tend to have open minds and no personal agendas to protect. They do not have a personal philosophy of how to transform emotionally disturbed and delinquent children. They do not feel they are giving up cherished beliefs, nor are they experiencing the daily impact of these ideas. It even makes sense to management when they hear ideas and philosophies of Transformation Education. However, the honeymoon is over when executive management staff begin to understand they must transform their mindsets and rethink how they manage and spend their time. The honeymoon phase lasts about three months.

Sort-Out Phase

The initial problem surfaces with top management. When management meets for an extended period to discuss the implementation of Transformation Education, there is always a key member of the team who cannot adopt its basic assumptions.

They will enter into an ideological battle to preserve existing practice based on the medical, social control or current educational model. They are threatened by workplace expectations, believe growth (transformation) can occur without pain, and are greatly upset by the questioning of their assumptions. They become angry and say they feel "devalued." This reaction relates to the challenge of their expertise and from the loss of acceptance of the rationales they utilize to justify how they manage and problem solve.

Transformation Education throws into doubt the knowledge passed down to them through professors, former mentors and books they have studied. They are tripping over a new paradigm. The ideological issues deflate them. When implementation is expected, the manager will not or cannot execute.

Resistance forms. Adopting a new culture is compared to "cult" thinking. They do not believe we should expect employees to "transform." These recalcitrant member(s) of the management staff will try to maintain the status quo and avoid their own transformation.

They will argue that it does not make a difference if everyone "buys into the philosophy." They will say one's philosophy is not important as long as the results are good. They will insist that philosophies come and go. They will say we need to attract good people, and good people do not want to be micromanaged.

Their theme song is: "Let's just say what needs to be done and permit everyone to carry it out in whatever way they prefer. This is true leadership. We are all professionals." You can imagine the confusing messages and lack of alignment between values and practice that occur. They perceive the leader's job as obtaining the funds necessary so everyone can practice what they believe.

These managers will most likely resign and share the reason for their resignation with their supporters or a member of the board of trustees. A common tactic is to write a letter and send it to each member of the board of trustees. Their rationale for doing this "...is to prevent good staff from leaving the agency and for the best interest of the children." Whether the person resigns or is fired for making the end run–the result is the same. Fear is instilled in the staff: If you don't agree, you will be forced out or fired. This phase lasts for about six months. However, the fear of being fired is likely to become imbedded in the culture until the organization is truly transformed.

Development Phase

Implementation begins when the management team coalesces around the ideas of Transformation Education. The management team is energized by the challenge and intellectual stimulation resulting from the intensity and awareness of the discussions. Examined are the assumptions and hidden messages buried in policy statements, the program, physical environment and work processes.

Executive management relationships with one another grow. Managers are honest with one another; they challenge their colleagues and the CEO's perceptions. They feel the freedom to question, to innovate and to risk. They also experience great satisfaction as they witness the agency growing. Yet, they also are frustrated when they see the long road ahead and report that they lack the energy, time and staff necessary to accomplish the level of transformation they are being asked to bring about.

During management retreats, it will be easy to identify those who are willing to adopt the principles of Transformation Education. Within three months, the CEO will know the extent of commitment of each manager, the level of understanding they have of Transformation Education and his/her ability to implement it in their sphere of organizational influence. In this phase, they will have the willingness to implement Transformation Education, but they will lack a true understanding of how to implement it. If they are open to learning, this is not a problem. This phase is ongoing.

Launch Phase

Be aware when the launch phase starts, there may be some backlash. It could be an office move, a program change, a schedule change or a performance review system. This will cause someone on the staff to act out, blatantly resist or become insubordinate. This will eventually happen no matter how much you prepare the staff.

When a staff member acts out you will be forced to deal with it. If you discipline an employee who is popular with the staff, be prepared for a battle. It is not out of the realm of possibility that the employee, or those who are sympathetic to his/her cause, will call the news media, or send a letter to one of the regulatory bodies complaining about the organization. Or, they might try to organize a strike or invite in a union, send a letter to the board, organize parents against the agency or take action to motivate an investigation to discredit the agency. You will of course have to discipline or discharge this person and/or his/her accomplices, and unfortunately, this may create fear and distrust throughout the staff. The Launch Phase lasts for about 18 months.

Passive Resistance Phase

In the next phase, a strong and supportive executive management team is in place, seasoned by overcoming the various trials and tribulations. The executive management team can make many things happen, but they will find that middle management and many of the staff retain old ideas. For middle management, this is the passive resistance phase.

Middle management and a sizeable number of the employees will be infected with what Davis Balestracci refers to as "victimitis" [Balestracci, 2003]. Staff members tend to resist by whining and avoiding true accountability through blaming, feigning confusion, denying responsibility, explaining why something can't be done and stonewalling.

Middle management responds by treading lightly around certain issues or avoiding them altogether. Many of the middle managers will want to maintain their relationships with their staff. They may report that they do not feel free to suggest specific solutions. They may complain bitterly about the employees' tactics, but take no action. They see new options as too complicated to implement and dance around responsible action. This static situation will continue for the length of time it takes management to train and gain the support of middle management staff. Passive resistance can last six months or until the program director becomes committed actively to implementing Transformation Education under his/her sphere of influence.

Transformation Phase

Once this problem is resolved, dramatic changes occur in staff and children. Staff turnover becomes minimal, and staff members become enthusiastic learners. Their competence builds daily. A minimum amount of time is spent dealing with discipline problems or out-of-control children. Ongoing, steady improvement of the program takes place. Upper management is freed from over involvement in crisis management issues and can now engage in program development and refinement. Staff members acknowledge that they have changed. The imprint of Transformation Education has made a positive impact on their personal lives.

The statement above is not intended to convey an end state or nirvana. It is true that management spends less time dealing with discipline problems or out-of-control children. However, management will continue to face resistance and struggle related to maintaining the transformational culture established and trying to make it more powerful and consistent. This is because entropy is real. The moment you cease contributing to move the culture of a child-serving organization toward being more child-centered and transformational it begins to revert back toward being more adult centered. The all-staff e-mail presented below provides an everyday example of organizational life encountered in this phase.

> *This morning I arrived at my office at 5:45 a.m. I noticed an orange lying by the curb by the door to enter the school. I decided to leave the orange there to determine if anyone would pick it up. I left the building at 6:45 a.m. and returned at 8 a.m. and the orange was still there. If your name is on the list below you walked past that orange, which sends one or more of these messages to me:*

1. *You support environments that convey neglect and low expectations.*
2. *You have an "It's not my job attitude!" and are deliberately undermining the philosophy of the organization.*
3. *You believe work begins once you enter the building rather than when you enter the parking lot.*
4. *You were taught never to pick up anything off the street and follow this expectation blindly rather than thinking in context.*
5. *You paid no attention to what you were taught in pre-service training about environmental messages. If you did pay attention, you do not believe messages in the environment have much of an impact on children.*

I'm asking for your help in being more vigilant and to counter messages of neglect and poverty at the school the moment you see them. Maintaining the culture is an important aspect of everyone's job. If a student is with you it is important that you pick up trash and interpret the meaning of the word commitment. By commitment we mean we are dedicated to maintaining a clean environment and doing a job right. Tell the student we want them to grow up and be an employee with high expectations who takes initiative to do the job right.

—Andy Ross

The adult centeredness is revealed in the comments received by 3 of the 80 employees who took the time to e-mail back a response.

Dorie: *Mr Ross, I really did take offense to those comments. I have never been treated with such disrespect. I feel as though my hard work was undermined.*

Sandra: *With all due respect, I must share my feelings.*

It saddens me greatly to think that my level of commitment, caring and dedication to The Guild is judged by an orange in the gutter and not by the effort displayed every day as I enter the doors of the school. I do my best to promote the philosophy of The Guild and in so doing support and encourage your leadership and would hope you know that by now. These are difficult times at The Guild. Unfortunately I believe this communiqué sets us back even further as we persevere; encouraging a positive environment, and appreciating the staff who continue to work very hard on behalf of the kids.

Vince: *Your comments about the orange have certainly stirred a lot of discussion at The Guild this morning. Picking up an orange is something that would go beyond the basic job responsibilities of most employees of the Guild other than Operations. If an organization wants its employees to go "beyond the basics," it has to create a climate in which the employees believe the organization goes "beyond the basics" in meeting their needs as well. This is known as Social Exchange Theory.*

Let me give you my situation as an example. Let's begin with salary. ... Given that I have an earned doctorate and more than 30 years of experience, my salary would be as follows:

Baltimore County School System $71,300
Baltimore City School System $68,534
Children's Guild..$57,157

In addition to salary, let us look at my employment. Since the beginning of the school year, I have worked part-time, but made it known that I wanted full-time employment. Can you understand why I might feel The Guild has not gone "beyond the basics" with me? While my circumstances are unique, it gives you something to think about. What does the Guild do to make employees want to go beyond the basics and pick up that orange?

The orange situation provides excellent material for growing the management staff. It is obvious that if 80 employees, including maintenance staff, walked past the orange, the importance of the physical environment is not being emphasized by department heads and supervisors. It also signals that executive management's attempts to train middle managers in environmental awareness are ineffective. The example also provides executive management with an everyday experience to use in training middle management how to foster a transformational culture in a child-serving organization.

The staff memos and comments will seduce the middle managers and department heads into appeasing the staff and identifying with their concern that the tone of the e-mail was inappropriate. They will view the problem from the perspective of process, i.e., "The way the e-mail was stated was critical and insensitive." "It did not need to list names; the complaint should have been forwarded to the department head and the department head could have brought up the issue at a staff meeting." "The sending of the e-mail created such an unnecessary negative reaction among staff and it took a great deal of time out of the day to deal with the reaction."

The executive staff will view the problem as middle managers and department heads making the following errors: 1) empathizing and identifying with adult-centered concerns rather than focusing on the neglected environmental message being sent to the child; 2) using undifferentiated management intervention and thinking, i.e., employing a managerial intervention that sustains a culture (empathy) rather than one that has the power to transform the culture (fostering anxiety); 3) failure to use the opportunity to emphasize paying attention to detail in their work, anticipating consequences of unwanted messages and helping employees understand the opportunities that exist in the environment for teachable moments.

This example also can be used to help middle managers diagnose the root cause of the problem. Possible diagnoses are any one or combination of the following staff mindsets:

1. Picking up trash is someone else's job.
2 Work begins after employees get to their posts, not on the way to them.
3. Staff need equipment to make trash pickup easier, such as gloves or graspers, to minimize direct contact with the trash.

4. Middle managers and department heads are not focused on organizational culture, just completion of work tasks.
5. Middle managers fear employee reactions to pointing out environmental messages that would create more work for employees.

The Etiology of Cultural Resistance

We were raised under the power of culture to believe and think in specific ways. There was impressed on our conscious awareness a right way to teach, learn and think about organizations and their construction. In examining the expectations of various organizational cultures (social service, education, businesses) we began to understand why it is so difficult to reshape the basic organizational operating assumptions that guide child-serving organizations.

It is difficult at first to consider the legitimacy of other ways of operating organizations. Once a person has been acculturated with the beliefs and modus operandi of a culture, it is extremely difficult to do anything but repeat the same instilled beliefs and approaches. The rare few break the mold. They undertake the challenge if they truly feel the necessity to adopt different beliefs and approaches, and a new methodology opens for the rest of us. We must be frank. There is a definite bias against the basic assumptions of Transformation Education held by the clinical and education staff that inhabits and inhibits child-serving institutions. There is a physiological and evolutionary rationale for their resistance.

The Way the Brain Operates

Neuroscience has taught us that "the neuron is the principal cellular unit of the central nervous system (i.e., the brain). These cells are the units that receive, integrate and transmit electrochemical signals in neural networks that produce body movement and mental activity. Indeed, all human behavior is the result of communication among neural cells." [Dickman and Stanford-Blair: 2002]

As mentioned in chapter 1, if we learn a response to something through practicing it over and over again, the neurons (our brain's communication agents) trigger an electrical impulse to a receiving neuron that tells us how to act. So, if we extensively speak another language in another culture for a lengthy period of time, speaking English will not be lost to us. When we learn how to speak English again, we can recall the English words instantaneously and use them to make puns and jokes, and create different meanings by using them in different contexts and with different tones.

As mentioned in chapter 2, a myelin sheath (see Figure 1 in chapter 2) grows over this neural pathway like a conduit or tunnel through which this electrical impulse is transmitted. The conduit makes sure the electrical signal stays on the path. It becomes thicker the more times we use the information. In essence it becomes a superhighway with no exit to get off. The thickness of the myelin sheath increases the more times we use the information and the response as a means of making sure we have instantaneous recall of it. This serves us well until something new is discovered, or we want to learn Japanese. Now we need to think differently.

So English gets in the way and the sheath prevents you from building an "off ramp" so you can respond differently. To think in a different language requires much practice to create the neural pathways that permit you to do so. You really can't until you have a transformation experience of living in Japan and speaking Japanese daily.

To incorporate new ways of thinking in the staff, the first thing that needs to be done is to motivate them to want to adopt new beliefs and approaches. Along with the motivation, the organization has to provide a different culture and repeated opportunities for practice and correction before new neural pathways develop and a new myelin sheath thickens. This is obviously a lot of work for the staff. They will resist unless they have no alternative but to give up old ideas and take on new ones. Positive motivation makes the learning easier. All of us really should want to learn and discover more effective ways of practicing our craft.

Davis Balestracci, in his article "Handling the Human Side of Change," points out that there is a deliberate process to individual learning and culture change. First, adults must achieve awareness of what is being asked. Then they must experience a breakthrough in knowledge. Following the intellectual understanding, adults need to choose to make a breakthrough in thinking, and finally choose a breakthrough in acting consistently with the knowledge and the thinking the organization expects. Balestracci goes on to say that the traditional linear, stimulus-response education model is useless when employees need to make fundamental changes as to how they think and act in an organization. [Balestracci: 2003]

Evolutionary Forces

Being aware of Darwin's theory of "the survival of the fittest" will generate an understanding of the resistance to the cultural approach. Just like animals will fight to pass on their genes to preserve the fittest of the species, humans do the same thing with ideas. Once ideas reach the level of assumptions and beliefs, they become ideals we are willing to die for so we can pass them on to the next generation. Consider such concepts as democracy and Islam. Employees and bosses try to pass on their philosophies so the organization operates in conjunction with their clinical practice philosophy, or enforcing their concept of a fair day's work.

The concept that it is the individual or family who is the prime determiner of our society's values is one of our nation's strongly held beliefs. This entrenched concept prevents organizational culture from being the primary authority to educate and treat emotionally disturbed children. To believe otherwise has been un-American. Therefore, it is the parent's fault that the child misbehaves or is not interested in school. As professionals, we should not be held responsible for the actions of the family if we cannot make the child behave.

We have heard staff in our group homes and schools use the measure of their own families repeatedly. "If I did that, my mother would have grounded me for a year!" Everyone has heard a public school teacher say when confronted with unruly students: "I came to teach not to baby-sit!" If we can blame the families for a child's behavior, what is the staff's motivation for the child learning or adopting more socially appropriate behavior? Hence, there is staff resistance to give up their self-protecting beliefs for the accountable beliefs of a Transformation Education organization.

Too many child-serving institutions and schools are rooted in segmentation. We have been seduced into the belief that effectiveness is achieved through delineating tasks and departmentalizing responsibilities. From Henry Ford's assembly line to McDonald's hamburgers, organizations rely on the principles of segmentation and specialization to achieve economic efficiency and bottom-line results. By breaking tasks and responsibilities down into sequential steps, efficient systems are created that can produce more for less.

To achieve segmentation and efficiency, we have constructed "education factories." These factories come complete with rooms to hold children of the same age. Students sit at the rows of desks and learn the same standardized information. The students are taught by individuals, who were taught by college professors, who were taught using the same structure and methodology since the early 20th century. The education factories have the same bottom-line intent of producing workers for other organizations in the culture. It is a closed-loop system with a self-fulfilling philosophy.

The structure for evaluating performance is also linear: A, B, C, D, E/F. Naturally, those who achieve "A" are considered successful and those who do not are less successful and even failures. If you fail on a continuous basis, you are labeled. The labeling is due to individual peculiarities such as "sub-normal" IQ, behavioral/emotional "disorders," learning "disabilities," or perhaps most degrading, "unmotivated!" Unmotivated to do what? Absorb information or live a meaningful life? The assumption that perhaps the rigidity of the system is inappropriate for the child is seldom questioned. Even when it is, no real change can result. We continue to operate without vision and fail to ask "what if" we approach education differently.

One of the greatest tragedies of this linear extension is our cultural belief that schools should not teach values. Do we honestly believe values can be separated and taught apart from the daily interactions of society? To suggest that schools do not already teach values is blindness. To prevent them from developing and teaching from a common value base is to foster mindlessness. It is not the responsibility of the nonsectarian child-serving organizations and schools to teach religion. It is their responsibility to consciously develop a child's character. What do we value more than teaching the importance of caring for one's self and others, for one's family, school, community, state, country and the world?

Despite our grave concerns about the moral decay of our current culture, we persist in believing that what we learned and how we learned it is the truth. What is true is that our culture has certainly been effective. We now have great corporations and technology. We also have large and noble churches. But we are also left grasping for meaning.

Professional Bias

In a workshop given in 1993 at the Family Service of America Biennial in Madison, Wisconsin, Dr. Robert W. Terry illuminated our thinking regarding staff resistance to change. He described the various mindsets, which help people identify their worldviews and their prejudices. He suggested we see life primarily as one of the following metaphors: life is a Gift, a Market, a Body, a Struggle, a Journey or Art.

Professionals in human service professions and education have been acculturated to view life as a Body. The Life is a Body metaphor finds it very difficult to accept that the key stimulus for growth is "death" (of an idea, a way of doing things) and renewal. Life is a Body is focused on the avoidance of pain. This concept of no growth without pain is misleading. We can be sidetracked by the outcry from those who believe that "if you do it right, it doesn't have to be painful."

Struggle and change are not valued commodities among direct care staff who deal with emotionally disturbed and behavior-disordered children. Their primary focus is on compliance and control–the dominating cultures of child-serving organizations. This emphasis on ensuring absence of conflict is an ingrained obsession. The goal is managing and preventing out-of-control behavior through its policies, rules, procedures and the design of its building and activities.

Any attempts to empower children by operating without clearly defined consequences for aberrant behavior sends shivers down the backs of the staff. Without strict controls in place, the direct care staff consider themselves impotent and endangered. That is the fear that prevents change.

The aforementioned beliefs are not congruent with the basic tenets for promoting growth and transformation of children who populate group care agencies serving emotionally disturbed or delinquent youth. Nor do such control tactics apply to schools serving the socially and economically deprived children.

When we talk about children who are emotionally disturbed, delinquent or socially and economically deprived, let's take a pass on the Life as a Body metaphor. The metaphor that fits this population is Life is a Journey. The basic belief of this metaphor: Life is a continuous series of comings and goings, the opening of new paths of discovery. You can't control life but you can control your response to it. Chaos and order exist at the same time. When it comes to conflict and change, flexibility is essential and rigidity is bad. Change is constant and crises present opportunity for change and growth. Discovery results from "bumping" against ideas and people. The goal is personal knowledge and moral growth.

Unfortunately, the mental health and education professionals that populate child-serving institutions and schools are unwilling to separate themselves from the Body metaphor. They have been acculturated by their professions to exercise control as the underlying principle.

Business and health professionals and most of the technical and support staff will operate from the other metaphors i.e., Life is a Market (acquisition is the goal); Life is a Gift (goal of life is accept what you get); Life is a Struggle (goal of life is power); or Life is Art (goal of life is freedom and expression of individuality). With these mixed metaphors, you can expect resistance and a reluctance to adopt values and beliefs consistent with the journey metaphor.

M. Scott Peck began his book *The Road Less Traveled* with these words, "Life is difficult." The children in our care cannot escape struggle, suffering and pain. They have to journey through struggle until they are ready to "die" or surrender the self-imprisoning behaviors that bind them. On the journey's path through the pain and suffering, all of us have the capacity to grow in sensitivity, caring and service. We believe the organizational culture sets the stage for this redevelopment process to occur.

What we have seen happening in child-serving organizations is the growth of psychodynamic therapeutic approaches and a disregard for the impact the organizational culture has on a child. This perspective has resulted in an unspoken assumption that the design of the organization's culture has little bearing on the treatment of the child.

Along with this assumption is the belief that the ingredients necessary to help youth change and grow are: structure, consistency, behavioral contracts, life space interview, physical crises management, locked facilities, family therapy, medication, psychotherapy and counseling. When there are problems with the child, it naturally follows that the solution is to increase staff and psychiatric time, change medication and change structure. If such adjustments to the existing system do not obtain the appropriate response, the problem is then assumed to be with the child; that s/he is not amendable to treatment.

As we know from the *Hardwired to Connect* study, many child-serving organizations are not designed to foster change and growth, even though they think they are. The assumptions that the professionals hold to be true to promote growth are necessary, but not optimal. In some cases, they are not sufficient. We find an organizational culture and design that places its demands on the children, but does not model behaviors encouraging growth and purpose. In essence they model: "Do as I say!" not "Do as I do!"

Unfortunately, the overriding bias of many administrators and professionals is that the organization is separate from treatment. Administration in child-serving organizations, actually in all of human services, is expected to concentrate on the maintenance needs of the organization and its political function [Miringhoff 1980]. The result is an overwhelming emphasis on the organizational goal of compliance with the demands of funding bodies, regulatory and accrediting agents and the needs of the professional staff. When management takes on the role of fostering change, growth, wisdom and contextual thinking of the staff and the children, it is viewed as entering the turf of the professionals.

One of the main reasons Transformation Education concepts find difficulty taking root in group care has been the belief that the concept of the therapeutic milieu has already been well developed and thoroughly understood. Therefore, the milieu is separate from the organizational culture. It is believed that the children and the staff, not the organization, create the milieu. This is far from a proven fact, however. This splitting off from organizational culture is at the core of resistance when trying to implement Transformation Education in a group care setting.

If we re-read Fritz Redl's paper "The Concept of the Therapeutic Milieu," we quickly come to the realization that Redl did not understand how the milieu actually worked. He states: "Just what goes on when we claim that any one of those milieus given did something to your youngster? This puts us into one of the most noteworthy gaps in all our theory of personality, and frankly, I don't think even our most up-to-date models are quite up to it." Redl goes on to state: "I, for one, would want to explain loudly what I didn't dare whisper at the start of my paper, or I would have scared you off too soon. I would like to find out not only what milieu is and how it operates, but also how we can describe it, how we influence it and by what actions...created or molded. At the moment I am convinced of only one thing for sure, we all have quite a way to go to achieve either of those tasks." [Whitaker & Trieschman: 1972]

Minimizing the Natural Resistance to Transformation Education

The Board of Trustees

There are two prerequisites to the adoption of Transformation Education. One is that the governing body operates in such a way that it is not involved in day-to-day management of the organization, i.e., it governs through policy and assessment. The other is that the mission and vision statements are current and supported by the governing body. If these two prerequisites are in place, gaining the governing body's active support for Transformation Education is no different than gaining the support of the governing body for any project.

The CEO discusses the need for implementing Transformation Education with the board chair. Then the CEO develops a presentation for the appropriate board committee to review a new direction for the child-serving organization. The plan includes presenting the problem and the proposed solution (adoption of Transformation Education); and introducing a summary of the research that led to the conclusion to adopt Transformation Education, along with an analysis of the research supporting it, the issues to be addressed and the plan for funding and implementation.

Following the board committee's approval of the adoption of Transformation Education, it is brought to the governing body's executive committee for review and discussion. Finally, a presentation is made to the governing body for its final approval. Throughout all the discussions with the governing body, it is important for the CEO to remember that a major transformation of all the organizational systems is being proposed. Therefore, it is important to reiterate during the presentation process that the adoption of Transformation Education will result in a major change in how the organization operates. Employees who are unable to work effectively under the new model will leave on their own accord and some will be terminated.

With the adoption of Transformation Education, the CEO has to provide regular reports on the implementation process. Although necessary, the regular updating is not sufficient by itself in maintaining the support of the governing body through the transformation process. To ensure the support of the governing body during the implementation process, the CEO will need to do three things:

1. Continue to operate with a balanced budget or surplus, and agree upon measurable outcomes indicating success such as academic scores, number of discharges to less restrictive environments, decrease in medication errors, etc. This is essential. The dramatic process of change to incorporate Transformation Education unleashes chaotic conditions that give the appearance of an organization out of control. In reality, this is the fallout from a change process.

2. Hire a public relations consultant to generate the positive coverage your organization requires prior to the implementation of Transformation Education. There needs to be increased visibility of the organization in the community through feature stories, radio and TV coverage of fundraising events and increased communication with employees, parents and referral workers. Prepare the board and referral sources for the launch and fallout that can occur through implementing Transformation Education. Make sure you do not under-communicate. If anything, try to over-communicate. Send out monthly newsletters promoting successes to staff, parents and referral workers. It is important to continue this effort throughout the implementation process to counter any employee attempts to undermine or discredit the change process.

3. Establish performance goals and measures. Rate the degree of achievement in attaining the goals set with the governing body such as renovating the physical plant to be consistent with Transformation Education, achieving national accreditation or re-accreditation, implementing the Baldridge System or some other goal that sanctions the review and alteration of policy, procedures and processes. These management actions require some urgency in rewriting policies, procedures, processes and mission statements in a way that is consistent with Transformation Education concepts. This provides a rationale to review the basic assumptions of how the organization operates and sets needed deadlines for training the entire organization in the transformation effort. It also provides a clean audit and support for what the CEO is doing from an outside independent source.

Expect a typhoon effect when implementation occurs. That is why the CEO needs to prepare the governing body and community for massive changes. Key staff may resign, and high turnover may occur. Disgruntled managers and employees may attempt to engage the board in an effort to undermine the cultural changes.

The Executive Management Staff

For starters, the CEO develops a three- to four-day management retreat with the top leadership. The CEO uses the retreat to educate the key management staff about the concepts underpinning Transformation Education. The CEO helps them understand how the adoption of these principles will have an impact on the daily operations of the organization. Next, the organization's mission and vision statements are reviewed to determine if they should be changed or restated. The third component is to identify organizational changes needed.

When the discussion turns to key organizational changes such as eliminating departments, changing reporting relationships and who supervises whom, moving people to improve communication and efficiency, etc., the plan will bog down. The CEO will need to reflect on the rationale presented for maintaining the status quo in any particular area. It is good to reconvene the group within four weeks to rediscuss these issues, following reflection and individual discussions with key management staff.

The CEO may want to use a consultant for the second retreat to help the group develop a draft of the implementation plan. Undoubtedly, there will be a number of issues not resolved. These should be listed at the end of the retreat. The CEO should then meet with the executive management group to resolve these issues and create the implementation plan.

Any resistor who is a member of the executive management group should not be involved in the creation of the implementation plan. That will only waste time and create battles. When the plan is drafted, share it with the entire executive management group for reactions and suggestions.

It is extremely important not to attempt to alter the mindsets of the strongest resistors to the plan. They will continue to battle, be "hurt" and feel their opinions are devalued if the CEO disagrees. The ongoing battle with these individuals is what fuels active resistance. They will depart the organization; some will attempt to discredit the CEO and the organization. It is best to discuss the resistance with the chair of the governing body and gain support and understanding for their departure from the organization. Then recruit quietly for their replacements prior to terminating them so their replacements are ready to start work the day after the resistors are terminated.

Then the CEO meets with the resistors and explains why they will be happier working for an organization that is more consistent with their philosophical beliefs and expectations. Likely, a severance payment to cover a three-month period will be arranged. Fortunately there will be other organizations that match their philosophies. Keep in mind the understanding that there is no way to send them away happy. Strive nonetheless to minimize the amount of effort they will expend being publicly critical of you, the organization and Transformation Education.

Bring the plan back to the retreat group for final review and comment. Explain the reasons for the departure of some members of the management group. This will do two things: Transmit the message that the CEO is serious about implementing Transformation Education, and emphasize that management is expected to be actively involved in the implementation process.

However, the CEO should hold off the initiation of Transformation Education until replacements are on board. The evidence for this was garnered by Jim Collins, a professor in the Stanford Graduate School for Business, and his research team of 21 top graduate students. They studied the companies in America that had gone from good to great. [Collins: 2001]

> *The executives who ignited the transformations from good to great did not first figure out where to drive the bus and then get people to take it there. No, they first got the right people on the bus (and the wrong people off the bus) and then*

figured out where to go. . . . The good-to-great leaders understood these simple truths. First, if you begin with "who," rather than "what," you can more easily adapt to a changing world. If people join the bus primarily because of where it is going, what happens if you get ten miles down the road and you need to change direction? You've got a problem. But if people are on the bus because of who else is on the bus, then it's much easier to change direction: "Hey, I got on this bus because of who else is on it; if we need to change direction to be more successful, fine with me." Second, if you have the right people on the bus, the problem of how to motivate and manage people largely goes away. The right people don't need to be tightly managed or fired up; they will be self-motivated by the inner drive to produce the best results and to be part of creating something great. Third, if you have the wrong people, it doesn't matter whether you discover the right direction; you still won't have a great company. Great vision without great people is irrelevant.

In determining who should and should not be on the bus, one needs to have a guideline. Collins found out in his research that the moment the CEO or his key managers feels the need to manage an employee tightly, that is a hiring mistake. The best people don't need to be managed. However, one needs to make sure that a person is in the right seat on the bus. Great companies spend time moving their people around if they feel they possess the talent to do the job better in another position. They were just in the wrong job. [Collins: 2001]

The departure of these management staff does not ensure the end of resistance. As the implementation process moves forward, there will be dissenting managers who indicated initial support for these ideas. They will not be able to adopt them. Their decisions and positions will be inconsistent with Transformation Education. This is to be expected. There is a difference between those who need more education and those who are not motivated to change. The telling points are the amount of effort they put into trying to implement components of Transformation Education and their success doing it. The absence of effort or even minor progress means resistance.

Working with the Professional and Support Staff

It is delusional to believe that intensive training and logic will overcome old habits and beliefs when threatened by a new idea. Balestracci [Balestraci: 2003] postulates that an individual's mindset and workplace behaviors are shaped by the first 20 years of life.

The result is unconscious, predictable adult behavior patterns that are changeable only by significant emotional events—either personal (birth, death, illness, marriage), societal (the Great Depression, WW II, the Kennedy assassination, 9/11) or the sudden realization (through appropriate feedback) that some of these behaviors will sabotage organizational success. In other words, job security.

Our emotions alert us and protect us. So if the brain's amygdala perceives a threat, it will trigger an emotion that gets us to act first and think later, resulting in predictable defensive patterns. Research has shown that emotion is very much in charge of human behavior.

Staff Selection

If it is true that an individual's mindset and workplace behaviors are shaped within the first 20 years of life, staff selection has a great deal to do with minimizing or overcoming resistance to the Transformation Education model. But selection is an unpredictable process. Picking the Heisman Trophy winner or a number one college football draft choice is no guarantee of success in the National Football League. But if you use a disciplined and consistent approach to selecting staff and things don't work out, it is easier to analyze comparative data. Comparative data helps us understand the interview's degree of effectiveness. It helps you determine if a question assessed the life theme you were evaluating, or if the selection was right but the supervision or training was inadequate.

Besides the interview, credentials and reference checks, and work history, the Transformation Education approach calls for an assessment of talent and of applicants' values to see if they are congruent with those of the organization. Many selection companies can assist an organization in evaluating a prospect's innate talent to perform the role of a practitioner, membor of support staff, supervisor or administrator. We have found the Gallup Organization's Perceiver instruments are highly reliable for this purpose. Readers who would like more information regarding this methodology should refer to the articles written by Ross and Holtke in the bibliography.

Life themes, as they apply to applicants, are considered crucial to the hiring process for Transformation Education. Life themes emanate from what is known as Theme Theory and are defined as recurring patterns of thought, feeling and behavior. We learned of Theme Theory from Dr. Donald O. Clifton's work at the University of Nebraska. He later used the theory to launch a major corporation that assists businesses in identifying highly talented people. His firm, Selection Research, Inc., proved so successful that he later purchased and now operates the Gallup Poll.

Each person possesses different sets of themes. These themes are not always dominant, but are easily and spontaneously aroused and thus characterize the behavior of the person. The following constellation of life themes we found to be helpful in identifying those candidates with a mindset compatible with Transformation Education:

- *Courage* – Persons with courage have the ability to express their own emotionality in a positive, genuine way. Without attacking anyone, they "speak out" when necessary to give difficult feedback to a coworker or to management. They are willing to risk rejection from others for their beliefs. They set and maintain limits and deal directly with young people in an open, straightforward manner.

- *Kinesthetic Work Orientation* – These persons are physically active and are always involved in their work: be it working around the house, shopping, gardening, reading, volunteering, traveling, socializing. They are always doing something. They tend to have a good deal of stamina and enjoy spending long hours working. A person with strength in this theme area sees work or physical activity as positive and personally satisfying.

- *Developer* – These individuals have the capacity to receive satisfaction from the growth of others in a vicarious manner. The developer gives time, talents and resources to bring about the greatest change for the good in others. Helping others be successful is more satisfying to this individual than his or her own performance. Developers are essential for those in management/supervisory positions and who directly work with children or in training others.

- *Relationship* – Those who are good at building relationships fit well in management/supervisory positions and can directly work with children or in training others. The individual likes young people and expects them to reciprocate. These are employees who work with children and see relationships as a favorable and necessary condition for human growth.

- *Mission* – These employees embrace success in the cultural model. That is their mission. Mission refers to the staff beliefs and assumptions that determine to a large degree what is possible. They understand that they are engaged in facilitating or directly carrying out important work, i.e., providing an opportunity for children to grow and change so they will be successful in life.

- *Discernment* – These are the contextual thinkers. This is important particularly for the management and clinical staff, since the Transformation Education organization operates on principles and norms rather than rules. Take the principle of caring. In one context, if an employee is late for work because a child is ill, it requires some understanding. In another situation caring may mean that the employee should receive a written reprimand or be terminated for regularly not showing up on time. Ideally you would want every employee to possess this theme, but at a minimum it is essential that the management and clinical staff possess discernment.

Questions during employment interviews should assess these themes to determine compatibility of the candidate with the organization. Assistance on how to do this effectively is provided in the book *First Break all the Rules: What the World's Greatest Managers Do Differently* by Marcus Buckingham and Curt Coffman.

Our experience indicates that the employees who demonstrate the six key themes will have the greatest success in helping children change and grow and will enjoy the challenge of a Transformation Education approach. The result of hiring people with this constellation of traits is best described in a brochure advertising a human resource publication. An excerpt attributed the concept of Peak Performers to Charles Garfield.

Peak Performers differ from workaholics in many ways, but the philosophy all boils down to the idea of balance. As a group, peak performers are fascinating to study. In studying peak performers in health care, education, athletics, business and creative arts, we have identified many common characteristics. Here are some characteristics that contrast peak performers with workaholics.

Peak Performers derive their motivation from commitment to a very personal set of goals; workaholics are motivated primarily by fear of failure. Early in their careers, workaholics tend to be seen as up-and-coming people who will contribute, and in fact, they often do. They rise quickly in their organizations or professions but end up managing details, becoming attached to a multitude of status-related symbols, events and circumstances, rather than to creative work.

Peak Performers, on the other hand, derive their motivation from a very personal commitment. While they, too, may work very long hours, they often experience their work as replenishing and nourishing, rather than debilitating and toxic. Peak Performers understand the need for systematic relaxation and reflection. They tend to look upon vacations and breaks as a source of creative stimulation. As a group, they tend to get away from their office work far more than the workaholics.

Peak Performers are frequently deeply committed to some physical activity. Often the optimal performers play tennis or golf, jog or lift weights, hike or garden. They have some powerful attachment to physical expression and an innate understanding of the mind-body connection. They realize that for the mind to perform optimally, the body must be conditioned to perform optimally.

Peak Performers develop and nurture strong family and friendship networks, unlike the workaholics who tend to devastate family-friendship networks by going through a series of relationships that deemphasize and often deteriorate them. Peak performers build quality personal relationships. Workaholics, married to work more than to anyone, destroy friendships and neglect their personal lives.

Peak Performers practice mental rehearsal. They rehearse in their mind's eye any incident or event that is important to the organization. Mental rehearsal is a talent of Peak Performers—one that the former Soviets and East Germans developed extensively in their athletic programs. Business executives can benefit by rehearsing specific events in the mind's eye, including all the possible outcomes and surprises that can materialize.

Peak Performers challenge popular notions and their own limiting beliefs. They are fond of "turning the world on its head." They challenge popular notions about what's healthy and what isn't, what's real and what isn't, trusting their judgment instead of prevailing opinions.

Peak Performers develop the core competencies necessary for excellence and success in their fields. Top athletes, executives and artists determine what capabilities lead to success in their fields – whether it be memory, a specific skill, interpersonal relations, manual dexterity or any number of others. They identify the Peak Performers in their fields and examine their successes while developing their own unique styles.

Peak Performers have a keen sense of the use of time. They divide all of their activities and tasks into three separate categories: A, B and C. In category C are interesting possibilities that don't fit their game plan or specific goals. In category B are important activities, given their goals and game plan, which can be delegated to others. In category A are important activities that only the Peak Performer can do. Peak Performers tend to reject category C, delegate items in category B and spend as much time as possible on activities in category A.

Peak Performers know how to commit. A prominent corporate executive once shared with me this quote, which had been his credo for a number of years: "Until one is committed, there is hesitancy, a chance to draw back, always ineffectiveness. Concerning all acts of initiative and creation, there is one elementary truth, the ignorance of which kills countless ideas and splendid plans. The moment one definitely commits one's self, then providence moves, too."

Cultivating a Climate of Trust and Support

Management can minimize the emotional reactions that are labeled as resistance. That can be accomplished by having a safe and supportive social environment to ensure survival interests in an employee. This can be done by [Dickman and Stanford-Blair: 2003]:

> *... facilitating an environment that generates a spirit of collaboration, values diversity in perspective and experience, fosters camaraderie and collegial relationships, promotes individual and organizational confidence in the capacity to learn and achieve, honors and celebrates positive events and achievements both of the individual and the organization and operates with a no-blame policy.*

It bears repeating: Transformation Education is all about transforming the children through transforming the staff. This is achieved by management treating the staff in the way they would like the staff to treat the children. Below are vehicles we have used successfully to bring this about.

Leadership Development Team (LDT) – We found that the biggest barrier in implementing Transformation Education was the performance of middle management staff. They simply were not cooperating with the beliefs and principles of Transformation Education. First and foremost, many of the middle managers lacked the skills and system savvy to supervise their staff successfully. Their introduction to Transformation Education came through the filter of department heads, who themselves lacked skill and understanding of Transformation

Education. Quite frankly, our early department heads were overwhelmed trying to implement its program components.

Realizing this, we initiated the LDT. The LDT includes anyone who is in a management, supervisory or coordinating role and those staff members with the promise of future promotion to one of these roles. Executive management, the CEO and each vice president are responsible for creating the training for these two-hour, once-a-week sessions.

LDT training uses live examples of what is going on in the organization to demonstrate the beliefs and values of Transformation Education. These are called "how-to" sessions, which teach how to:

- Conduct a good performance review
- Give feedback to an employee
- Use the recognition system
- Run an effective team meeting
- Determine the need for middle management's involvement and attendance at organizational functions
- Use the culture card system
- Discipline an employee properly with a written warning
- Do anything that has to do with the field of management and supervision

We work hard on making training interactive and experiential. We apply the principles of Transformation Education in context with the topic discussed.

The LDT has a personal side. Each week, a member of the group gives a 15-minute presentation on him/herself. Managers bring in pictures of their families and themselves in elementary school, high school and college. They share hobbies, family history and their journey to our organization.

By having the executive management communicate directly with the middle management, we eliminate confusion over what is expected by the organization. Everyone knows what transformation is, and is not.

LDT gives the executive management an opportunity to challenge inconsistencies in the manner Transformation Education is implemented, and allows for collaborative work on problem solving. This has led all managers to understand the use of core program components that comprise transformation. It helps executive management figure out the gaps in services. In this training, the executive management team gains an understanding for the skill, talents and limitations of those serving in supervisory positions.

Limiting Job Responsibilities – Management clearly needs to analyze and design jobs in ways that are doable. We found that most of the positions in our residential and school programs were filled with so many responsibilities they were undoable. We remedied the situation by limiting each position's responsibilities:

1. *Group home director* – Manages day-to-day operations, staff recruitment and hiring, training, supervision, budget and regulatory compliance

2. *Group home school counselor* – Provides therapy, contact with parents and referral workers and supervises the student coordinator

3. *Group home student coordinator* – Maintains clinical records, takes students to appointments and assists school counselor as needed

4. *Youth life educator* – Carries out daily life activities and program curriculum as directed by shift supervisor

6. *Youth life education shift supervisor* – Carries out daily living and program activities, as well as directing and coaching youth life educators on the job

7. *Program and design specialist* – Designs program curriculum activities, trains youth life educator supervisors on how to conduct these activities and designs the aesthetic look of the physical environment

8. *Principals* – Provide instructional leadership, chair individual education plan meetings and guide curriculum implementation in the school environment

9. *Instructional coordinator* – Trains teachers in the classroom on how to teach and implement lesson plans

10. *Director of school counselors* – Oversees clinical records, supervision of related service staff (occupational therapy, speech and language, social work), behavior motivation system and MSD room training

11. *School business manager* – Manages budget, transportation, purchasing and maintenance, and provides administrative supervision of the psychiatrist and nursing staff

Assigning Expertise – Trainers with expertise are the key to good practice. We make certain that our management staff know how to execute the job they are training others to do. These manager-trainers are expected to observe those they trained while they are carrying out their function to see firsthand if the staff are implementing what they were taught. Often implementation is not consistent with expected practice, which brings the managers and staff together to review what was missed.

Rubrics – Rubrics are used in education to assist a teacher in judging the quality of a student's work based on a preestablished set of criteria. Rubrics are used extensively in everyday life when a waitress asks: "How do you like your steak, and what type of dressing do you want for your salad?" When you say "medium rare" and "blue cheese dressing on the side" that is the restaurant's rubric. If the waitress returns with a well-done steak and blue cheese on the salad, the restaurant did not pass.

Providing guidelines and samples proves very supportive and helps make the job doable. Managers who establish rubrics create a supportive environment. See Appendix 7 for the rubric for our group home growth plan that is consistent with the Transformation Education approach.

Rubrics guide staff behavior. They can be as simple as a checklist or as elaborate as the growth plan. The length is not important. What is important is that management identifies how activities are to be carried out. That might be a procedure for returning a van following a field trip, or how to evaluate an employee. Rubrics establish expectations for quality. They help management understand what may be misunderstood in verbal communication. Their use develops consistency throughout our programs, departments and sites.

Own It First Policy – We found a "no-blame" policy fosters a supportive and trusting environment. Of course, even if management does not blame it needs to hold staff accountable. One of the principles of Transformation Education is: "Own It." In plain language, no excuses. Everyone is taught that "The only person I can change and speak for is myself." In order to assist employees with "owning," we teach them how to use the problem-solving process presented in chapter 5.

Data Notebook – Another evaluation tool is the student Data Notebook. Data Notebooks use Run Charts. A Run Chart is a line graph that shows data points plotted in the order in which they occur. They are used to show trends and shifts in a process or variation over time, or to identify decline or improvement in a process. The students maintain Run Charts on their attendance, academic performances and extracurricular activities.

Recognition System – Our system approaches recognition in a different way than most organizations. Our approach is designed to educate employees to align their expectations with the reality of Transformation Education. A detailed discussion of our recognition system can be found in chapter 5. We consider the recognition system a valuable tool to encourage teamwork.

Cultivating a Climate of Challenge and Passion

Simply put, if the brain does not become emotionally excited about something, it is not going to engage efficiently and effectively in social interaction, construction of knowledge, reflective reasoning or productive thinking disposition–all of which are stimulating to the physiological growth and refinement of neural networks. The arousal and focusing of the multidimensional capacity of human intelligence, therefore, is responsive to a clear and meaningful sense of purpose. The engagement of intelligence is also emotionally motivated and maintained by novel and challenging tasks that are related to significant purpose. Again, there is a strong tie between emotion and social experience here, in that clarity of shared purpose becomes an emotional rallying point for collaborative endeavors, and collaboration sparks a contagious exercise of intelligence. [Dickman and Stanford-Blair: 2003]

Our management intentionally creates a climate of challenge and passion. We enter into dialogue about beliefs and values, visioning and referencing organizational purpose. We model passion for the work. We get involved in creative and analytic reflection and we involve staff in planning, implementation and assessment. Our preservice training program and management-led meetings help generate a climate of challenge and passion.

Preservice Training– Remember the biggest challenge our employees confront. We present to them an expectation to adopt a mindset most employees are never asked to adopt in other workplaces. No matter how much experience an employee brings to a job with The Children's Guild, all employees must undergo two weeks of training to know how to approach their jobs. In our workshops, they review material that is entirely new to most of them. They have to learn concepts, practices and approaches they never expected to face in their previous training or places of employment. Workshops include these topics:

- Culture as an educational methodology
- The way the brain operates and learns
- Understanding messages in the physical environment
- Workplace expectations
- The behavior management system
- Contextual thinking

It is our practice to have every key member of the management staff present in at least one workshop during the training period. The managers will reflect the expectations and competence of the organization during the training, and hopefully high expectations will be set. A detailed discussion of the preservice training program is presented in chapter 5.

Management Meetings– The search for truth is essential for obtaining a meaningful and fulfilling life. The search is what ensures that the organization will operate in a mindful way. Management models this belief through the way meetings are conducted and issues on the agenda are discussed. Management must value the concept of searching. This example will make the case.

> *The director of residential services met with the supervisors of our residential programs to discuss the expectations of dress for the students and the staff. The fashion craze at the time was blue jeans with rips and holes. These jeans were designated as unacceptable by the agency. For three meetings the supervisors hotly debated the issue. They based their case on the students' need for freedom of expression, their need to be a part of the youth culture and their need to make decisions about their clothes.*

> *The director of residential services let this discussion continue for three meetings. He thought it was important to hear from each supervisor. What was not discussed in the meeting was how these jeans negatively reinforced the background and mindset of the students. The jeans send the message of rebellion and nonconformity. In group care, our students have a tremendous problem with rebellion. They often dress in a way that highlights this aspect of*

their personalities. The style of the jeans also counteracts the concept of caring we try to convey to the students.

The vice president of programs intervened to resolve the issue by stating that ripped jeans were unacceptable. The vice president of programs suggested the director of residential services develop, with the help of the supervisors, a "dress for success" picture book that would guide clothing purchases and the dress code. Dressing for success is now defined as an L.L. Bean, J.C. Penney look for students.

A common occurrence in organizations serving troubled children is the management meeting, where the agenda never is completed. Managers try everything: making it shorter, keeping the meeting on task, asking other members to stay focused, allotting a certain amount of time for each agenda item and rotating the chairmanship of the meeting. Nothing seems to work.

The problem is not a time management issue. What we discovered is that the assumptions and philosophy of certain agenda items are in conflict with the goal of the organization, which is change.

Several organizations we worked for wanted 100% staff participation in the United Way campaign. We received no funds from United Way. Every year one of the management team members was put in charge of running the agency solicitation of the staff. As an agenda item, it should have taken no more than five minutes to discuss.

However, most of the managers never contributed to charities. They didn't really want to give or to ask for money. The feeling was that the United Way supports Boy Scouts and Girl Scouts more than organizations that really help needy people. They also felt that we worked many hours overtime without pay; our salaries were low and the agency should not expect everyone to give to the United Way.

This would result in a discussion about giving and the responsibility our staff has to support social services. Questions would be raised, "How can we model giving to the kids if we don't show that we give to help others?" or "Who made the rule social workers and child care workers shouldn't have to give because they aren't as rich as businessmen?"..."Is that a caring stance?" As a result, a five-minute agenda item turns into an hour-and-forty-five-minute lesson on what it means to be selfless.

There is a tendency when running a meeting "to get it done" and avoid or minimize conflict. We tend to engage in what Scott Peck calls "pseudo community "or conflict avoidance. [Peck: 1992]

Tc belong to a change-oriented organization, everyone should understand the basic principles behind how decisions are made. Our purpose is to create a cohesive team and a mindset consistent with change. Once the principles and process are understood and everyone is on the same wavelength, the right answer will result. If we design a meeting to problem-solve specific issues, the chances are the right problems will be solved either at the meeting or subsequently.

Your Goal: The Tipping Point

Everyone in the organization will be called on periodically to change and grow. Transformation for you, the staff, the children or the organization will always be required. Each year the support for Transformation Education will increase. To be a successful Transformation Education organization, it is not necessary to have 100% of the staff in sync with the culture of change and growth. But you need to strive toward this goal. The mere striving for the goal will result in your organization reaching what Malcolm Gladwell calls the "tipping point."

The tipping point refers to that one dramatic moment when everything changes at once. It is the time when transformation actually enters a culture. An organization suddenly becomes what people accept as the thing to do, talk about, buy, use, watch out for, wear, hear, be at or see.

In essence, management needs to understand how epidemics work and how to create one to overcome resistance. Gladwell [Gladwell: 2002] came to understand that:

> *Epidemics are a function of the people who transmit infectious agents, the infectious agent itself, and the environment in which the infectious agent is operating. And when an epidemic tips, when it is jolted out of equilibrium, it tips because something has happened, some change has occurred in one (or two or three) of those areas. These three agents of change I call the Law of the Few, Stickiness Factor, and the Power of Context.*

> *Economists often talk about the 80/20 Principle, which is the idea that in any situation roughly 80 percent of the "work" will be done by 20 percent of the participants. In most societies, 20 percent of criminals commit 80 percent of crimes. Twenty percent of motorists cause 80 percent of all accidents. Twenty percent of beer drinkers drink 80 percent of all beer. When it comes to epidemics, though, this disproportionality becomes even more extreme: a tiny percentage of people do the majority of the work.*

The Law of the Few means that a few individuals with social connections, energy, enthusiasm and personality can create the tipping point. Gladwell backs this up with a story about Paul Revere and a man named William Dawes. Both started out with the same news that "The British are coming!" However, Revere rode through towns where he had relationships and was known; Dawes went through towns where he was not known and lacked relationships. The colonists showed up for Revere but hardly anyone came or passed on the news where Dawes rode.

To bring about change or make something happen that allows an organization to reach that tipping point, ask the ones with personality and connections to the staff to support your motives. Resistance will be not only minimized, but your organization will move toward transformation.

Once it occurs, you need to have a stickiness factor to keep the transformation going forward and gathering momentum. Gladwell reminds us that the advertisement known for its ability to stick in people's heads was: "Winston tastes good. Like a cigarette should!" To maintain the ground gained and to gather momentum, develop an advertising campaign to recognize the adopters and encourage others to adopt.

The Power of Context is the basic thinking behind Transformation Education. In New York City paying attention to the little stuff decreased crime. The messages of lawlessness in the form of jaywalking, jumping turn styles in subways to avoid fares, littering, loitering, etc. resulted in arrests and changed the nature of the culture about crime.

In this context, communities came to understand that crime and the lack of it are contagious in the same way as is fashion or disease. Broken windows and abandoned houses breed crime. Muggers understand they reduce their chances of being caught or identified if they operate on streets where potential victims are already intimidated by prevailing conditions. Galdwell's argument says that behavior is primarily a function of social context. There is a great deal of research to back him up on this.

The lesson that leaders and managers need to draw from this is: Resistance is overcome in an organization through a word-of-mouth epidemic. Management supports adopters and gains more converts through establishing an advertising campaign. This campaign should recognize those employees in sync with the culture. Management needs to spend time dealing with the small stuff that sends loud messages, such as dress code, language, physical environment, being on time, cleanliness and the way meetings are conducted, to strengthen and build the messages in the culture.

However, arriving at the tipping point doesn't mean new employees automatically buy in. It is just harder for them not to. It is important to remember transformation is a new concept. There are hardly any employees who have worked for an organization that operates with the transformation model. Even though very qualified and successful individuals will want to work for your organization–attracted by its beliefs, values, freedom to be creative, lack of rules, vision and the way it looks and operates–these employees will struggle and resist when they need to transform. For their hearts are with the idea, but their mindsets and knowledge are firmly anchored in what made them successful.

Their fear of change can result in whining, avoiding true accountability through blaming, feigning confusion, denying responsibility, explaining why something can't be done and explaining that their staff members are overwhelmed. They will try to do things one at a time, and never get to innovations and new programs that need to be implemented. This is unintentional in most instances. It is a fear reaction and an indicator of lack of integration with the work and the ideas of Transformation Education.

While they will agree it is possible to breath and tie your shoes at the same time, they will not believe it is possible to innovate while carrying out basic job responsibilities. They have difficulty incorporating change as a part of everyday life. Keep in mind that this is natural, and have patience. Also remember the tipping point concept. Use the Law of the Few.

Pilot innovations in other parts of the organization, and then have the staff share their experience. Assign some of your best people to them as coaches. Good coaching can help them achieve aspects of their responsibilities. Use the stickiness factor. Publicly recognize those who are in sync with the organizational expectations and beliefs. Believe in the power of context. Their supervisors will hold them accountable for their need to transform. Their transformation will take 18 months to two years. As long as they are moving the organization forward in some way, stick with them. If they are basically in business for themselves to do what they want to do rather than what you need done you have a mishire who you need to get out of the organiztion quickly.

CHAPTER 10
Measuring the Impact of Transformation Education

Principle: All life on this planet is connected in profound and countless subtle ways.

> *We focus on what we measure. In God we trust . . . all others bring data!*
> – *W. Edwards Demming*

Every leader needs to assess key data. Are our strategic goals being achieved? Is our program effective?

A child-serving organization has little time and dollars to dedicate to ongoing assessment. Our methodology for evaluating success is based on several central concepts: Is our culture aligned with our avowed values and beliefs and do they express meaning? Are we achieving the outcome we stated in the mission statement? Are the students actually being taught the values and life skills needed to be successful in life?

By assessing the answers to these questions, we continuously improve the effectiveness of our service to children. Based on positive findings, we market and justify the program to referral sources. We will conclude our discussion on assessment by detailing the procedures to assess job competence and the level of support for the organization's goals and culture.

Assessing Organizational Effectiveness as a Change- and Growth-Oriented Culture

Since Transformation Education is rooted in the belief that culture is an effective agent in motivating transformation of behavior and mindsets in staff and children, how do we assess the effectiveness of the organization (i.e., culture)? The method we have found useful is the Baldridge National Quality Program for Education. The Baldridge System is too extensive to explain comprehensively. A brief explanation of what comprises the system will provide an understanding of the assumptions behind it.

The Baldridge System assesses seven areas of organizational behavior:

Leadership–A major emphasis of this evaluation component is to review: (1) how the organization's senior leaders set and deploy organizational values and expectations; (2) how they communicate these values and expectations to all employees; and (3) how well top management and the board of trustees work together to become more effective leaders and ensure ethical behavior and good citizenship. While there are many other dimensions of leadership assessment measured by the Baldridge System, these aspects are directly related to evaluating the effectiveness of a growth-producing culture–an integrated culture that has beliefs and values that express meaning.

Strategic Plan–Does an organization's strategic plan address student and stakeholder needs in both the external and internal environments the organization operates? This assessment also measures if the organization successfully executes its strategic plan, and if it makes a difference in outcomes, such as student achievement and behavior.

Organizational Design–It measures the relevance of the organization to the needs of the children served. It also rates the needs of those who refer the children and gauges their satisfaction with the service provided. Is the organization operating as it is designed to operate?

Data Collection and Analysis–Does the organization actually know how effectively it is operating? Does the organization's efforts at improvement really make a difference in performance outcomes?

Staff Alignment–How well is the staff aligned with the organization's objectives and action plans? How effective is the organization in creating a growth- and change-oriented culture? Baldridge looks to see if the staff members are sharing their skills across departments, jobs and locations. If good succession planning is in place, organizational depth ensures quality if someone departs the organization. It assesses the training of the staff. Does staff training translate into demonstrable performance outcomes of students? How satisfied is the staff? What is the staff's level of well-being?

Service Delivery–Does the organization's technology, lesson plans, treatment plans, structures and routines, recreational program and therapies meet the students' needs? Are the services provided as they are planned; if so, to what degree of skill?

Performance Results–How is the organization's performance and improvement in student learning/growth/transformation? What is the organization's financial performance and position in the marketplace?

The measurement indicators for the Baldridge Assessment System:

• Staff members throughout the organization know the values and beliefs of the organization and can state them, if called upon to do so. Can they give an example of what they mean?

- The outside reviewers, such as accreditation teams and licensing reviewers, are able to report experiencing organizational values and beliefs throughout the program.
- There is a demonstrated upward trend line indicating achievement of the strategic plan. There is a high degree of satisfaction with the services reported by parents and referral sources.
- The presence and applicability of data used by management and line staff to make decisions are evident.
- Consistency of service quality throughout the organization's programs and services is apparent.
- There is an identified system for evaluating work processes. It is known by management staff, and there is written evidence that it is used on a regular basis.
- Program outcomes reflect effective service.

We will attempt to demonstrate how the Baldridge System evaluates the effectiveness of our organization.

Assessing Achievement of the Mission

Alignment is a foundational principle of the Baldridge system. Alignment is the harmonization of plans, processes, information, resource decisions, actions, results, analysis and learning to support key organization-wide goals. Effective integration is achieved when the individual components of a management system perform as a fully interconnected unit. [Education Criteria For Performance Excellence 2003, p. 36] Given assessment should be aligned with an organization's mission. We have used our organization as an example of how to achieve this. We began by establishing our outcome measures by reviewing our mission statement.

To teach children the values and life skills necessary for a successful life—one filled with caring, contribution and commitment, empowering each with:

- *The vision to see* opportunity within adversity and the value of setting ideals to reach
- *The courage to try* and the value of accepting obstacles as challenges to meet
- *The will to succeed* and the value of making the commitment to persevere

The core outcome of the mission is to teach children the values and life skills necessary for a successful life. We aligned our assessment program to measure the success we were achieving each year teaching values and life skills. There are two methods used to achieve this outcome.

1. Establish an organizational culture that demonstrates connectedness that emotionally disturbed and behavior-disordered children lack. Using the six Baldridge assessments, this was our process measure. It is our assumption that culture is the most powerful force available for transforming and educating behavior-disordered and emotionally disordered youth. We had to create and maintain a change- and growth-oriented culture to generate the outcomes we postulated.

2. The other method for teaching a child values and life skills needed to live a successful life is the child's individualized education/growth plan. The indicators for assessing the child's adoption of these values are related to good citizenship.

The indicators assess socially appropriate behavior and the life skills. They are: the acquisition of daily living skills such as eating healthy, personal hygiene, proper nutrition and exercise, functional knowledge associated with using the transportation system, operating a check book and the academic skills necessary to gather information to make good decisions and to earn a living consistent with one's talents, abilities and interests.

We used the United Way of Central Maryland's outcome model for measuring the impact that our organization had on a student's progress. The model is comprised of outcomes, outcome indicators, measurement tools, activities and outputs. The definitions of these components are stated below:

- *Outcomes*–Benefits or changes to students during or after participation in activities reported as initial, intermediate and long-term gain e.g., acquisition of values, life skills, academic skills.
- *Outcome Indicators*– The specific characteristics or behaviors measured to track a program's success in achieving outcomes e.g., scores on skill streaming checklist, number of crises intervention reports, grades, Woodcock Johnson Mini Battery scores.
- *Measurement tools*– The method used to measure the outcome indicators i.e., individualized education plan, growth plans, student portfolios, standardized tests, grades.
- *Activities*– How the program fulfills the mission of teaching children the values and life skills to lead a successful life e.g., speech and language, therapy, teaching strategies, service learning, activities, trips.
- *Outputs*–Direct products of the program activities e.g., hours of service delivered, people helped during service learning, number of trips exposing children to broader world view and number of students transitioned to less restrictive environments.

Assessing the Acquisition of Citizenship

Citizenship assesses how each child adopts the values needed to live a successful life. Success in life is defined as moving from being selfish to selfless. A good citizen is aware that life is lived to benefit the greater community. For example, good citizens obey just laws; maintain the environment for the next generation; are willing to give their lives for their country; work to make their communities stronger through political advocacy, building family, promoting commerce and volunteerism and are willing to engage in public service.

Good citizenship is expressed by the student's willingness to pursue a cause larger than him/herself, to make the world a better place through caring for others, caring for one's family and supporting a cause that will benefit one's community, environment, state, nation and/or the world. The student demonstrates caring through the contributions s/he makes and the frequency and degree of contribution made over time (commitment) to a person, group, organization or cause.

Our indicators signifying citizenship development are the tools we use every day to assess a child's progress in our school and group home program. Citizenship is taught through the activity of the service learning program and is the spiritual component of the curriculum.

Success is measured via a quarterly review of a child's work portfolio. Are there work samples having to do with caring, contribution and commitment, such as involvement in a supportive caring relationship with others – peer tutoring, cooperative learning activities, group projects?

- How frequently are service learning projects in classroom, school, community, nation and/or world reflected in the portfolio document?
- Does the portfolio reflect that the child has been assigned responsibility to care for a plant or animal at home or in the classroom/group home, or has taken responsibility to complete a job for the benefit of the school or group home?
- Are character education themes imbedded in the curriculum and the assignments?
- How extensive and sophisticated are the planning of the social skills activities in the group homes?
- How meaningful, frequent and integrated with a student's daily life is the student government program?

If in fact we are being successful in generating good citizens who exhibit caring, contribution and commitment we should witness:

- Community service hours earned
- Community improvements, e.g., beautification projects, service learning projects, a recycling program
- Reported increase in student's pride for the environment in the school, community and/or home

There are two life skills that are important for a child. One is the adoption of prosocial behavior and the other is academic mastery.

Assessing the Acquisition of Prosocial Behavior

Prosocial behavior outcomes are realized when a child is placed in a less restrictive environment based on an increase in frequency and duration of socially appropriate behavior.

The activities designed to bring about prosocial behaviors are the individualized educational/growth plan and the behavior motivation system identified in chapter 5, and the skill-based component of the program curriculum identified in chapter 8 (career, wellness, cultural arts, enrichment, individual and group therapies and the daily routine).

At The Children's Guild, each student experiences the need to learn and acquire life skills on a daily basis. The student must engage in these experiences frequently enough to practice the life skills taught.

We measure the effectiveness of these activities to produce prosocial behavior with:

1. A child's individual education/growth plan's quarterly assessment and quarterly progress summary
2. Work orders to repair property damage per child and cost of property damage
3. Positive Behavioral Intervention and Supports (PBIS)* activities and incentive program
4. Skill Streaming Check List** scores
5. Functional Behavior Assessment
6. Intervention Reports (indicate need for crisis intervention and physical restraint)
7. The child's return to least restrictive environment statistics

The signs indicating progress toward obtaining the outcome of prosocial behavior are:

- A trend toward mastery of goals related to increase in prosocial behavior in a child's individualized education/growth plan
- Frequency of utilization of crisis intervention services, primarily physical restraint
- Number of work orders for property destruction generated by a student and property repair destruction costs due to student destruction for the organization
- On-task behavior in the classroom
- Percentage of students discharged to a less restrictive environment

The current goal of government agencies such as the Departments of Mental Health, Child Welfare, Department of Special Education and Juvenile Justice for child-serving organizations is the child's return to a less restrictive environment.

In the eyes of government stakeholders, a key indicator of service effectiveness is return of a child to a less restrictive environment. Therefore, the goal is not to cure a child, but to ensure the child has the ability to function effectively in a less intensive and expensive service. Consequently, all the aforementioned measures of prosocial behavior are subsumed under one major variable—return to least restrictive environment.

Our system for determing the success we have at returning a student to a less restrictive environment is calculated by establishing the average length of stay needed before we return a child with a given diagnosis to a less restrictive environment. Then we determine how many children were returned to a less restrictive environment after the course of our program intervention. This makes sense because the withdrawing of any child from the service prior to the average length of stay (by the family or the referring agency) needed to successfully educate the student did not provide us with adequate time for our intervention to work. Therefore, students who exit prior to the average length of staff are not included in the calculation for return to a less restrictive environment.

---

*PBIS is a school-wide discipline procedure for fostering prosocial behavior; maximizing opportunities for teaching, student engagement and academic attainment; and decreasing the occurrance of disruptive, problematic behavior. School-wide prosocial behaviors are routinely taught and modeled to all students and then consistently monitored and reinforced.

**Skill streaming is a psycho-educational approach to teaching prosocial skills, through social scripting, on a step-by-step basis that compares frequency of exhibited prosocial behavior on a quarterly basis to baseline at inception of the intervention.

If our organization unsuccessfully discharged the child to the same or higher intensive service prior to the average length-of-stay period, this child was included in the less intensive service statistic. This provides us with an understanding of the effectiveness of our service in the eyes of the referring agency.

We realize sometimes discharging a child to a higher level of service or to the same level of service is not necessarily a failure of the service being provided. However, by only counting students who return to a less restrictive environment as a success it provides us with the data needed to review how we can improve service delivery.

Assessing the Acquisition of Academic Skills and Knowledge

Our school is designed for behavior-disordered/emotionally disturbed children. We are not provided the opportunity to work with a child until s/he achieves grade level. Our mission is to restore the child's availability for learning and to motivate the child's interest in the acquisition of academic skills and knowledge. The academic skills are acquired through establishing an environment in which each student can learn at a rate appropriate to his/her capabilities.

The activities used to bring about this outcome are:

- Implementation of integrated curriculum instructional delivery format
- Implementation of experiential learning opportunities to enhance the student's ability to see the connectedness between classroom instruction and its relevance to society
- Diagnostic/prescriptive classroom and individualized instruction designed to meet the learning styles of the student
- Exposure of students to contextual problem-solving strategies to implement throughout the curriculum
- Use of brain-based instructional strategies to maximize student engagement in the learning environment
- Integration of technology into daily instruction
- Use of differentiated curriculum implementation to expose all students to grade level learning

The indicators one would look at to determine progress are:

- Academic progress on individualized education plans and achievement of learning outcomes
- A decrease in frequency of acting-out behavior, task-avoidant behavior and crisis intervention
- Demonstrated improvement in reading, math and written language performance levels

The tools for measuring this improvement are the Woodcock Johnson Mini Battery Assessment, the state's school assessment test, report card grades, assessment of student portfolios and the outcomes of Individualized Education Plan meetings.

Assessing the People

Until now we have been discussing the alignment of the outcomes with the mission statement. If we are truly going to have an integrated organization, it is essential that every component that comprises the culture be aligned with the mission statement.

As indicated previously, cultures are comprised of people, the physical environment, systems and program activities. The employees are one of the most important sources expressing cultural values. Even the assessment instrument itself should express expectations that are consistent with the mission. We must determine if our employees are aligned with and focusing their efforts on the strategic goals of the organization, supporting and expressing the values and beliefs of the organization and possessing the skills and talent needed to perform their tasks.

We have developed a performance review system that is consistent with each employee's job task. The performance review is designed to accomplish the following:

- Ensure that each job description is current and accurate
- Evaluate job performance as it relates to the achievement of strategic plan goals
- Rate how each staff member fits with the philosophy and values of the organization
- Assess the employee's performance in achieving his/her job tasks and the level of sophistication of job skills
- Identify performance goals and the means to achieve them
- Formulate an individual staff development plan that meets the needs of each employee

This is a good time to share the aspects of our performance review process and summarize our current strategic plan. We use these tools to assess each job position. The evaluation packet is comprised of the strategic plan goals form. This form was developed by each senior manager and asks the question, "What do the staff members need to accomplish for the senior manager to achieve his/her goals and objectives in the strategic plan?" This approach makes sense because management works through others to achieve organizational goals and objectives. Likewise, each staff member, who is supervised by a senior manager, repeats the process for the employees s/he supervises. This process continues until it filters to every level in the organization.

Our strategic plan goals are disseminated throughout the organization and made clear and meaningful to each employee through the performance review system. Our strategic plan has three goals:

1. Refining how we carry out and evaluate the Transformation Education Model. This objective is achieved by implementing the Baldridge System, focusing on staff training, program execution and manualizing/packaging program components into training modules.
2. Exploring diversification of our funding. This objective will be achieved by expanding fundraising, marketing our services to other organizations and transporting our services to other settings such as public schools.

3. Completing the transformation of the physical environment of our facilities and implementing the recommendations of the information technology consultant. This is achieved by replicating the design of the physical environment of our flagship campus at our other campuses and implementing the management information plan prepared by our information technology consultant.

The executive management staff are evaluated, in part, on their success in moving the strategic goals forward. We provide examples of how this is done in appendix 4.

CHAPTER 11
From a Threat to a Promise

Principle: In virtually every choice is a moral dilemma and we must decide which choice is the most right. Each dilemma one faces provides the opportunity to grow in wisdom and experience.

Moriality, like art, means drawing a line somplace. —Oscar Wilde

Working with the children, no matter how difficult they are, is seldom the problem that causes the staff to burnout, to be frustrated or take another job. The staff frustration and the lack of success appears to result more from a dysfunctional organization. Even though we understood this, we tended to ignore the obvious and directed our energies toward hiring better staff, and more staff, selecting children who were easier to work with, blamed the home situation or we believed we needed to increase the pay and training of the staff. We tried all this but the problem of teacher and direct care turnover did not improve that much. Besides that, the discharge, expulsion or psychiatric hospitalization or imprisonment of difficult children continued.

In the organizations we worked and managed, we preached the need for growth to occur in our staff and the children. What happened? All of our organizational systems, people, physical environment and policies radiated social control. We were teaching youth that we could get them well, if we could get them to agree that they were sick. We could make them good, if they would agree that they were bad. We continuously emphasized our power over them as the means to empower them. Like most of our colleagues, we were delusional. We believed we were involved in promoting personal growth and transformation. In reality, we were mere agents of social control. Our organizations perpetuated the delusion that our approaches and our theories were right. In our distorted view, the professionals knew what they were doing. We were not the problem. The problem always was the difficulty of the children.

Our journey began when we redesigned the organizations we led to foster personal growth and transformation. We began to infuse them with systems, environments and people who inculcated meaning in the lives of children and the people whom the organization employed. This opened our eyes to the understanding of how unaligned and under-deployed our systems were to achieve the ends we sought. This encouraged us to work harder; we gained a true understanding of what is meant by the saying, "The road to success is to fail faster and try new things." We were rewarded for our efforts when a visiting alumnus returned to the first child welfare agency we transformed and said, "Wow! You have changed this place from a threat to a promise."

The Children's Guild

The Children's Guild had an excellent reputation, employed 90 staff members and had a budget of $4 million when we arrived in 1995. It operated one school serving 114 emotionally disturbed children, a satellite program that served 12 children, a group home for adolescents and three clinical staff who provided an intensive family therapy service.

The Guild was in the midst of reorganizing itself to resolve the turf battles between the clinical and the education staff. The school was organized to please the staff, whose needs generally superseded those of the children. This was manifested in many ways, but none more explicit than by the school start time.

The children, age preschool to grade eight, were bused to The Guild from all over Baltimore City. This required children to be on the bus anywhere from a half-hour to an hour and fifteen minutes. The school buses were scheduled to arrive at 8:15 a.m. but usually arrived around 7:30 a.m. After a long bus ride, the children couldn't manage the 30- to 45-minute wait on the bus without fighting. Despite that condition, the staff continued to arrive at 8 a.m. and open the doors at 8:15 a.m. The professional staff maintained that a change of the starting time would cause problems with their child care arrangements and personal lives. When asked to change the start of the school day to 7:30 a.m., the professional staff refused.

The issue of classroom management was another way of catering to the staff's prerequisites. Children were constantly being sent out of their classes to isolation rooms. There were so many children in the isolation rooms that the halls were lined with staff. They were physically controlling the children outside the doors of the classrooms.

The employees were frustrated; meetings were continuously held on how to manage behavior problems and how "sick" the kids were that were being referred. The school served 114 children and was well funded. It employed a full-time psychiatrist, five school psychologists, five speech and language therapists, 10 clinical social workers, two dance therapists, a full-time occupational therapist, a full-time nurse and a special education teacher and assistant teacher for every nine children. Upon request, the staff had use of one-to-one aides. The Guild also provided an intensive screening of referrals to determine the children they could best serve. The children had an average length of stay of over five years and returned 38% of the children commencing from the program to public school.

Nine years after our arrival, The Children's Guild employs 280 staff, serves 280 children in three schools at any one time and 640 children in a given year. The Children's Guild also operates two group homes, an outpatient mental health center and has a $15 million budget.

The Guild no longer screens the children it admits, has cut its average length of stay from over five years to two years and two months and returns between 50% and 86% of its students to public school most every year. The isolation rooms are closed, children are engaged in their classrooms and the hallways are quiet. The community is actively engaged in its support. The school environment is so inviting that visitors comment, "Every school should look and be like this!"

We have also had great results over the years in returning children to a public school with an average length of stay being 26 months. (See figure below.)

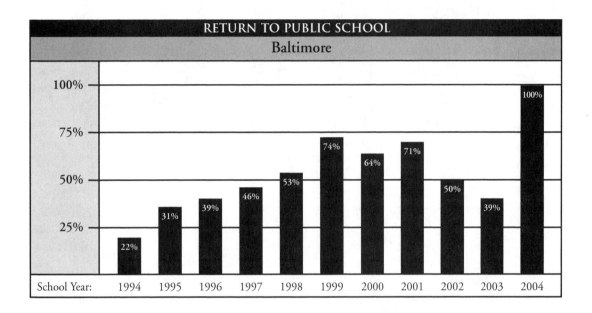

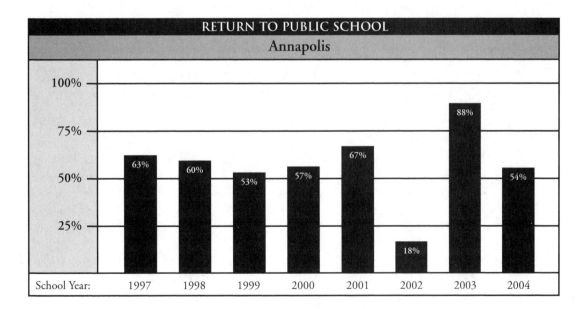

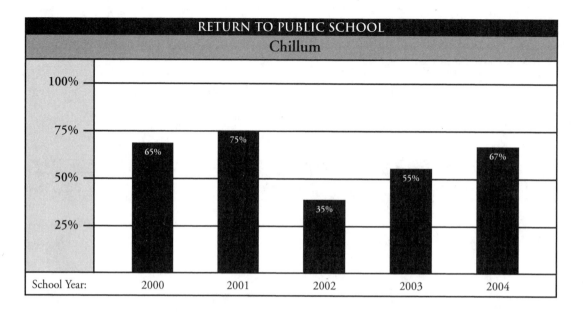

The results tell an interesting story. The latest results from the National Association of Private Special Education Centers survey indicate that prior to the 2002-2003 school year, the national average for return to public school of emotionally disturbed students was 43% and following 2002-2003 school year, it has been 56%. However, the population who did so was comprised of a more socially and economically advantaged group – 60% were Caucasian, 29% were African American and 11% were Hispanic, Asian or others; 45% qualified for subsidized school lunches.

In contrast, The Children's Guild serves 17% Caucasian, 83% African American, Hispanic, Asian or others; 78% of the students are qualified for free or subsidized school lunches. Yet, The Children's Guild generally met or far exceeded these results even with more troubled and disadvantaged students. Prior to the initiation of Transformation Education, The Children's Guild returned less than the national average of students to public school. But with the initiation of Transformation Education in 1995, The Children's Guild showed consistent improvement.

The national study places students into five categories: Preschool Disorders Pervasive Developmental Disorders, Medical Disorders, emotional/Behavioral Disorders and Learning Disorders. The Children's Guild data includes in its emotionally/behaviorally disturbed population: Pervasive Developmental Disorders, Preschool Disorders and multiple handicapping conditions such as students who are emotionally disturbed and mentally retarded.

On a year-by-year basis, the road to complete implementation is not a consistent upward trend in success. Based on our experience, the ebb and flow of success has much to do with our inability to develop a strong, well-trained middle management staff. Where leadership was strong, results were strong. Where leadership was weak, there was a tendency to put aside Transformation Education and return to traditional teaching approaches. In essence, entropy set in.

We have been trying to track academic achievement for six years. It took us four years to get the school administrators to agree on the test to assess academic progress, and to get them to actually give the test to all the children within the same two-week period at the beginning of the year and the end of the year. During the last two years, we were able to achieve this and have had consistent scores. (See figure below.)

What the tests reveal are significant gains in reading, writing, math and factual knowledge at the .05 level of significance with the exception of the Baltimore Campus in 2004.

It is not difficult to understand the lack of academic gain in 2004. We were not able to employ effective leadership in 2004, and had a great deal of turnover in the school's administrative team. Consequently, academic progress suffered.

In 2002, Transformation Education was successfully implemented at The Guild's group home program. Previously, it was a very rule-oriented, rigid place for children. The results were dramatic.

Direct care staff turnover dropped from 188% in 2001 to 86.4% in 2002, to 24% in 2003, to 13.8% in 2004.

A visible indicator of the impact of Transformation Education is the decline of property destruction and "wear and tear" on the physical plant in our group home program. In 2001,

EMPOWERMENT IN WOODCOCK JOHNSON MINI BATTERY SCORES OVER 2002 - 2003 SCHOOL YEAR																
	Reading				Writing				Mathematics				Factual Knowledge			
ANNAPOLIS	Test 1	Test 2	Differ-ence	T Test	Test 1	Test 2	Differ-ence	T Test	Test 1	Test 2	Differ-ence	T Test	Test 1	Test 2	Differ-ence	T Test
FY '02-'03	87.85	91.32	3.47	.017	77.32	76.79	-.53	0.368	89.35	90.94	1.59	.255	92.79	91.91	-.88	.292
FY '03-'04	96.04	102.77	6.73	.025	78.04	83.27	5.23	.008	84.81	90.00	5.19	.047	94.38	97.50	3.12	.021
BALTIMORE																
FY '02-'03	64.62	72.68	8.06	<.001	55.14	61.63	6.49	<.001	58.91	66.99	8.08	<.004	74.41	79391	5.52	<.001
FY '03-'04	70.77	72.17	1.40	.0291	61.15	59.62	-1.53	.17	63.92	63.75	-.17	.464	78.08	79.02	.94	.277
CHILLUM																
FY '02-'03	4.1	4.91	.81	.007	3.01	3.29	.28	.023	4.51	5.51	1.00	.002	n/a*	n/a*	n/a*	n/a*
FY '03-'04	82.32	83.82	1.50	.016	70.21	72.99	2.78	.009	76.78	81.39	4.61	.007	81.48	84.64	3.17	.003
ALL PROGRAMS																
FY '02-'03	**	**	.00	**	**	**	.00	**	**	**	.00	**	*	*	.00	*
FY '03-'04	80.32	82.59	2.27	.074	68.18	69.80	1.62	.033	73.428	76.423	3.00	.007	82.262	84.69	2.43	.004

*   * Factual knowledge test scores were not available due to an employee who resigned and took scores with her.
*   ** Chillum Campus turned in scores based on grade level equivalent comparison and did not turn in factual knowledge scores in FY '02-'03. This made it impossible to compare the scores with the T scores submitted by Annapolis and Baltimore Campuses for FY '02-'03.

maintenance and repair costs were $101,881 and in 2002 they dropped to $43,447. In 2003 they dropped to $29,002 and in 2004 they were reduced to $10,500. Another indicator used to determine the impact of Transformation Education was the cost of newspaper ads to recruit staff. In 2001 it was $33,800 and was $4,800 in 2002. In 2003 staff recruitment cost increased by $58 to $4,858 due to the focus on recruiting substitute staff to cover shifts during call-outs and holidays but was reduced to $2,347 in 2004.

During these years, occupancy increased from 89.8% in 2001 to 91.25% in 2002, to 100% in 2003 and went down to 94% in 2004. Total cost savings and revenue generation due to increased occupancy for a 16-bed operation (not including management time, opportunity time, workers' compensation claims and time spent dealing with community problems and licensing) for 2002 revenue over 2001 was $157,652, for 2003 over 2002 it was $107,800 and for 2004 over 2003 it was $80,004 or a total savings of $345,456 for the three-year period.

We should also mention that prior to the implementation of Transformation Education, it took weeks and sometimes months to fill a staff position. This resulted in the remaining direct care staff working a great deal of overtime hours with no time off. Now, we have a pool of workers willing to work if someone quits or is terminated, ill or on vacation. We can fill a vacant position on the day that we know a direct care staff person is leaving.

Even though the yearly comparisons show an overall decline in maintenance cost, beginning in 2002, when compared to the first three years the decline is greater than depicted. This is so because during 1991 through 2001 we had one eight-bed group home. All the expense is due to that one home. In 2002 through 2004 we operated two eight-bed group homes. Transformation Education was introduced in 2002 and the staff's ability to deploy all aspects of Transformation Education has not been realized.

However, the true achievement of any group care program is how many children were returned to a less restrictive environment. In 2002, seven out of eleven boys (64%) who were discharged moved to a less restrictive environment, with three of those seven returning to their biological families and four to less intensively staffed group home settings. In 2003, nine out of ten (90%) boys discharged returned to a less restrictive environment. Three reunited with biological families, two to less intensively staffed group homes, four to independent living and one to a higher level of care. In 2004, fifteen out of fifteen boys discharged were returned to a less restrictive environment. Four reunited with biological families, ten to a less intensively staffed group home and one to independent living. These results were achieved for any student who remained in the program for nine months or longer, and all students referred were acting out, challenging, aggressive, emotionally disturbed youth ages 13 to 18.

Other indicators of the success of Transformation Education were a perfect licensing report and medication errors dropping from 69 in 2002 to five in 2003 to zero in 2004, with 90% of the population on medication. Incidence of runaway behavior has become almost nonexistent since the implementation of Transformation Education, and our group homes are located on a residential street in Northwest Baltimore. Specifically, there were 15 runaways in 2002, 10 in 2003 and one in 2004.

The True Payoff - Organizational Wisdom

It is true that under the Transformation Education banner, we can point to sizeable increases in our budget and staff. The physical environments are more sophisticated and appealing; accolades are bestowed upon us by the community and our boards of trustees. But what really counts is the personal growth and way of thinking of the executive management team and the children. It has been dramatic and meaningful.

Executive management came to realize that they did not need experts to tell them what to do. Our management team learned they needed to engage in reflective self-examination. Management took the time to observe how the organization really operated. When confronted with problems or struggling with dilemmas, they came up with effective solutions. They became wise enough to investigate how the basic truths or assumptions were being violated.

By squarely facing problematic relationships, organizational inequities, lack of resources, absence of talent and other pitfalls, the management grew in wisdom. This spirit of seeking wisdom was infused into the organization and generated major changes in service quality and effectiveness. The bottom line is that this wisdom principle created a culture that makes it possible for the organization and the children to change and grow.

Executive management came to realize an important truth about itself. Management is more than the voice of authority and control. By using the organization as a vehicle to radiate messages that were consistent with growth and change, management became a guiding force for promoting personal growth. The staff and students learned basic truths that permit them to take more responsibility for their lives.

By honing our mission, we have constantly gained talented and effective employees who are at one with the mission and have a desire to grow and discover wisdom. These individuals who encourage like-minded friends to apply to work with us. Employees who prefer rule-oriented approaches and reductionism tend to leave, since they feel uncomfortable and out of place.

With success comes a bountiful harvest. It generates enthusiasm among the board of trustees. This exuberance has spurred them on to recruit talented and well-connected individuals to the board. It has spurred a willingness by the board to be involved in fund-raising. The number and size of gifts by the trustees continues on the upswing. Board expectations are raised for both trustee performance and participation, thus, a stronger, more effective board evolved. There is a synergy flowing in our organization thanks to Transformation Education. It makes things happen, things that never happened previously.

We are not trying to sell anyone a tonic when we say that in a Transformation Education culture, an average person can raise his/her performance from just a bit above average to good. And, it can mitigate against the negative impact that department heads, supervisors and professionals who value social control can cause in an organization. Implicit with Transformation Education is a routine process of examination by a team or individual of the actions taken and even the message inherent in an action taken. This frustrates anyone who operates without thinking in context. Needless to say, employees depart if they refuse to look at each child within the context of the situation and the stated principles and beliefs of the organization.

The biggest difference was observable in the children. Their natural curiosity was rekindled. They became easier to teach when management focused on itself and its employees. The more the organization and the employees grow and change, the more the children are willing to change.

Toward the Future

As mentioned earlier in chapter 9, Dr. Robert W. Terry [Terry: 1993] illuminated our thinking by using metaphors to describe how people identify their worldviews and their prejudices. He suggested that each of us saw life primarily as one of the following metaphors: Life as a Gift, a Market, a Body, a Struggle, a Journey or Art.

When he outlined the characteristics of each metaphor it became clear that those of us in the human services generally fit the "Life is a Body" metaphor. This is in sharp contrast to the ideology of Transformation Education. We use the metaphor we added to Terry's Organizational Mindset metaphor's chart, Life is a Bumper Car. We are not implying that the Bumper Car metaphor is different, but rather is another way of articulating the Journey metaphor.

ORGANIZATIONAL MINDSET METAPHORES

Metaphor of Life	Basic Beliefs	Conflict & Change	Solutions to Problems	Who Decides the Cultural Values	Goal
Gift	All life is a gift–the good, bad, joyful and tragic. Life is to be faced and embraced even when not understood.	Diversity is a fact, not an option. It simply is, accept it.	Get along by going along.	Fate.	Acceptance.
Market	Life is a constant series of decisions at the margin separating the more desirable from the less desirable. Some people win, others lose but society wins.	Competition is good, stagnation is bad. Markets are real, they determine outcome. Freedom is necessary.	Whatever works and what contributes value.	Winners, those who know how to win best.	Acquisition.
Body	The whole is greater than the parts; e.g., one part ill, the rest is ill.	Harmony is ideal and conflict is minimized, i.e., antibodies are sent to challenge intruders.	Intervention by professional experts. Processing differences leads to solutions.	No one, we are all equal and have equal say.	Unity.
Struggle	Life is a constant interplay of polar opposites joined in inevitable struggle.	Conflict drives history; it is the center of life. Struggle is good.	Wrest power, become an "up."	Those in power.	Power.
Journey	Life is a continuous series of comings and goings, the opening of new paths of discovery.	Flexibility is essential, rigidity is bad. Only by bumping up against differences can we know others and ourselves.	Education of self and others is required, insight is important.	Leadership, which emerges, based on the situation.	Personal growth and knowledge.
Bumper Car	Life is a happening. You can't control life but you can control your response to it. There is order in chaos. Chaos and order exist at the same time. The natural order is that everything in the universe is interconnected.	Change is constant and crises are positive. Discovery results from "bumping" against ideas and people. Implicit in tension is the potential for new insights.	Understand the context and decide accordingly. Truth is in shades of gray.	The leaders of the organization.	Moral growth and selflessness.
Art	Life is an interpretation; it does not interpret itself.	Transformation is good; stagnation is bad.	Creativity. Connecting what others don't connect.	Collective responsibility results from individual responsibility.	Freedom and expression of individuality.

Each belief has its strengths and flaws. These metaphorical beliefs are part of every organization. Even so, we need to determine the primary goal we have designed our organization to achieve.

The Market metaphor makes sense in the world of business and the Struggle metaphor makes sense in the world of politics. Likewise, the Journey metaphor makes sense for child-serving organizations. Our goal is to develop the concepts of citizenship and prosocial responses in behavior-disordered children, while bringing about a major transformation of employee mindsets and the organization's culture. Transformation is not an end in itself, nor is it a one-time event. It is an unending process. Even the most effectively operating organizations need to understand what will be the next required transformation. This is where "Life as Art" comes in.

We no longer need a crystal ball to anticipate what will happen. Organizational leaders must interpret life and in doing so create the future. Knowing this means that the most profound result of our journey is yet to come. This book is an attempt to create the future by establishing a movement to transform child-serving organizations and schools. It is essential that universities train professionals in the fields of human service and education with the concepts of Transformation Education. We want foundations to rethink how they use their resources to improve outcomes in child-serving organizations.

We want the child welfare system and institutions to care for delinquent youth using this philosophy. We want to generate a new way of thinking among school administrators and not-for-profit executives about their work. And, it is a way to move our organization to a point where we are less dependent on government dollars to operate our mission.

We will begin this endeavor by sponsoring a one-day conference to heighten the lay and professional community's awareness of the *Hardwired to Connect* study and Transformation Education. We will initiate an Institute of Transformation Education to spread these ideas and to study the results of those who adopt this philosophy of teaching values and life skills to children in child-serving organizations.

The Institute will bring together those who are interested in the use of culture to foster transformation and meaning. The Institute will work hard to bring those interested in our work to The Children's Guild, where they can witness Transformation Education in action and become involved in supporting the development of new systems and approaches to help behavior-disordered children. And of course there is this book to help guide the transformation of your organization to becoming more child centered. We welcome your reactions and comments. E-mail us at ross@childrensguild.org or krosf@childrensguild.org.

BIBLIOGRAPHY

Allport, G. (1961). *Pattern and Growth in Personality.* New York: Holt, Rinehart and Winston, p. 246.

Balestracci, David. (2003). "Handling the Human Side of Change." *Quality Progress.* November, pp. 42-44.

Bennis, W. & Nanus, B. (1985). *Leaders: The Strategy for Taking Charge.* New York: Harper & Row, p. 21.

Buckingham, Marcus and Curt Coffman. (1999). *First Break All the Rules.* New York: Simon and Schuster, pp. 59-63.

Burns, James McGregor. (2003). *Transforming Leadership.* New York: Atlantic Monthly Press, pp. 24-25.

Campbell, Joseph. (1988). *The Power of Myth.* New York: Doubleday.

Case, C. C. (1977). *Culture the Human Plan: Essays in the Anthropological Interpretation of Human Behavior.* Washington, DC: University Press of America, pp. 16-17, 28.

Cash, Carol; Glen Earthman & Eric Hines. (1997). "Building Conditioned Tied to Successful Learning." *School Planning and Management.* January, 21 (1): pp. 48-53.

Centers for Disease Control and Prevention. (2004). *Surveillance Summaries.* May 21, MMWR 2004:53 (No. SS-2).

Chicago Statement on Education, adopted by 80 holistic educators. (1990). Conference near Chicago, IL, June 3.

Clark, B. (1975). "The Organizational Saga in Higher Education." *Managing Changes In Educational Organization.* Edited by J. V. Baldridge & T. E. Deal. Berkeley, CA: McCutchan, pp. 98-108.

Clark, E. (1990). "A Search for Wholeness." *Holistic Education Review.* pp. 5-7.

Clifton, Donald. President of Gallup Organization, Lincoln, NE.

Cohn, D.C. Editor. (1991). *The Circle of Life, Rituals from the Human Family Album.* San Francisco: Harper.

Collins, Jim. (2001). *Good to Great.* New York: Harpers Business, pp. 41-42, 56-57

Dickman, Michael H., Nancy Stanford-Blair. (2002). *Connecting Leadership to the Brain,* Thousand Oaks, CA: Corwin Press, pp. 39, 201-202.

Druckheim, K. (1990). *Parabola.* Fall, 7.

Durkin, R. (1983). "The Crisis in Children's Services: The Dangers and Opportunities for Child Care Workers." *Journal of Child Care.* 1 (5): pp. 1-13.

Durkin, R. (1961). *The Generation and Dissipation of Aggression in a Residential Treatment Program for Disturbed Children.* Unpublished Masters Thesis. Seattle, WA Department of Anthropology, University of Washington.

Eccles, Jacquelynne and Jennifer Appleton Gootman. (2002). *Community Programs to Promote Youth Development.* National Research Council and Institute of Medicine (Eds.). Washington, D.C.: National Academic Press.

Education Criteria For Performance Excellence. (2003). Baldridge. National Quality Program. NIST. Gaithersburg, MD.

Festinger, L. (1957). *Theory of Cognitive Dissonance.* Evanston, IL: Row Peterson.

Follet, M. P. (1982). (see Weiner). p. 33.

Foster, H. (1988). "Personal Dress and Grooming; Something to Consider in Staff Development." *Journal of Experiential Education.* Summer, pp. 31-32.

Frank, D.A. & M.E. Greenberg. (1994). "A Mediator of Long-Term Memory from Mollusks to Mammals." *Cell,* 79 pp. 5-8.

Fuller, R. B. (1932). *John Bartlett Familiar Quotations.* sixteenth edition 1992. Boston: Little Brown & Company, p. 691.

Gannon, M. J. (1979). *Organizational Behavior.* Boston: Little, Brown & Company, p. 81.

Gladwell, Malcolm. (2000). *The Tipping Point.* Boston, New York, London: Little, Brown & Company, pp.19-29.

Glasser, W (1965). *Reality Therapy.* New York: Harper & Row.

Gleick, J. (1987). *Chaos: The Making of a New Science.* New York: Viking Penguin, Inc.

Greenleaf, R. K. (1977). *Servant Leadership.* Ramsey, NJ: Paulist Press, pp. 65-67.

Greenspan, Stanley I., MD & J. Salmon (1995). *The Challenging Child.* Reading, MA: Perseus Books.

Halpin, A.W., & D. B. Croft. (1962). *The Organizational Climate of Schools.* St. Louis, MO: Washington University.

Herchong, Lisa. (1999). *Daylighting In Schools: An Investigation Into the Relationship Between Daylighting and Human Performance.* A study performed on behalf of the California Board for Energy Efficiency as part of Pacific Gas & Electric contract 460-000. For a copy, e-mail: Lisa Heschong at info@h-m-g.com.

Houston, Jean. (1989). Comment made at Sacred Psychology Workshops held in Waterloo, IA.

Iraneous of Lyons. (Bishop Iraneous of Lyons) source unknown.

Jensen, Eric. (2000). *Brain-Based Learning,* The New Science of Teaching and Training.

Jung, C. G. (1978). *Psychological Reflections.* edited by Jolande Jacobi & F. F. C. Princeton, NJ: Hull, Princeton University Press, pp. 81-82.

King, Keith. (1988). "The Role of Adventure in the Experiential Learning Process." *Journal of Experiential Education.* Summer, pp. 4-6.

King, Martin Luther, Jr. (1964). Speech accepting Nobel Peace Prize. December 11.

Kopp, S. B. (1972). *If You Meet the Buddha on the Road,* Kill Him! New York: Bantam Books.

Kuo, Francis E. (2001). "Coping With Poverty: Impacts of Environment and Attention In the Inner City." *Environment and Behavior.* 33 (1), pp. 5-34.

Langer, E. (1989). *Mindfulness.* Reading, MA: Addison-Wesley Publishing Co., Inc., pp. 35, 124.

Lewin, K. (1939). "Field Theory an Experiment in Social Psychology." *American Journal of Sociology.* May, 44, pp. 868-896.

Manasse, L. A. (1989). "Vision and Leadership: Paying Attention to Intention." *Peabody Journal of Education.* pp. 2-22.

May, R. (1989). "The Chaotic Rhythms of Life." *New Scientist.* November 18, 124 (1691), pp. 37-41.

McDill, E. & I. Rigsby. (1973). *Structure and Process in Secondary Schools.* Baltimore, MD: John Hopkins University Press.

McGinley, D. (1989). Editorial. *Caring.* Washington, DC: National Homes for Children Fall, 2.

McPherson, G. (1972). *Small Town Teacher.* Cambridge, MA: Harvard University Press.

Mental Health: A Report of the Surgeon General. (1999). Rockville, MD: US Department of Health and Human Services, Substance Abuse and Mental Health Services Administration, Center for Mental Health Services, National Institute of Mental Health, p. 123.

Miller, Lisa. (2002). "Spirituality and Resilience in Adolescent Girls." Commission On Children At Risk. Working paper 8. New York: Institute For American Values, p. 6.

Miller, R., P. S. Gang, & E. T. Clark. (1988). "What is Holistic Education?" *Holistic Education Review*. 1(6), pp. 3-30.

Miringhoff, M. L. (1980). *Human Service Organizations*. New York: Prentice-Hall, pp. 9-10.

Peck, Scott. (1992). *The Different Drum*. New York: Simon & Schuster, p. 62, pp. 88-89.

Peck, Scott. (1985). *The Road Less Traveled*. New York: Simon & Schuster.

Percival, I. (1989). "Chaos: A Science for the Real World." *New Scientist*. 124 (1687), pp. 42-48.

Pirsig, R. M. (1974). *Zen and the Art of Motorcycle Maintenance*. New York: William Morrow & Company, Inc.

Postman, N., C. Nystrom, L. Strate, C. Weingartner. (1987). *Myths, Men and Beer: An Analysis of Beer Commercials on Broadcast Television*. Falls Church, VA: AAA Foundation for Traffic Safety.

Renato, T. & G. Litwin. (Eds.). (1968). *Organizational Climate-Explorations of a Concept*. Boston: Harvard University, p. 27.

Rodman, T. A. (1984). "Make the Praise Equal the Raise." *Personnel Journal*. Costa Mesa, CA.

Rogers, C. R. & B. F. Skinner. (1956). "Some Issues Concerning the Control of Human Behavior: A Symposium." *Science Magazine*. November 30, 124 (3231), pp. 1057-1065.

Rogers, E. M., & G. M. Beal. (1957-1958). "The Importance of Personal Influence in the Adoption of Technological Changes." *Social Forces*. May, 36, pp. 330-331.

Ross, A. and G. Holtke. (1985). "A Tool for Selecting Residential Child Care Workers: An Initial Report." *Child Welfare*. January-February, LXIV, (1), pp. 46-54.

Ross, A. & G. Holtke. (1987). "An Interview Tool for Selection of Residential Child Care Workers: A Follow-up Report." *Child Welfare*. LXVI. (2), 175-183.

Rutter, M., P. Maughan, P. Mortimore, J. Ouston, & A. Smith. (1979). *Fifteen Thousand Hours*. Cambridge, MA: Harvard University Press.

Sarason, S. (1971). *The Culture of the School and the Problem of Change*. Boston: Allyn and Bacon, pp. 227-228.

Savit, R. (1990,)."Chaos on the Trading Floor." *New Scientist*. August, 11127 (1729), pp. 48-51.

Siebert, A. (1990). in Siege, Bernie. (1986). *Love Medicine and Miracles*. New York: Harper Perenial.

Simon, S. B., Howe, L. W., & Kirschenbaum. (1972). *Values Clarification*. New York: Hart Publishing Company, p. 13.

Stilwell, Barbara M. (2002). "The Consolidation of Conscience In Adolescence." Commission On Children At Risk. working paper 13. New York: Institute for American Values, p. 2.

Suomi, Stephen J. (1999). "Developmental Trajectories Early Experiences and Community Consequences." in Keating and C. Hertzman (eds.) *Developmental Health and the Wealth of Nations: Social Biological and Educational Dynamics*. New York: Guilford Press, pp. 189 -200.

Suomi, Stephen J. (1999). "How Mother Nurture Helps Mother Nature: Scientific Evidence for the Protective
  Effect of Good Nurturing on Genetic Propensity Toward Anxiety and Alcohol Abuser."
  Commission on Children at Risk, Working Paper 14 (New York: Institue for American Values,
  2002) pp. 18-19. See also Attachment, "Theory, Research, and Clinical Applications."
  New York: The Guilford Press, pp. 181-197.

Terry, R. W. (1993). *Authentic Leadership.* San Francisco: Jossey Bass.

The Commission on Children at Risk. (2003). Hardwired to Connect: *The New Scientific Case for
  Authoritative Communities.* New York, New York: Institute for American Values, pp. 5, 9.

Thompson, J. D. (1967). *Organizational Design and Research.* Pittsburgh, PA: University of
  Pittsburgh Press, p. 35.

Thurman, Robert. (1976). *The Holy Teaching of Vernalahicti.* University Park, PA: Penn State
  University Press, p. 47.

Treischman, A., J. Whittaker & L. Brendtro. (1969). *The Other 23 Hours.* Chicago, IL:
  Adline Publishing.

Vaill, P. B. (1982). "The Purposing of High Performing Systems." *Organizational Dynamics.*
  Autumn, pp. 23-39.

Waller, W, (1932). *The Sociology of Teaching.* New York: Wiley.

Weiner, M. E. (1982). *Human Service Management: Analysis and Application.* Homewood, IL:
  Dorsey Press.

Whitaker, J., A. Trieschman. (1972). *Children Away From Home.* Chicago, IL: Aldine-Atherton, Inc.,
  pp. 68, 70.

Wolfe, Patricia. (2001). *Brain Matters: Translating Research Into Classroom Practice.* American Society
  for Curriculum Development. ISBN: 0-87120-517-3, 1-12.

The Children's Guild — Culture Card

The Nine Wisdom Principles

The Personal Values
"What are the values needed to access personal growth?"

Caring
As an organization and as individuals, we need to be caring.

Contribution
Caring does not exist without action.

Commitment
Commitment is contribution over time.

The Life Skills
"What are the skills needed to achieve growth?"

Vision
The ability to see what you can become.

Courage
Pursuing one's vision despite adversity.

Will
Will is the application of courage over time.

The Growth Processes
"What is the process through which growth occurs?"

Struggle
Struggle is required for growth.

Transformation
Growth requires a change of thinking and behavior.

Enlightenment
A broader awareness of one's responsibilities and moral obligations.

Purpose

"To serve children not achieving their full capability in academic, emotional, social or life skills by establishing programs and discovering more effective methods to promote growth and change in the levels of achievement of those we serve."

Mission

"To teach children the values and life skills necessary for a successful life, one filled with caring, contribution and commitment, empowering each with:

The Vision to See

opportunity within adversity and the value of setting goals to reach;

The Courage to Try

and the value of accepting obstacles as challenges to meet;

The Will to Succeed

and the value of making the commitment to persevere."

Vision

"To create, implement and replicate an organizational culture that produces documented growth and change in the academic, emotional, social and life skills of the children we serve."

The Children's Guild, Inc.
6802 McClean Boulevard
Baltimore, Maryland 21234
www.childrensguild.org
March 2005

Transformation Education

Transformation Education is an organizational philosophy that guides the creation of a culture for transmitting the value and life skills necessary for a successful life.

Foundational Beliefs

1. Life is a journey of personal growth ascending from a focus on self to a focus on family, community and world.

2. Culture is the most powerful force available to child-serving organizations for transmitting pro-social values and transforming one's mindset.

3. All life on this planet is connected in profound and countless subtle ways.

4. In virtually every choice is a moral dilemma and we must decide which choice is the most right. Each dilemma one faces provides the opportunity to grow in wisdom and experience.

5. Chaos is the norm, not the exception in a child-serving organization. The key to managing chaos is to embrace it, not fight it.

6. A child-serving organization is more than a host for the professions. The organization is the critical component for transmitting values and fostering emotional and intellectual growth.

7. The focus of management efforts is on transforming the disparate individual beliefs and values into alignment with the foundational beliefs and values of the organization.

Workplace Expectations

1. **Norms Not Rules**
   Understand the situation and act in context.

2. **Spinning Plates**
   Often we must manage a myriad of tasks with insufficient time and resources.

3. **Be a Brinksman**
   We come to know our true potential when we are pushed to the brink of the impossible.

4. **Change is Constant**
   Expect change because we live in a dynamic environment that calls for constant re-evaluation of decisions and assumptions.

5. **Decide! Then Re-decide!**
   Don't stick to the old decisions when you have new information.

6. **Own It!**
   When you're looking for the problem, start with yourself.

7. **Be True to Your School
   (Talk the Talk & Walk the Walk)**
   Model the values you espouse.

8. **A Master Teacher and a Master Learner**
   Teach by example and always be open to grow personally and professionally.

9. **Count Using Mission Math**
   Value mission, not recognition.

10. **Don't Sign It Until the Quality is in it**
    Do it over until it is right!

11. **Work is Fun!**
    Working where our talents lie brings joy and enriches life.

12. **There is No Growth Without Pain!**
    Accomplishments are attained through struggle and self-discipline.

13. $1 + 1 = 3$
    In problem solving, the sum is greater than the parts.

14. **Ready-Fire-Aim**
    Assess the risk, begin to act and then make the adjustments along the way.

15. **Say No With Compassion**
    Develop the courage to deliver a difficult message with respect and compassion and then do it.

16. **Make the Covert, Overt**
    When there are unstated issues between individuals and groups, bring them to the surface of discussion.

PRE-SERVICE TRAINING PROGRAM SYLLABUS

The Children's Guild
Pre-Service Training Program
Master Schedule
Baltimore Campus

Week A - Tuesday

9:00 a.m.   Introduction to Transformation Education and Culture
Dr. Andrew L. Ross, President

12:00 p.m.   Lunch

1:00 p.m.   Promoting and Teaching Guild Values: the Culture Card System
Frank Kros, Executive Vice President

2:30 p.m.   Executing TransZed: The Children's Guild Vision and Strategic Plan
Dr. Andrew L. Ross and Frank Kros

3:45 p.m.   Closing and Evaluation

4:00 p.m.   Adjourn

An invincible determination can accomplish almost anything, and in this lies the great distinction between great [people] and little [people]. –Thomas Fuller

PRE-SERVICE TRAINING PROGRAM SYLLABUS

The Children's Guild
Pre-Service Training Program
Master Schedule
Baltimore Campus

Week A - Wednesday

9:00 a.m.   Team-Building Workshop
Claire Tuberville, VP of Administration

12:00 p.m.   Lunch

1:00 p.m.   Teamwork Primacy
Terry Manning, VP of Programs

2:30 p.m.   Service Leadership: The Importance of Professionalism,
Hospitality, Etiquette and Appearance
Claire Tuberville, VP of Administration

3:45 p.m.   Closing and Evaluation

4:00 p.m.   Adjourn

*Thoughts have power; thoughts are energy. And you can make
your world or break it by your thinking.* —Susan Taylor

PRE-SERVICE TRAINING PROGRAM SYLLABUS

The Children's Guild
Pre-Service Training Program
Master Schedule
Baltimore Campus

Week A - Thursday

9:00 a.m.   Safety Comes First: An Introduction to Brain-Compatible Learning
Frank Kros, Executive Vice President

12:00 p.m.   Lunch

1:00 p.m.   Brain Matters: The Neuroscience of Emotional Disturbance,
ADHD and Conduct Disorder
Frank Kros, Executive Vice President

3:45 p.m.   Closing and Evaluation

4:00 p.m.   Adjourn

*First say to yourself what you would be; and
then do what you have to do.* –Epictetus

PRE-SERVICE TRAINING PROGRAM SYLLABUS

The Children's Guild
Pre-Service Training Program
Master Schedule
Baltimore Campus

Week A - Friday

9:00 a.m.   Data, Data Everywhere But What Does It Mean?
Claire Tuberville, VP of Administration
Frank Kros, Executive Vice President
Dr. Wilmer Cozens, CQI Consultant

10:30 a.m.   Continuous Quality Improvement at The Guild
Frank Kros, Executive Vice President
Dr. Wilmer Cozens, CQI Consultant

12:00 p.m.   Lunch

1:00 p.m.   P.B.I.S. Overview
Guild Educational Leaders

3:45 p.m.   Closing and Evaluation

4:00 p.m.   Adjourn

*In seeking wisdom, the first step is silence, the second
listening, the third remembering, the fourth practicing,
the fifth is teaching others.* –Ibn Gabirol

PRE-SERVICE TRAINING PROGRAM SYLLABUS

The Children's Guild
Pre-Service Training Program
Master Schedule
Baltimore Campus

Week B - Monday

9:00 a.m.   Personnel Handbook Review
John Moore, Director of Human Resources

10:30 a.m.   Human Resources Orientation and Benefits Enrollment
Wendy Peterson, HR Generalist

12:00 p.m.   Lunch

1:00 p.m.   Tour of Baltimore Campus
History of The Children's Guild
The Children's Guild Video, Annual
Events, Publications and Public Relations
Chris Siciliano, Director of Development

3:45 p.m.   Closing and Evaluation

4:00 p.m.   Adjourn

*Imagination was given to man to compensate for
what he is not. A sense of humor was provided
to console him for what he is.* - Horace Walpole

PRE-SERVICE TRAINING PROGRAM SYLLABUS

The Children's Guild
Pre-Service Training Program
Master Schedule
Baltimore Campus

Week B - Tuesday

9:00 a.m. Safety, Security and Emergency Response
Greg Victor, Director of Operations

10:30 a.m. Credentialing, Tuition Assistance and Professional Development
Wanda Chaney, Credentialing & Compliance Coordinator

12:00 p.m. Lunch

1:00 p.m. Funding, Budgeting and Finance
Steve Baldwin, CFO

2:00 p.m. Orientation to Information Technology Services
Clint Isett III, IT/Computer Support

3:45 p.m. Closing and Evaluation

4:00 p.m. Adjourn

The foundations of character are built not by lecture, but by bricks of good example, laid day by day. –Leo Blessing

PRE-SERVICE TRAINING PROGRAM SYLLABUS

The Children's Guild
Pre-Service Training Program
Master Schedule
Baltimore Campus

Week B - Wednesday

9:00 a.m.   Therapeutic Options Training (Concepts and Knowledge)
Stan Jacobs and Thomas Gunter
Guild Certified TherOps Trainers

12:00 p.m.   Lunch

1:00 p.m.   Therapeutic Options Training (Concepts and Knowldge)
Stan Jacobs and Thomas Gunter
Guild Certified TherOps Trainers

3:45 p.m.   Closing and Evaluation

4:00 p.m.   Adjourn

Lerners who live under stress, anxiety or a constant
threat of some kind don't receive the all-important brain
rest needed for optimal functioning. Without it, learning
and thinking are impaired. –Eric Jensen

PRE-SERVICE TRAINING PROGRAM SYLLABUS

The Children's Guild
Pre-Service Training Program
Master Schedule
Baltimore Campus

Week B - Thursday

9:00 a.m.   Therapeutic Options Training (Physical Skills)
Stan Jacobs and Thomas Gunter
Guild Certified TherOps Trainers

12:00 p.m.   Lunch

1:00 p.m.   Therapeutic Options Training (Physical Skills)
Stan Jacobs and Thomas Gunter
Guild Certified TherOps Trainers

3:45 p.m.   Closing and Evaluation

4:00 p.m.   Adjourn

Violence is the language of the unheard.
–Rev. Martin Luther King, Jr.

PRE-SERVICE TRAINING PROGRAM SYLLABUS

The Children's Guild
Pre-Service Training Program
Master Schedule
Baltimore Campus

Week B - Friday

9:00 a.m.   Commitment to Regulatory Excellence
Terry Manning, VP of Programs (Educational staff)
Walter Alston, Director, Therapeutic Group Home (TGH staff)

10:30 a.m.   Child Abuse Reporting Policies and Procedures
Guild Clinical Services Leaders

12:00 p.m.   Lunch

1:00 p.m.   Writing Student Intervention Reports
Guild Clinical Services Leaders

2:30 p.m.   Profile of Students Served and Admissions Process
LaMar Williams, Director of Admissions

3:30 p.m.   Commencement

4:00 p.m.   Adjourn

*It is doing the little things well that can transform a good
person into a great person; a good school into a great school.*
–Lowell W. Biller

CREDENTIAL STATUS REPORT

Revised March 10, 2004 - WMC

Teacher's Name	Campus	Certificate/License	Status	Notes
A. Alicia	Baltimore	*Advanced Professional Certificate*	Pending	Renewal mailed to MSDE 05/23/03
A. Peter	Chillum	Conditional Degree Certificate	Pending	Submitted 07/23/04
B. Latoya	Baltimore	Conditional Degree Certificate	Pending	Submitted 10/17/03
B. Claudia	Annapolis			Waiting to receive application and transcripts
B. Rosa	Chillum	Conditional Degree Certificate	Pending	Submitted 02/14/03
B. Audry	Baltimore	LCSW-C	10/31/04	
C. Georgia	Chillum	Conditional Degree Certificate	Pending	
C. Jefferson	Chillum	Conditional Degree Certificate	Pending	Submitted 01/17/03
C. Kay	Annapolis	Conditional Degree Certificate	Pending	Renewal submitted
C. Cliff	Baltimore	Conditional Degree Certificate	Pending	Submitted 01/17/03
D. Bob	Chillum	Conditional Degree Certificate	07/01/03	Waiting on transcripts for renewal
D. Ann-Marie	Baltimore	Conditional Degree Certificate	07/01/05	Met and advised on what courses she must take 11/05
F. Tom	Chillum	*Standard Professional Certificate*	Pending	Submitted 10/30/03
H. Sandy	Annapolis	Conditional Degree Certificate	Pending	Submitted 12 /22/03
H. Stillman	Baltimore	*Standard Professional Certificate II*	07/01/08	
J. Robert	Baltimore	Conditional Degree Certificate	Pending	Submitted to MSDE 11/14/03
J. Lance	Baltimore	Conditional Degree Certificate	Pending	Submitted 12/18/03
M. Anthony	Baltimore	Conditional Degree Certificate	07/01/03	Met and advised on what must be done to renew certificate
M. Lydia	Baltimore	Conditional Degree Certificate	07/01/05	Waiting on certificate
M. Tess	Baltimore	Conditional Degree Certificate	Pending	Submitted
Masarov, Mika	Baltimore	Conditional Degree Certificate	Pending	Enrolled in Master's Program
M. Brian	Chillum	Conditional Degree Certificate	Pending	Submitted 11/10/03
N. Jan	Chillum	*Standard Professional Certificate*	Pending	Submitted 11/10/03
O. Joseph	Chillum	*Standard Professional Certificate*	Pending	Submitted 01/20/04
C. Leigh	Chillum	Conditional Degree Certificate	Pending	Submitted 04/19/03
R. Lisbeth	Annapolis	*Standard Professional Certificate*	07/01/04	
S. Gwendolyn	Chillum	*Advanced Professional Certificate*	07/01/07	
T. Beth	Chillum	Conditional Degree Certificate	07/01/07	
W. Ron	Chillum	Conditional Degree Certificate	Pending	

COURSE LEVELS				
Job Classification	Orientation	Required	Intermediate	Advanced
Staff and management are interviewed to develop a menu of training needs, opportunities and priorities for each job classification.	*Orientation is competence based; preemployment training offered three times per school year.*	*Required training is either licensing or a basic best practice.*	*Intermediate courses are designated to build knowledge and competency in agency's philosophical and theoretical approach.*	*Advanced courses are talent and classification driven and are designed to develop a specialty.*
- Special Education Teacher	- Standard Operating Procedures - Universal Precautions - Medical Policies and Procedures - Workplace Expectations - Crisis Prevention Institute Training - Intervention Reports - Child Abuse Reporting - MSDR Utilization - Confidentiality and Record Keeping - Behavior Motivation	- The IEP Process - Integrated Curriculum - Transition Services - Pharmacology - Information Technology - Service Learning - Parent and Community Relations - Team Building - Assessment and Quality Improvement - Violence Prevention	- Brain-Based Learning - Experiential Learning - Team-Focused Learning - Creating the Upside Down Organization - Change Insurgency Training - Community of Character - The Process of Culture - Design Maintenance and Utilization of the Physical Environment - Greenspan Development Model	- Diagnostic Assessment - Emotional Intelligence - Using Technology to Transform Learning for Students with Special Needs - The Experience Economy - Small Group Research and Pilot Study - Content Refreshment - Peer Review - Teaching Moral Development - Mentoring Your Teachers - The Balderidge System and Improving Education

Competencies of Youth Life Educator

1. Teach daily living skills – staff person is able to:

- Identify daily living skills – list them
- Properly set a table
- Help a child to dress for various situations
- Shop and buy clothes that send positive messages and are appealing to body shape
- Present food in an appealing way at the table
- Execute wake-up and bedtime routines
- Execute shower routines
- Do laundry
- Clean a house and know chemicals to use and what clean means
- Demonstrate basic understanding of nutrition – cooking without grease, eating vegetables and healthy snacks
- Demonstrate what to do when a student won't do a chore and model participation in chores
- Respond to property destruction
- Care for a lawn, shrubs, flowers, houseplants, fish, hamsters, furniture, clothing, recreational equipment, tools, etc.

2. Participate and lead curriculum activities – staff person is able to:

- Execute the activity program as it is planned
- Create an experience rather than an activity
- Understand what to do when things go wrong in an activity
- Articulate goal of activity or trip and motivate child to participate in an activity
- Read a map and follow directions
- Understand logistics of an activity
- Handle money and receipts on a trip

3. Documentation – staff person is able to:

- Demonstrate how to take pictures so students have an album to document their childhoods
- Fill out crisis intervention reports, daily logs, and medication logs correctly

4. Transportation – staff person is able to:

- Abide by traffic laws
- Make sure van is clean of refuse upon return
- Fill out van inspection report
- Ensure seat belt useage
- Fill out mileage report
- Understand how to manage a fight or out-of-control behavior in a vehicle

5. Communication and relationship skills – staff person is able to:

- Understand how verbal and nonverbal behavior is communicated and influence children through actions such as words, tone of voice, dress, physical appearance, understanding what confidentiality is and is not, cleanliness of physical environment, expressing opinions consistent with organizational values
- Understand and be aware of boundary issues between staff and children gift giving, borrowing and lending, touching and hugging, self-disclosure, personal use of agency equipment
- Understand the concept of life space interviewing and execute it
- Understand supportive counseling and execute it as needed
- Use the etiquette of how to answer phone and represent the organization
- Demonstrate understanding of rituals and their importance, such as how to decorate for secular and religious holidays, present gifts, structure birthday parties
- Understand values expressed in movies, TV, videos and music, and turn them into learning events while watching and listening

6. Observation skills – staff person is able to:

- Understand basic childhood illness symptoms
- Identify medication side effects
- Identify symptoms associated with suicide, depression, sexual acting-out behavior
- Identify symptoms of substance abuse
- Identify potential risks at child's home, school, community outings and report them

7. Behavior management skills – staff person is able to:

- Demonstrate ability to appropriately use therapeutic holds
- Stay out of battle of wills or be aware when engaged in battle of wills
- Identify cues that lead to out-of-control aggressive or provocative behavior
- Demonstrate conflict-resolution skills
- Keep children challenged and engaged in activities
- Participate in activities and assist children to do the same
- Utilize natural and logical consequences so child learns from his/her mistakes
- Manage runaway or elopement situations
- Welcome (host) visitors, activity teachers, parents, volunteers and neighbors, and teach children to do the same
- Provide direction to staff or visitors who do not know the program
- Ensure visitors are displaying values and limits consistent with residential program

8. Physical health – staff person is:

- Certified in CPR, first aid
- Knowledgeable about water safety

9. Assists clinical intervention – staff person is able to:

- Identifiy situations that warrant notification of supervisor, school councelor or on-call person – a lawyer asking for information, a parent who doesn't know what to do with a child's behavior
- Understand the child's growth plan and is aware of each child's goals

10. Provides a safe and secure environment – staff person:

- Takes universal precautions training and demonstrates knowledge by passing test
- Knows exit plan and passes test on what to do in case of disasters such as tornadoes, floods, electrical wire down, fire, electricity off, gun in the house
- Understands how and when to conduct room searches and personal searches
- Completes training on abuse and neglect and is able to follow protocol for suspected abuse or neglect

11. Provides educational assistance – staff person:

- Passes a study skills course and can execute contents
- Passes course on learning disabilities and how emotional disturbance impacts learning and can execute contents
- Understands teaching strategies, use of computer programs that remediate math and academic subject gaps and can execute contents
- Possesses the skill to help the nonreader study

12. Participates in admission and discharge of residents – staff person:

- Demonstrates how to orient and welcome child, create welcome party, clothing, inventory, review day-to-day structure of the program, shop for clothing, provide hygiene supplies, determine favorite food, secure welcome gift, help child set up his/her room, purchase suitcase
- Demonstrates understanding of transition planning and issues related to transition
- Demonstrates basic understanding of child's emotions regarding leaving, court dates, etc.

13. Group skills – staff person:

- Demonstrates use of Roberts Rules of Order and can run house meeting
- Knows how to run activity group
- Is able to facilitate group meeting
- Understands group dynamics and group development theory

Appendix 4A: *Instructions for Conducting Employee Performance Reviews*

Instructions for Conducting Employee Performance Reviews

Performance reviews are performed for each staff member after the six-month period from the date of hire and annually thereafter on the anniversary of the date of hire. The purpose of the performance review is to accomplish the following:

- Ensure that each job description is current and accurate
- Confirm that each job description is in alignment with the goals set forth in the strategic plan
- Evaluate job performance as it relates to the achievement of strategic plan goals
- Assess the performance of job tasks and skills
- Rate the fit of each staff member with the philosophy and values of The Children's Guild
- Acclimate the new employee to the culture and expectations of The Guild

What You Will Need

1. You will need a copy of the job description of the staff person that you are evaluating.

2. You will need a copy of the Strategic Plan Goals & Achievements.

3. You will need the Performance & Competency Rating paperwork specific to the position for evaluation such as management level, teaching staff, counseling staff, etc., as well as the Performance & Competency Rating Measures document.

4. You will need the Organizational Fit Assessment paperwork to assess the cultural performance and organizational fit.

The Strategic Plan Goals Achievement Form

This section is designed to identify and rate strategic plan goal achievement for the person that you are supervising. You will need to compare your responsibilities for achieving the strategic plan to what this position needs to do so that you (the supervisor) can achieve your goals. When the strategic plan changes, it is possible that the strategic plan goals of your supervisee will also change. You may need to add, delete or rework the entire strategic plan objectives that currently exist to align the strategic plan objectives you listed previously with the most recent strategic plan.

Use the rating key located on the Strategic Plan Goal Attainment Form to determine progress made toward strategic plan goals.

The Job Review Competency Form

In this section you will evaluate the supervisee's job tasks and skills performance competence. You will need to check the competency rating against the competency requirement listed on the appropriate form (i.e., management competency, teacher competency, support staff competency, psychiatrist competency, nurse competency, etc.) to determine the actual rating. The definition of each performance measure is on the Performance Rating Explanation document. A solid rating in any area is an "A," given it is a full and complete job of that area. The next two highest ratings are really A+ (Superior) and A++ (Exceptional). The two lower ratings are a "C" (Inconsistent) and a "D" (Marginal).

The Organizational Fit Performance Assessment Form

This portion of the performance review is designed to assess the supervisee's fit with the organization. You will need to rate your supervisee's performance in the areas of attitude, flexibility and teamwork by using the Organizational Fit Performance Assessment Form. You may add comments if you like to the comment section.

The Employee Growth Plan Form

The Employee Growth Plan Form identifies the plan for improvement in each of the three components of the performance review process. The supervisor works with his/her supervisee to identify the performance objective in the strategic plan, job task or skill and organizational fit areas that need improvement. Then the supervisor and supervisee develop the plan for improvement and how it will be measured. Last but not least, a credential review is conducted and training needed is identified and documented in the performance review. The individual's staff development plan is forwarded to and maintained by the executive vice president's assistant.

Each employee should have a plan of action geared toward his/her own personal growth and development in relation to the respective job description. A plan of action is achieved through the appropriate staff development using The College of Transformation Education, seminars and outside workshops.

Starting the Process

1. Schedule a meeting with the employee to be evaluated. At the meeting, share all the paperwork required to perform the evaluation with that staff member. Be prepared to answer the employee's questions. Ask the staff member to meet with you at a later date after s/he has read all the paperwork and compared it to his/her job description. This will provide both of you the opportunity to perform a preliminary evaluation of the employee's performance.
2. At the second meeting, share your evaluation as a manager with the employee and listen to the evaluation the employee provides. Discuss where you are in agreement and where you may be in disagreement. Discuss strengths and areas for improvement. Allow for open communication.

One of three outcomes will result from the second meeting:

- You are both in agreement.
- The manager may concede points by the employee during the discussion and rework portions of the evaluation.
- You and the employee are in substantial disagreement.

Completing the Process

1. If you are both in agreement, then the manager finalizes the evaluation and signs both copies of the evaluation form. One signed copy is to be filed with Human Resources and one copy is for the employee.
2. If the employee has made valid points and the manager agrees to incorporate or revise a portion or portions of the evaluation, the manager makes the revision and the evaluation is now ready to be finalized as outlined in #1.
3. If the manager and the employee cannot agree and the manager is secure in his/her evaluation, then the evaluation stands and is finalized as outlined above. The employee who is in disagreement may document his/her concerns and areas of disagreement. This documentation becomes a part of the evaluation and is filed with Human Resources.

STRATEGIC PLAN GOALS ACHIEVEMENT FORM

Employee Position: _____ Vice President of Finance _____

Rater's name: _____

Date of Review: _____

Key:

TCI	=	Thoroughly and consistently implemented
GI	=	To great extent it is implemented
SI	=	Somewhat implemented
L/NI	=	To little or no extent is it implemented

PERFORMANCE OBJECTIVE	RATING			
I. Program Refinement	TCI	GI	SI	L/NI
Consistent Implementation of: • Baldridge System in areas of responsibility				
- Finance				
- Information technology				
- Human resources				
• Develop and deploy human resources plan				
- Recruitment				
- Retention				
- Hiring				
- Temporary pool				
- Recognition				
- Compensation				
• Maintain information technology program that supports program and operational needs				
II. Diversify Funding	TCI	GI	SI	L/NI
• Support partnerships with private and public entities				
• Develop business plans to support marketing of programs and Transformation Education				
• Create budget projections for new programs and ventures as requested				
III. Transformation of Physical Environment	TCI	GI	SI	L/NI
• Manage cash and cash projects				

Comments (if any):

STRATEGIC PLAN GOALS ACHIEVEMENT FORM

Employee Position: ____Vice President of Programs____

Rater's name: _____

Date of Review: _____

Key:
TCI = Thoroughly and consistently implemented
GI = To great extent it is implemented
SI = Somewhat implemented
L/NI = To little or no extent is it implemented

PERFORMANCE OBJECTIVE	RATING			
I. Program Refinement	TCI	GI	SI	L/NI
Consistent implementation of:				
• Basic school				
• MSDR manual				
• Kiosk concept				
• Transformation Station manual				
• Integrated curriculum concept				
• Economics of staying in school				
• Cognitive theory approaches				
• Integration of art, drama, music & physical education in academic program				
• PBIS				
• McGraw Hill				
• Success maker				
• Therapeutic group home manual				
• Inculcation of contextual thinking				
II. Transformation of Physical Environment	TCI	GI	SI	L/NI
• Implement Baldridge throughout program				
• Staff involvement in QI & UR				
• Execute business manager system in schools				
• Execute instructional coordinator in schools				
• Execute design team				
• Execute IEP system				
• Execute Guild's performance review system				
• Implement Guild's behavior motivation system				

(continued on next page)

PERFORMANCE OBJECTIVE	RATING			
III. Environment	TCI	GI	SI	L/NI
• Execute library as hub of school				
• Execute group home as boarding school (i.e., rooms used as defined in TGH Manual)				
• Kiosk & Transformation Station changed quarterly				
• Therapeutic group home manual				
• Inculcation of contextual thinking				
• Articulate therapeutic approach for OMHC staff				
IV. People	TCI	GI	SI	L/NI
• Program staff desmostrate support for Guild's sponsored lectures and events				
• Retain highly qualified staff				
• Well-planned and appropriate training of staff development days				
V. Diversify Funding	TCI	GI	SI	L/NI
• Implement and execute after-school grant as written				
• Baltimore Campus pre-school to 12 certified				
• Expand OMHC to viable program				
VI. Outcomes	TCI	GI	SI	L/NI
• Meet student census projections for program				
• Trend toward achieivng overall returns to less restrictive of 60% or better				
• Meet testing goals time frames				
• Use QI data and outcomes information to improve and operate program				

Comments (if any):

STRATEGIC PLAN GOALS ACHIEVEMENT FORM

Employee Position: ___Director of Group Homes___

Rater's name: _____

Date of Review: _____

Key:

TCI	=	Thoroughly and consistently implemented
GI	=	To great extent it is implemented
SI	=	Somewhat implemented
L/NI	=	To little or no extent is it implemented

PERFORMANCE OBJECTIVE	RATING			
I. Program Refinement	TCI	GI	SI	L/NI
Consistent implementation of: • Deployment of group home manual				
• Weekly training in group home manual				
• Community-based training				
II. Systems Refinement	TCI	GI	SI	L/NI
• Implement Baldridge training throughout TGH program				
• Responsible to ensure QI of program is being coordinated				
• Implement behavioral management in accordance with the agency philosophy				
III. Environment	TCI	GI	SI	L/NI
• Implementation of group home boarding school philosophy				
• Facilities management environment meets or exceeds the organization's expectations				
IV. People	TCI	GI	SI	L/NI
• Responsible for staff participation in Guild lectures and events				
• Staff training needs identified and deployment of group home manual				
V. Diversify Funding	TCI	GI	SI	L/NI
• Support program expansion				
VI. Outcomes	TCI	GI	SI	L/NI
• Support preparing students for less restrictive environments				
• Meet regulatory compliance				
• QI outcome information shared				

Comments (if any):

STRATEGIC PLAN GOALS ACHIEVEMENT FORM

Employee Position: ___Youth Life Educator Supervisor___

Rater's name: _____

Date of Review: _____

Key:

TCI = horoughly and consistently implemented
GI = To great extent it is implemented
SI = Somewhat implemented
L/NI = To little or no extent is it implemented

PERFORMANCE OBJECTIVE	RATING			
I. Program Refinement	TCI	GI	SI	L/NI
Consistent Implementation of: • Deployment of group home manual				
• Weekly training in group home manual				
• Community-based training				
II. Systems Refinement	TCI	GI	SI	L/NI
• Participate in QI program				
• Responisble to ensure QI of program is being coordinated				
• Implement behavior system management in accordance with organization's philosophy				
III. Environment	TCI	GI	SI	L/NI
• Implementation of group home boarding school philosophy				
• Facilities management environment meets or exceeds the organization's expectations				
IV. People	TCI	GI	SI	L/NI
• Responsible for staff participation in Guild lectures and events				
V. Diversify Funding	TCI	GI	SI	L/NI
• Support program expansion				
VI. Outcomes	TCI	GI	SI	L/NI
• Support preparing students for less restrictive environments				
• Meet regulatory compliance				
• QI outcome information shared				

Comments (if any):

STRATEGIC PLAN GOALS ACHIEVEMENT FORM

Employee Position: _____Youth Life Educator_____

Rater's name: _____

Date of Review: _____

Key:

TCI	=	horoughly and consistently implemented
GI	=	To great extent it is implemented
SI	=	Somewhat implemented
L/NI	=	To little or no extent is it implemented

PERFORMANCE OBJECTIVE	RATING			
I. Program Refinement	TCI	GI	SI	L/NI
Consistent Implementation of: • Weekly training in group home manual				
• Community-based training				
• Implementation of TGH manual with students				
II. Systems Refinement	TCI	GI	SI	L/NI
• Reponsible for collection of QI data				
• Implement behavioral management in accordance with organization's philosophy				
III. Environment	TCI	GI	SI	L/NI
• Implementation of group home boarding school philosophy				
• Facilities management environment meets or exceeds the organization's expectations				
IV. People	TCI	GI	SI	L/NI
• Responsible for staff participation in Guild lectures and events				
V. Diversify Funding	TCI	GI	SI	L/NI
• Support program expansion				
VI. Outcomes	TCI	GI	SI	L/NI
• Meet regulatory compliance				
• Support preparing students for less restrictive environment				

Comments (if any):

PERFORMANCE & COMPETENCY RATING FORM FOR YOUTH LIFE EDUCATOR

Employee Position: _____ Youth Life Educator _____

Supervisor's Name: _____

Years of experience in the field: _____ Date: _____

COMPETENCIES	MARGINAL	INCONSISTENT	SOLID	SUPERIOR	EXCEPTIONAL
Program Refinement					
• Identifies daily living skills: _____ _____ _____					
• Properly sets a table					
• Teaches how to help a child to dress for various occasions, to shop and buy clothes that send positive messages and are appealing to body shape					
• Knows how to present food in an appealing way					
Activities Program					
• Executes the activity program as planned					
• Creates an experience rather than an activity					
• Understands what to do when things go wrong in an activity					
• Knows to articulate goal of activity or trip and motivate child to participate in an activity					
• Knows how to read a map and how to follow directions					
• Knows logistics of an activity					
• Knows how to handle money and receipts on a trip					
Documentation					
• Demonstrates how to take pictures to document childhood					
• Fills out crisis intervention report appropriately					
• Fills out medication log					
• Fills out daily log					

(continued on next page)

COMPETENCIES	MARGINAL	INCONSISTENT	SOLID	SUPERIOR	EXCEPTIONAL
Transportation					
• Makes sure van is clean of refuse upon return					
• Abides by traffic laws					
• Fills out van inspection report					
• Ensures seat belt usage					
• Fills out mileage report					
• Knows how to manage a fight, out-of-control behavior or smoking in the van					
Communication and Relationship Skills					
• Knows how verbal and nonverbal behavior is communicated and influences children through actions such as words, tone of voice, dress, physical appearance					
• Knows the meaning of confidentiality and options consistent with organization's values					
• Aware of boundary issues between staff and children: gift giving, borrowing and lending, touching and hugging, self-disclosure, personal use of agency equipment					
• Knows concept of life space interviewing					
• Knows supportive counseling techniques					
• Knows etiquette of how to answer phone to positively represent the organization					
• Demonstrates understanding and importance of rituals such as how to decorate for holidays, gift giving, how to structure birthday parties, religious holidays and national holidays					
• Demonstrates ability to use watching and listening to movies, TV, videos and music into learning events related to values and beliefs					
Conduct Assessment					
• Knows basic childhood illness symptoms					
• Identifies medication side effects					
• Knows first aid					
• Knows symptoms of suicide, depression, sexual acting-out behaviors (predators or victims)					

(continued on next page)

COMPETENCIES	MARGINAL	INCONSISTENT	SOLID	SUPERIOR	EXCEPTIONAL
Conduct Assessment (continued)					
• Knows symptoms of substance abuse					
• Can identify potential risks at child's home, school, community outings and how/who to report them to					
Behavior Motivation					
• Can demonstrate ability to execute preventive measures taught in Therapeutic Options Training					
• Can demonstrate ability to appropriately use therapeutic holds					
• Can stay out of battle of wills					
• Identifies cues that lead to out-of-control, aggressive or provocative behavior					
• Demonstrates conflict-resolution skills					
• Keeps children challenged and engaged in activities					
• Participates in activities and assists children to do the same					
• Utilizes natural and logical consequences so children learn from their mistakes					
• Knows how to manage AWOL situation					
Supervisory Assistance					
• Welcomes (hosts) activity teachers, parents, volunteers and neighbors and teaches children to do the same					
• Provides direction to staff or visitors who do not know the program					
• Ensures visitors display values and limits consistent with residential program					
Safe and Secure Environment					
• Identifies the basic childhood illness symptoms					
• Identifies medication side effects					
• Knows first aid					
• Knows symptoms of suicide, depression, sexual acting-out behavior (predator or victims)					
• Knows symptoms of substance abuse					
• Takes universal precautions training and demonstrates mastery of information					

(continued on next page)

COMPETENCIES	MARGINAL	INCONSISTENT	SOLID	SUPERIOR	EXCEPTIONAL
Safe and Secure Environment (continued)					
• Identifies situations that warrant notification of supervisor, social worker, on-call person, such as a lawyer asking for information, a parent who doesn't know what to do with a child's behavior					
• Knows exit plan, what to do in case of disasters (e.g., tornados, floods, fallen electrical wire, fire, power outage)					
• Knows how and when to conduct room and personal searches					
Educational Assessment					
• Passes study skills course					
• Passes course on learning disabilities and how emotional disturbance impacts learning					
• Knows teaching strategies, use of computer programs and academic subject gaps					
• Knows how to help the nonreader study					
Regulatory Requirement					
• Attends child abuse training and knows protocol to follow for suspected abuse					
• Knows how to identify and report child abuse					
• Receives passing grade on regulatory compliance competency exam					
• Demonstrates awareness of meeting regulatory compliance mandates					
Intake Process					
• Demonstrates how to orient and welcome child through creating a welcome party; conducting clothing inventory; reviewing day-to-day structure of the program, and shopping for hygiene supplies, favorite foods, welcome gift, room set-up, etc.					
• Demonstrates understanding of transition planning and issues relating to transition					
• Demonstrates basic understanding of child's emotions regarding leaving, court dates, etc.					
Household Management					
• Demonstrates how to do laundry					
• Demonstrates how to clean house and knowledge of cleaning products					
• Demonstrates understanding of nutrition					

(continued on next page)

COMPETENCIES	MARGINAL	INCONSISTENT	SOLID	SUPERIOR	EXCEPTIONAL
Household Management (continued)					
• Demonstrates what to do when student lacks participation in house jobs					
• Knows how to respond to property destruction					
• Demonstrates proper care of pets, plants, furniture, clothing and recreational equipment					
Other Activities					
• Demonstrates use of Roberts Rules of Order					
• Knows how to develop an agenda and run a house meeting					
• Demonstrates group facilitation skills to operate business or democratic meeting					
• Understands group dynamics and what a group can/cannot do based on stage of development					
Knowledge/Skills Required					
• Human growth and development, particularly child development					
• Human (child) psychology, family systems and dynamics					
• Socioeconomic factors that may place children/families at risk					
• Drug and alcohol abuse					
• Child welfare system – public and private resources, regulations that govern the child mental health care system					
• Educational processes to assist children with learning disabilities					
• Basic computer skills					
• Written and oral communication skills					
• Group dynamics					
• CPR and first aid instruction					
• Nutritional needs of children					
Comments (if any):					

PERFORMANCE & COMPETENCY RATING FORM FOR SEPECIAL EDUCATION TEACHER

Employee Position: _____Special Education Teacher_____

Supervisor's Name: _____

Years of experience in the field: _____ *Date:* _____

COMPETENCIES	MARGINAL	INCONSISTENT	SOLID	SUPERIOR	EXCEPTIONAL
Organizational Skills					
• Manages time effectively relative to assigned responsibilities					
• Completes and submits assigned reports in a timely fashion: lesson plans, IEPs, FBA/BIP report cards, integrated curriculum, QI data, etc.					
• Maintains student portfolio and grade book that is current and reflects student progress/regression					
• Classroom environment is neat and orderly					
Teaching Methodologies					
• Utilizes an integrated curriculum instructional delivery format					
• Teaching strategies exemplify a cognitive/experiential educational perspective					
• Differentiated instructional strategies are utilized to foster student achievement while recognizing individual student strengths and weaknesses					
• Student learning styles are recognized and incorporated into lesson plan development and implementation					
• Curriculum implementation is in alignment with MLO and TCG philosophy					
• Technology is incorporated into lesson plan and student research activities (Successmaker, etc.)					
• Cultural arts are integrated with monthly theme and current unit of study					
Classroom Management					
• Maintains classroom atmosphere conducive to personal growth and an absence of fear					
• Identifies and executes clear, concise behavioral expectations for all students					

(continued on next page)

COMPETENCIES	MARGINAL	INCONSISTENT	SOLID	SUPERIOR	EXCEPTIONAL
Classroom Management (continued)					
• Demonstrates an appreciation of diversity (cultures, lifestyles, personalities, talents, etc.) in relationships with students, parents and colleagues					
• Implements PBIS initiatives consistent with program goals and objectives					
• Collects and analyzes data regarding student performance					
• Utilizes various behavioral intervention strategies consistent with TCG philosophy and individual student IEP/BIP					
Teamwork					
• Employs a team-oriented approach to classroom/program daily operation					
• Presents with a competent, professional demeanor					
• Facilitates and participates in problem-solving discussions in a professional manner					
• Executes classroom/program goals in a consistent manner					
• Participates willingly and volunteers services in TCG activities					
• Effectively communicates with team members and colleagues					
• Seeks external support when needed					
Computer Skills					
• Utilizes basic computer skills to input data and complete assigned reports					
• Possesses knowledge of computer capabilities; e.g., word processing, Internet access, e-mail, spreadsheets, etc.					
• Participates and implements training on computerized IEP system, lesson plans and grade book					
Training					
• Embraces training/educational opportunities to enhance professional growth					
• Certification and continuing educational requirements are met					
• Active participation in scheduled supervision meetings					

(continued on next page)

COMPETENCIES	MARGINAL	INCONSISTENT	SOLID	SUPERIOR	EXCEPTIONAL
Training (continued)					
• Actively participates in campus and organization in-service trainings					
• Attendance at organization-sponsored activities, which may include weekend and evenings					
• Completion of Therapeutic Options training					

Comments (if any):

JOB TASK & SKILL PERFORMANCE RATING MEASURES

Marginal	Inconsistent	Solid Professional Performance	Superior Professional Performance	Exceptional Performance
Use of this performance category implies:	*Use of this performance category implies:*	*Use of this performance category implies:*	*Use of this performance category implies:*	*Use of this performance category implies:*
Has been on the job long enough to have shown better performance. Probably should be told time is running out.	This employee is doing the job reasonably well. Performance meets the minimum requirements for the position and many of the normal performance requirements.	This employee is doing a full, complete and satisfactory job. Performance is what is expected of a fully qualified and experienced person in the assigned position.	The employee exceeds the position requirements even on some of the most difficult and complex parts of the job. Takes the initiative in development and in implementation of challenging work goals. Normally, this individual will be considered for promotion.	Employee demonstrates knowledge that normally can be gained only through long periods of experience in this particular type of work.
Is creating a bit of a morale problem with those who have to help carry his/her load (including yourself).	The employee's performance is not really poor, but if all of your people were at this performance level, you would be in trouble.	You would not require significant improvement. If improvement does occur, it's a plus factor for your group's effectiveness. If it does not occur, you have no reason to complain.	You are getting more than you bargained for.	Recognized by all as a real expert in this job area.
Just doesn't seem to have the drive or the know-how to do the job. Would be better off with other job for which qualified.	You would like to see the employee improve but in the meantime, you really don't have too much to complain about.	If all your employees were as good, your total group's performance would be completely satisfactory. (In your judgment and your manager's too.)	You find the employee accomplishing more than you expect.	This employee can usually be a prime candidate for promotion when a higher level position in this or a related field becomes open.
The employee's work is holding up that of the other positions with which it interrelates.	May be the kind of employee who needs some pushing and follow-through, but does the job under close guidance.	You get few complaints from others with whom the employee's work interfaces.	Is able to take on extra projects and tasks without defaulting in other assigned activity fields.	This employee's actions show an understanding of work well beyond the assigned area. Outsiders seek the employee out because of knowledge of many facets of the department's work.
It is more than likely that the employee probably recognizes that the job is not getting done.	You may have to keep a close watch, otherwise you would consider the employee competent.	Errors are few and seldom repeated.	Each project or job tackled is done thoroughly and completely.	Requires little or no supervision or follow-up.
If performance continues at this level, the employee should be replaced.	The employee shows drive but needs to acquire more know-how.	Demonstrates a sound balance between quality and quantity.	The employee's decisions and actions have paid off to a higher degree than would be expected.	Shows unusual initiative and is self-started.
Just doesn't seem to get things accomplished.	You may have to plan the employee's programs or assignments step by step. After that, the job usually gets done.	Does not spend undue time on unimportant items, neglecting problems or projects that should have priority.	Often provides "extras."	Almost invariably takes the best approach to getting the job done.
The work keeps falling behind. If you keep the employee much longer, you will be in real trouble.	Some of your people have to "carry" the employee on occasion.	You feel reasonably secure in quoting the employee's inputs or recommendations.	Requires only occasional supervision and follow-up.	*Note: This level of performance must be looked at in terms of both quantity and quality. Use of this category shows you are recognizing really outstanding worth to the company within the level of this position.*
Seems to make one mistake after another and some of them are repeats.	Can't always depend on the employee to complete the assignments or the daily work unless you keep checking.	Requires only normal supervision and follow-up and usually completes regular work and projects on schedule.	Frequently exceeds objectives.	
Apparently does not have the background to grasp the work.		Has encountered almost all the activity of the position and has proved quite capable in each.	Does own planning, anticipates problems and takes appropriate action.	
You have had adverse comments from outsiders concerning the employee's performance.		You consider the employee a good, solid member of your team and feel reasonably secure in making any kind of assignment within the scope of the job and level.	Shows a good grasp of the big picture. Thinks beyond the details of the job, works toward the overall objectives of the department.	
			If you had four employees like this employee, you would only need three.	

Rodman, T.A. (1984) Make the Praise Equal the Raise. Personnel Journal. Costa Mesa, CA

ORGANIZATIONAL FIT ASSESSMENT

Employee Position: _____ Date: _____

Assessor's Name: _____

Attitude

☐ Resistor	☐ Negotiator	☐ Acceptor	☐ Embracer	☐ Seeker
• Demonstrates a negative attitude through actions and/or words • Blames others for his/her mistakes or errors • Finds the easy way to get things done rather than the right way • Looks for problems, not solutions	• Attitude is inconsistent depending upon the situation • Presents other's ideas rather than their own • Views work as a job, no more or less • Listens to other people's problems but offers no appropriate problem-solving advice (usually agrees with the problems for the sake of agreement)	• Attitude is consistent, neither positive nor negative • Does not get involved in other people's problems, one way or the other • Takes direction well, offers very little input to change or ideas involving possible improvement	• Attitude is consistently positive • Willing to champion the message • Exemplifies enthusiasm about work • Assists others who are experiencing problems by teaching and modeling appropriate problem-solving techniques and channels	• Attitude reflects understanding of wisdom principles and life expectations • Sees difficult situations as opportunities • Views all problems as solutions waiting to happen

Flexibility

☐ Resistor	☐ Negotiator	☐ Acceptor	☐ Embracer	☐ Seeker
• Unwilling to try new methods • Unwilling to adopt language of organizational culture • Unwilling to change ways or actions even when confronted with new opportunities for change	• Willingness to grow if there is no struggle or pain • Open to discussions about new ideas/models but only with certain limitations	• Accept things the way they are • Is usually task-focused and does exactly what is expected for the job and the workplace • Does job for today and does not look toward the future	• Willing to endure pain and struggle for growth • Demonstrates life expectations • Understands change and demonstrates willingness to change	• Searches for new approaches to his/her job as well as for the agency as a whole • Welcomes challenges; pushes him/herself to the brink and then goes a step further • Can overcome fear to take risks

Team

☐ Resistor	☐ Negotiator	☐ Acceptor	☐ Embracer	☐ Seeker
• Unwilling to confront others who are being unsupportive of the agency and/or management	• Avoids conflict simply to avoid conflict • Says something different depending on the audience (i.e., says what you want to hear)	• Is not argumentative and does not challenge ideas, but is not excited or passionate about work either • Is neither helpful nor hurtful • Does not challenge him/herself or others • Will assist with extra tasks or projects when asked; offers very little initiative • Does not look for problems or solutions	• Models behavior that is congruent with the mission of the agency • Challenges ideas and brings forth new approaches and ideas • Encourages others to do more • Is a morale booster	• Seeks out messages conveyed in how systems, people, program and environment operate • Demonstrates leadership qualities and willingness to confront difficult situations to become stronger and more knowledgeable • Seeks out truth and teaches it by example • Seeks out additional responsibilities to help move the agency forward

EMPLOYEE'S GROWTH PLAN

Employee Position: _____   Date: _____

A. Strategic Plan Areas in Need of Development

Performance Objective	Area for Improvement	Improvement Plan	Measure to Determine Growth

B. Competencies in Need of Development

Competency	Improvement Desired	Improvement Plan	Measure to Determine Growth

C. Organizational Fit

Areas of Fit to Address	Improvement Desired	Improvement Plan	Measure to Determine Achievement

D. Credential (if applicable) or Coursework in College of Transformation Education *(please inform Human Resources office of information below to ensure it is entered in individual's staff development plan.)*

Credential or Course to be Obtained or Completed	Time Frame for Completion	Activity to be Achieved to Determine Credential or Knowledge Gained

INDIVIDUAL REGULATION PLAN FOR THE HIGHLY SENSITIVE CHILD

Student Name: _____ ID# _____ DOB: _____ Clinician: _____ Date: _____

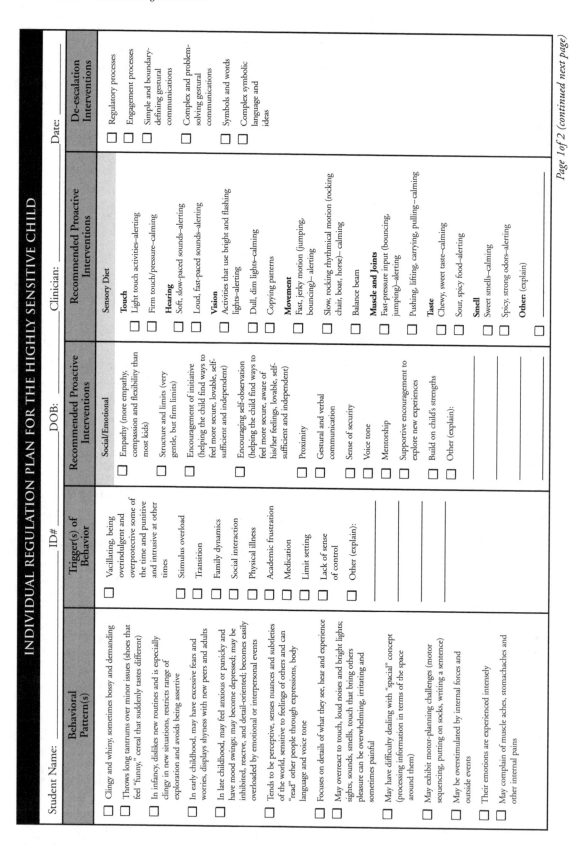

Behavioral Pattern(s)	Trigger(s) of Behavior	Recommended Proactive Interventions — Social/Emotional	Recommended Proactive Interventions — Sensory Diet	De-escalation Interventions
☐ Clingy and whiny, sometimes bossy and demanding	☐ Vacillating, being overindulgent and overprotective some of the time and punitive and intrusive at other times	☐ Empathy (more empathy, compassion and flexibility than most kids)	**Touch** ☐ Light touch activities–alerting ☐ Firm touch/pressure–calming	☐ Regulatory processes
☐ Throws long tantrums over minor issues (shoes that feel "funny," cereal that suddenly tastes different)	☐ Stimulus overload	☐ Structure and limits (very gentle, but firm limits)	**Hearing** ☐ Soft, slow-paced sounds–alerting ☐ Loud, fast-paced sounds–alerting	☐ Engagement processes
☐ In infancy, dislikes new routines and is especially clingy in new situations, restricts range of exploration and avoids being assertive	☐ Transition	☐ Encouragement of initiative (helping the child find ways to feel more secure, lovable, self-sufficient and independent)	**Vision** ☐ Activities that use bright and flashing lights–alerting ☐ Dull, dim lights–calming ☐ Copying patterns	☐ Simple and boundary-defining gestural communications
☐ In early childhood, may have excessive fears and worries, displays shyness with new peers and adults	☐ Family dynamics	☐ Encouraging self-observation (helping the child find ways to feel more secure, aware of his/her feelings, lovable, self-sufficient and independent)	**Movement** ☐ Fast, jerky motion (jumping, bouncing)– alerting ☐ Slow, rocking rhythmical motion (rocking chair, boat, horse)– calming ☐ Balance beam	☐ Complex and problem-solving gestural communications
☐ In late childhood, may feel anxious or panicky and have mood swings; may become depressed; may be inhibited, reactve, and detail-oriented; becomes easily overloaded by emotional or interpersonal events	☐ Social interaction	☐ Proximity	**Muscle and Joints** ☐ Fast-pressure input (bouncing, jumping)–alerting ☐ Pushing, lifting, carrying, pulling–calming	☐ Symbols and words
☐ Tends to be perceptive, senses nuances and subtleties of the world, sensitive to feelings of others and can "read" other people through expressions, body language and voice tone	☐ Physical illness	☐ Gestural and verbal communication	**Taste** ☐ Chewy, sweet taste–calming ☐ Sour, spicy food–alerting	☐ Complex symbolic language and ideas
☐ Focuses on details of what they see, hear and experience	☐ Academic frustration	☐ Sense of security	**Smell** ☐ Sweet smells–calming ☐ Spicy, strong odors–alerting	
☐ May overreact to touch, loud noises and bright lights; sights, sounds, smells, touch that bring others pleasure can be overwhelming, irritating and sometimes painful	☐ Medication	☐ Voice tone	**Other:** (explain) ☐ _____	
☐ May have difficulty dealing with "spacial" concept (processing information in terms of the space around them)	☐ Limit setting	☐ Mentorship		
☐ May exhibit motor-planning challenges (motor sequencing, putting on socks, writing a sentence)	☐ Lack of sense of control	☐ Supportive encouragement to explore new experiences		
☐ May be overstimulated by internal forces and outside events	☐ Other (explain): _____	☐ Build on child's strengths		
☐ Their emotions are experienced intensely		☐ Other (explain): _____		
☐ May complain of muscle aches, stomachaches and other internal pains				

Page 1 of 2 (continued next page)

INDIVIDUAL REGULATION PLAN FOR THE HIGHLY SENSITIVE CHILD

Student Name: _____ ID# _____ DOB: _____ Clinician: _____ Date: _____

Behavioral Pattern(s)	Trigger(s) of Behavior	Recommended Proactive Interventions	Recommended Proactive Interventions	De-escalation Interventions
☐ Clingy and whiny, sometimes bossy and demanding				
☐ Throws long tantrums over minor issues (shoes that feel "funny", cereal that suddenly tastes different)				
☐ In infancy, dislikes new routines & is especially clingy in new situations, restricts range of exploration and avoids being assertive				
☐ In early childhood may have excessive fears and worries, displays shyness with new peers and adults				
☐ In late childhood may feel anxious or panicky and have mood swings. May become depressed, may be inhibited, reactive, and detail-oriented. Becomes easily overloaded by emotional or interpersonal events				
☐ Tends to be perceptive, senses nuances and subtleties of the world, sensitive to feelings of others and can "read" other people through expressions, body language and voice tone.				
☐ Focuses on details of what they see, hear and experience				
☐ May overreact to touch, loud noises and bright lights. Sights, sounds, smells, touch that brings others pleasure can be overwhelming, irritating and sometimes painful				
☐ May have difficulty dealing with "spacial" concept (processing information in terms of the space around them)				
☐ May exhibit motor-planning challenges (motor sequencing; putting on socks, writing a sentence)				
☐ May be over-stimulated by internal forces and outside events				
☐ Their emotions are experienced intensely				
☐ May complain of muscle aches, stomachaches and other internal pains				

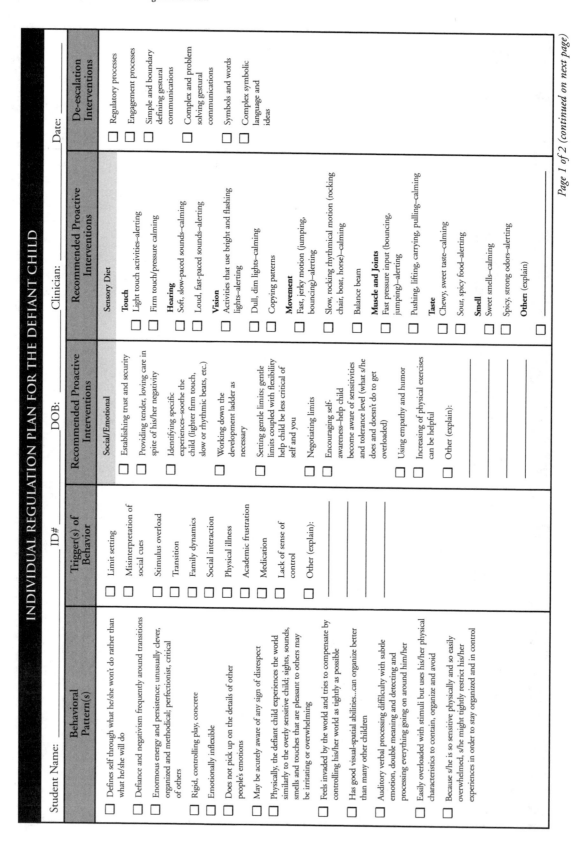

INDIVIDUAL REGULATION PLAN FOR THE DEFIANT CHILD

Student Name: _____ ID# _____ DOB: _____ Clinician: _____ Date: _____

Behavioral Pattern(s)	Trigger(s) of Behavior	Recommended Proactive Interventions — Social/Emotional	Recommended Proactive Interventions — Sensory Diet	De-escalation Interventions
☐ Defines self through what he/she won't do rather than what he/she will do	☐ Limit setting	☐ Establishing trust and security	**Touch** ☐ Light touch activities–alerting ☐ Firm touch/pressure calming	☐ Regulatory processes
☐ Defiance and negativism frequently around transitions	☐ Misinterpretation of social cues	☐ Providing tender, loving care in spite of his/her negativity	**Hearing** ☐ Soft, slow-paced sounds–calming ☐ Loud, fast-paced sounds–alerting	☐ Engagement processes
☐ Enormous energy and persistence; unusually clever, organized and methodical; perfectionist, critical of others	☐ Stimulus overload	☐ Identifying specific experiences–soothe the child (lighter firm touch, slow or rhythmic beats, etc.)	**Vision** ☐ Activities that use bright and flashing lights–alerting	☐ Simple and boundary defining gestural communications
☐ Rigid, controlling play, concrete	☐ Transition	☐ Working down the development ladder as necessary	☐ Dull, dim lights–calming	☐ Complex and problem solving gestural communications
☐ Emotionally inflexible	☐ Family dynamics	☐ Setting gentle limits; gentle limits coupled with flexibility help child be less critical of self and you	☐ Copying patterns	☐ Symbols and words
☐ Does not pick up on the details of other people's emotions	☐ Social interaction	☐ Negotiating limits	**Movement** ☐ Fast, jerky motion (jumping, bouncing)–alerting	☐ Complex symbolic language and ideas
☐ May be acutely aware of any sign of disrespect	☐ Physical illness	☐ Encouraging self-awareness–help child become aware of sensitivities and tolerance level (what s/he does and doesn't do to get overloaded)	☐ Slow, rocking rhythmical motion (rocking chair, boat, horse)–calming	
☐ Physically, the defiant child experiences the world similarly to the overly sensitive child; sights, sounds, smells and touches that are pleasant to others may be irritating or overwhelming	☐ Academic frustration	☐ Using empathy and humor	☐ Balance beam	
☐ Feels invaded by the world and tries to compensate by controlling his/her world as tightly as possible	☐ Medication	☐ Increasing of physical exercises can be helpful	**Muscle and Joints** ☐ Fast pressure input (bouncing, jumping)–alerting	
☐ Has good visual-spatial abilities...can organize better than many other children	☐ Lack of sense of control	☐ Other (explain):	☐ Pushing, lifting, carrying, pulling–calming	
☐ Auditory verbal processing difficulty with subtle emotion, double meaning and detecting and processing everything going on around him/her	☐ Other (explain):		**Taste** ☐ Chewy, sweet taste–calming ☐ Sour, spicy food–alerting	
☐ Easily overloaded with stimuli but uses his/her physical characteristics to contain, organize and avoid			**Smell** ☐ Sweet smells–calming ☐ Spicy, strong odors–alerting	
☐ Because s/he is so sensitive physically and so easily overwhelmed, s/he might tightly restrict his/her experiences in order to stay organized and in control			☐ **Other:** (explain)	

Page 1 of 2 (continued on next page)

INDIVIDUAL REGULATION PLAN FOR THE DEFIANT CHILD

Student Name: _____ ID#: _____ DOB: _____ Clinician: _____ Date: _____

Behavioral Pattern(s)	Trigger(s) of Behavior	Recommended Proactive Interventions	Recommended Proactive Interventions	De-escalation Interventions
☐ Defines self through what he/she won't do rather than what s/he will do				
☐ Defiance and negativism frequently around transitions				
☐ Enormous energy and persistence. Unusually clever, organized and methodical. Perfectionist, critical of others				
☐ Rigid, controlling play, concrete				
☐ Emotionally inflexible				
☐ Does not pick-up on the details of other people's emotions				
☐ May be acutely aware of any sign of disrespect				
☐ Physically, the defiant child experiences the world similarly to the overly sensitive child, sights sounds, smells and touches that are pleasant to others may be irritating or overwhelming				
☐ Feels invaded by the world and tries to compensate by controlling his world as tightly as possible				
☐ Has good visual-spatial abilities...can organize better than many other children				
☐ Auditory verbal processing difficulty with subtle emotion, double meaning and detecting and processing everything going on around them				
☐ Easily overloaded with stimuli but uses his/her physical characteristics to contain, organize and avoid				
☐ Because s/he is so sensitive physically, and so easily overwhelmed, s/he might tightly restrict his/her experiences in order to stay organized and in control				

INDIVIDUAL REGULATION PLAN FOR THE INATTENTIVE CHILD

Student Name: _____ ID# _____ DOB: _____ Clinician: _____ Date: _____

Behavioral Pattern(s)	Trigger(s) of Behavior	Recommended Proactive Interventions — Social/Emotional	Recommended Proactive Interventions — Sensory Diet	De-escalation Interventions
Has difficulty staying in one place at a time	☐ Focusing on child's inattentive behavior by drawing attention to it	**Social/Emotional** ☐ Help child develop sense of mastery around natural strengths	**Sensory Diet** **Touch** ☐ Light touch activities–alerting	☐ Regulatory processes
Restless, seeming to flit from place to place	☐ Using lots of do's and don'ts	☐ Note attentional problems as early as possible; work with abilities	☐ Firm touch/pressure–calming	☐ Engagement processes
Often misdiagnosed as having ADHD	☐ Downplaying the child's assets and stressing weaknesses	☐ Relate to child with respect to his/her strengths, either visually or auditory	**Hearing** ☐ Soft, slow-paced sounds–calming	☐ Simple and boundary-defining gestural communications
May appear forgetful and uninterested in conversation, shifts from subject to subject during conversation	☐ Overemphasizing the child's vulnerabilities and use the vulnerable areas as a mode of general communication	☐ Urge child to ponder behavior so s/he may figure out ways of concentrating on one subject	☐ Loud, fast-paced sounds–alerting **Vision** ☐ Activities that use bright and flashing lights - alerting	☐ Complex and problem-solving gestural communications
Variety of underlying reasons why child has difficulty paying attention, i.e., some children have visual or auditory processing difficulties, could be hypersensitive or hypo-sensitive to sound or sight, sensory integration difficulties, motor planning sequencing difficulties or visual problems	☐ Treating the child in a mechanical and inflexible manner by stressing rote approaches and fixed repetitive behaviors	☐ Attempt to maintain attention through behavioral or emotional interactions, rather than through just talking	☐ Dull, dim lights–calming ☐ Copying patterns **Movement** ☐ Fast, jerky motion (jumping, bouncing)–alerting	☐ Symbols and words ☐ Complex symbolic language and ideas
	☐ Humiliating or frustrating the child with unrealistic demands	☐ Encourage attention at each stage of development; reinforce strengths and present small challenges	☐ Slow, rocking rhythmical motion (rocking chair, boat, horse)– calming	
	☐ Demanding immediate conformity to be like other children	☐ Help child develop ability for self-observation and self-curing, so as to have internal dialogues	☐ Balance beam **Muscle and Joints**	
Usually has a lack of persistence of emotional interest	☐ Other (explain):	☐ Medication if appropriate	☐ Fast pressure input (bouncing, jumping)–alerting	
		☐ Empathy and nurturance	☐ Pushing, lifting, carrying, pulling–calming	
		☐ Present a calm presence	**Taste**	
Learning difficulties/disabilities		☐ Set limits so the child can stay focused and organized	☐ Chewy, sweet taste–calming	
		☐ Help child find a way to enjoy and achieve a sense of satisfaction from the work involved in mastering his/her vulnerable areas	☐ Sour, spicy food–alerting **Smell** ☐ Sweet smells–calming	
		☐ Other (explain):	☐ Spicy, strong odors–alerting	
			☐ **Other:** (explain)	

Page 1 of 2 (continued on next page)

INDIVIDUAL REGULATION PLAN FOR THE INATTENTIVE CHILD

Student Name: _____ ID# _____ DOB: _____ Clinician: _____ Date: _____

Behavioral Pattern(s)	Trigger(s) of Behavior	Recommended Proactive Interventions	Recommended Proactive Interventions	De-escalation Interventions
☐ Has difficulty staying in one place at a time ☐ Restless, seeming to flit from place to place ☐ Often misdiagnosed as having ADHD ☐ May appear forgetful and uninterested in conversation, shifts from subject to subject during conversation ☐ Variety of underlying reasons why child had difficulty paying attention, i.e., some children have visual or auditory processing difficulties, could be hypersensitive or hyposensitive to sound or sight, sensory integration difficulties, motor planning sequencing difficulties or visual problems ☐ Usually have a lack of persistence of emotional interest ☐ Learning difficulties/disabilities				

INDIVIDUAL REGULATION PLAN FOR THE AGGRESSIVE CHILD

Student Name: _____ ID# _____ DOB: _____ Clinician: _____ Date: _____

Behavioral Pattern(s)	Trigger(s) of Behavior	Recommended Proactive Interventions — Social/Emotional	Recommended Proactive Interventions — Sensory Diet	De-escalation Interventions
☐ Can't care for others because no one has consistently cared for them (attachment disorder)	☐ Limit setting	☐ Verbal prompting/warning	**Touch** ☐ Light touch activities – alerting	☐ Regulatory processes
☐ Can't purposefully communicate their desires, intentions and feelings. (Thwarted when attempting to communicate emotionally, nonverbally, cannot communicate emotionally using words and symbols.)	☐ Misinterpretation of social cues	☐ Practice and structure (consistency)	☐ Firm touch/pressure – calming	☐ Engagement processes
	☐ Stimulus overload	☐ Gestural and verbal communication	**Hearing** ☐ Soft, slow paced sounds–alerting	☐ Simple boundary defining gestural communications
☐ Can't construct internal dialogues. (Cannot visualize feelings and contemplate actions in advance.)	☐ Transition	☐ Proximity	☐ Loud, fast paced sounds–alerting	☐ Complex and problem solving gestural communication
☐ Craves physical input; needs a lot of noise, sound, touch or other sensations	☐ Family dynamics	☐ Sense of security	**Vision** ☐ Activities that use bright and flashing lights–alerting	☐ Symbols and words
	☐ Social interaction	☐ Warmth and engagement	☐ Dull, dim lights–calming	☐ Complex symbolic language and ideas
☐ May be less sensitive to pain	☐ Physical illness	☐ Limit setting	☐ Copying patterns	
☐ Inattentive, distractible	☐ Academic frustration	☐ Pretend play	**Movement** ☐ Fast, jerky motion (jumping, bouncing)–alerting	
☐ Difficulty with auditory processing and receptive language	☐ Medication	☐ Role playing	☐ Slow, rocking rhythmical motion (rocking chair, boat, horse)–calming	
☐ Motor planning difficulty	☐ Lack of sense of control	☐ Allow for choices	☐ Balance beam	
☐ Will likely become more aggressive when experiencing feelings of anxiety or embarrassment	☐ Other (explain): _____	☐ Voice tone	**Muscle and Joints** ☐ Fast pressure input – alerting (bouncing, jumping)	
☐ Enormous energy		☐ Label feelings	☐ Pushing, lifting, carrying, pulling–calming	
☐ Poor two-way communication		☐ Mentorship	**Taste** ☐ Chewy, sweet taste – calming	
		☐ Teach child how to read the body language and facial expresions of others	☐ Sour, spicy food–alerting	
		☐ Build on child's strengths	**Smell** ☐ Sweet smells - calming	
		☐ Other (explain): _____	☐ Spicy, strong odors - alerting	
			Other (explain): _____	

Page 1 of 2 (continued on next page)

INDIVIDUAL REGULATION PLAN FOR THE AGGRESSIVE CHILD

Student Name: _____ ID# _____ DOB: _____ Clinician: _____ Date: _____

Behavioral Pattern(s)	Trigger(s) of Behavior	Recommended Proactive Interventions	Recommended Proactive Interventions	De-escalation Interventions
☐ Can't care for others because no one has consistently care for his/her (attachment disorder)				
☐ Can't purposefully communicate his/her desire, intentions and feelings. (Thwarted when attempting to communicate emotionally, nonverbally, cannot communicate emotionally using words and symbols.)				
☐ Can't construct internal dialogues. (Cannot visualize feelings and contemplate actions in advance.)				
☐ Crave sphysical input; needs a lot of noise, sound, touch or other sensations.				
☐ May be less sensitive to pain				
☐ Inattentive, distractible				
☐ Difficulty with auditory processing and receptive language				
☐ Motor planning difficulty				
☐ Will likely become more aggressive when experiencing feeling of anxiety or embarrassment.				
☐ Enormous energy				
☐ Poor two-way communication				

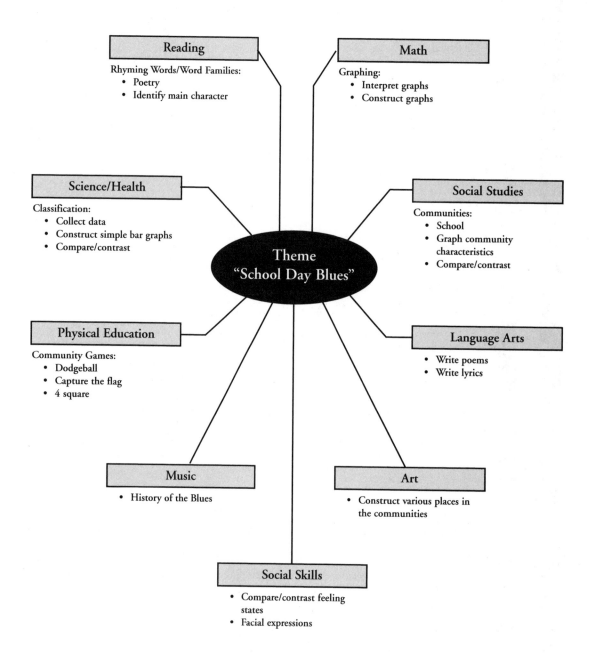

Reading

Rhyming Words/Word Families:
- Poetry
- Identify main character

Math

Graphing:
- Interpret graphs
- Construct graphs

Science/Health

Classification:
- Collect data
- Construct simple bar graphs
- Compare/contrast

Social Studies

Communities:
- School
- Graph community characteristics
- Compare/contrast

Theme "School Day Blues"

Physical Education

Community Games:
- Dodgeball
- Capture the flag
- 4 square

Language Arts

- Write poems
- Write lyrics

Music

- History of the Blues

Art

- Construct various places in the communities

Social Skills

- Compare/contrast feeling states
- Facial expressions

Individualized Growth Plan Rubric with Annotated Outline

Section I – Identifying Information

The content of this section of the plan is gleaned from the referral material and from conversations with the referring worker. This information is designed to provide a quick reference for all factual questions related to family, legal guardian, academic placement, etc. Use form 123.

Section II – Status at Admission

This section summarizes the reason for admission, the emotional/behavioral status at admission, immediate concerns that need to be addressed and the DSM-IVR referring diagnosis. When writing the discharge summary, one is able to look back and compare the status at discharge with the status at admission.

EXAMPLE: Sam is being admitted as an under-socialized, 17-year-old homeless boy with an alcohol problem who was found sleeping in an abandoned car in the inner city. He was recently arrested for assaulting a 14- year-old boy for stealing his clothes. He reads at the fourth-grade level. Three previous residential placements were terminated due to his running away, physically hitting staff and ripping a fire protection system out of the ceiling.

DSM-IVR Diagnosis

Axis I	Paranoid Ideation, Alcohol Intoxication
Axis II	Conduct Disorder (moderate)
Axis III	None
Axis IV	Stresses–homelessness, threat to personal safety, severity (4)
Axis V	Current GAF - 0 highest GAF past year - 31

Immediate Concerns:

a. Safety of peers
b. Safety of staff
c. Running away
d. Alcoholism
e. Inability to function in a classroom setting

Section III–The Profile

This section paints a profile or a character sketch of the student as a unique human being. It is not a social history but rather a description of the student as an individual or personality in positive terms that balance his character flaws with redeeming qualities.

EXAMPLE: Sam is a 17-year-old boy who is the product of the streets of Los Angeles. His stocky build, handsome features, charming personality and earnest tone of voice make one want to help him. While he possesses a fine talent as an artist and a great wish to obtain a GED, he lacks the self-discipline to use his talent or achieve his goal. Since he has been neglected most of his life, he has learned to survive through honing his skills in the area of "hustling" and "conning." He has witnessed a great deal of violence on the streets and in his home life. The result is that he does not feel safe in his neighborhood and at the same time he leans toward solving problems through physical force. His view of manhood is that of one who dominates women and who proves himself by being sexually active with many partners. Sam desires stability, family and safety but cannot attain these desires unless he is able to develop the self-discipline to advance his education, develop a work ethic and gain the social skills and values necessary to escape the life of the streets. Therefore, his struggle in life centers on making the commitment necessary to change. His artistic talent and salesmanship indicate he would do well in sales or an occupation that would tap his creativity. While he is an episodic drinker and has to live by his wits to survive, he has avoided any serious scrapes with the law. His strongest relationships are with a foster parent with whom he resided for three years and his grandmother who serves as his advocate.

Section IV – Implementation Strategy

This section of the plan is comprised of seven components and is designed to direct educator staff to intervene with the student in such a way that promotes normal growth and development.

1. Student Mindset

This area of the plan identifies the way a student perceives the world. By understanding the student's mindset toward change and growth, one is able to understand how behavior and problems will be interpreted by the student. Knowing this provides one a predictive indicator of how the student is likely to act under pressure. It also provides one with an understanding of the student's likeliness to manage effectively in a lower level of care in the community with available supports.

EXAMPLE: Sam perceives the world as hostile and life from a "short-term-get-your-immediate-needs gratified" perspective. His perceptions are due to the violence and death he has witnessed in the inner city and the fact that inner city African-American males have a short life span. He views relationships as something to be exploited for his own good. The more effective he is at exploiting people, the greater his status is amongst his peers on the street. He views women as sex objects, work as something to be avoided and violence as a fact of life. In summary, Sam views the goal of life as gratification of immediate needs and the process for fulfilling those needs with conning and hustling. The value he lives by is, "Don't do it if the police are watching."

2. Planning Focus

The planning focus establishes the context for the plan. It clarifies what one hopes to accomplish with the student. This component of the plan also serves as a reminder to the staff of the challenge or struggle(s) the student faces. For example, to learn to forgive his/her parents and love his/her enemies, or to achieve an age-appropriate developmental milestone, e.g., learn to share, separate from one's family; and/or specific outcomes such as to gain a GED, become employable, etc. The focus is stated in narrative form and identifies the issues blocking the student from overcoming the struggle or achieving the challenge.

The second component of the planning focus is identification of the messages to be sent to the child through the behavior of the staff toward the student. For example, constantly recognize caring actions, e.g., when taking the student to the zoo, point out how the monkey grooms or keeps the baby monkey close to her to protect it; ask the student at breakfast how he would like his eggs cooked, bring the student a gift or remembrance if you go on a trip, seek out the student's opinions, etc. The manner in which the staff interacts with the student based upon behavior observations, the student's learning style and talent assessment, personality, developmental history, previous experiences, student preference and referral source suggestions should be specific to the individual student.

EXAMPLE: The proper context of our work with Sam has to take into account his need to play to the street corner audience to project his manhood. Therefore, he should not be worked with in a large group. Given his lifestyle he will have a great need for excitement, yet will desire the safety and predictability of routine. His biological clock is set to rise at noon and to be in bed by 4 a.m. So adherence to the standard 7 a.m. to 11 p.m. schedule is alien to him. Therefore, one should anticipate difficulty awakening him in the morning, as well as getting him to follow the bedtime routine at night. He is likely to attack or interfere with staff when they are physically intervening with other students, as he will perceive this as aggression toward a friend. Staff will have difficulty in physically managing him should he get aggressive, belligerent or destructive as he operates from the view of the street. It is life threatening for him to appear vulnerable in front of staff or peers and he must be given a way out that demonstrates he has not lost face or appears vulnerable. If this is not done he will "fight to the death." Therefore, staff should try to move him or the other students out of the situation or provide him a face-saving way out of the situation while demonstrating lack of fear dealing with him. Manage him without physically restraining him if at all possible.

Sam cons and hustles people so he should receive no second chances and should experience the logical and natural consequences of his actions. He has been so deprived he will not function well in a group setting. Therefore he needs to be staffed with no more than a 1-3 ratio and tutored on a 1-1 basis. Given the narrowness of his worldview he should travel with a staff person away from the house rather than spend a great deal of time involved in group home activity programming. Given his lack of reading, math and writing skills the tutor needs to teach through extracting lessons from hands-on experiences. For example, teach distance by traveling in a car at rates of speed and having him anticipate how long it will take to arrive at a given destination. Teach fractions through cooking and recipe reading.

In summary, the general principles to keep in mind when working with Sam are:

- Work with him on a one-to-one basis as much as possible and in groups of no more than three or four.
- Be relentless in your efforts to hold him strictly accountable to counteract conning and hustling behavior.
- At least once a week, take him on an activity that meets his need for excitement and danger, e.g., roller coaster rides, skiing, jet skiing, wall climbing, etc.
- Expose him to people and careers in the sales and arts area that help build a vision of what is possible for him and the skills necessary for him to attain the vision.
- Be very giving to him, as he has never been nurtured.

- Teach him work skills and gradually increase his tolerance for work until he is able to work for eight hours.
- Remember his placement is guaranteed until he is 21, so view the need to work one-to-one with him to be for a minimum of a year.

Focus of Message Summary:

- Only chance is the first chance.
- There are many options and lifestyles to choose from in the world.
- Growth occurs through struggle.
- There are socially acceptable ways to meet one's need for excitement.
- We will nurture you.
- Education is a lifelong process.
- Nonviolence does not mean passivity.

EXAMPLE: Areas in Need of Special Attention

1. Special medical circumstances
   None
2. Restrictions on limiting telephone calls or visits from parents, guardian or visitors
   Do not accept calls or visits from those we do not know.
3. Student's difficulty in relating to, or taking direction from males or females
   None
4. Medications the student takes
   None
5. Allergies
   None
6. Special dietary needs
   Likes soul food—see he gets it at least twice a week.
7. Sleep difficulties
   Will take some time for him to adjust to 11 p.m. bedtime.
8. Encopresis/enuresis and how it is to be managed
   None
9. Special supervisor or monitoring needs
   If he is not engaged by staff he will get involved sexually and will leave the house to get involved in street life.
10. Suicide risks
    None
11. How to manage return from elopement
    Ask where he has been, meet current need and welcome him back, then put him right back in his program as if he never left. Do not give restrictions for running away, as he will have tremendous difficulty adjusting to an existence other than the freedom of street life.
12. Fire-setting risk
    None
13. Perpetration risk
    None

14. Rooming precautions
    Will bring females to his room to have sex if unmonitored.
15. Likelihood of cruelty or aggression toward peers, staff, small children, animals
    Will become physically aggressive—see mindset area of plan.
16. Substance abuse risk
    Will become paranoid if he drinks heavily; has tendency to wander off at night to buy wine or hard liquor. Should attempt to engage him in AA or substance abuse program.
17. Likelihood to shoplift
    Only if he needs to survive on the street.
18. Water/swimming risk
    Should be given swimming lessons, as he cannot swim.
19. Indificual Relulation Plan
    NA

3. Goals and Objectives

Student goals are established through the information gathered during the assessment period and through experience with the student throughout the placement. Objectives are developed from determining the steps a student needs to make on the way toward achieving the goal. Measurement of those steps result from assessing gains in skill competency in the curriculum areas, age-appropriate behavior and expansion of the student's worldview.

EXAMPLE: Goals

- Medical
  Goal: Complete AA treatment
  Method: Become member of AA
  Staff responsible: Youth life educators

- Health
  Goal: Competent understanding of AIDS prevention, birth control and preventive health care
  Method: Instruction by nurse, discussion groups, films, supervised volunteer experience in the organization's day care center with infants
  Staff responsible: Nurse, day care teachers and youth life educators

- Physical Fitness
  Goal: Pass physical fitness test
  Method: Develop fitness program of Sam's choice
  Staff responsible: Youth life educators

- Therapy
  Goal: Determine if paranoid ideation is result of realistic fear of living in violent environment or actual personality disorder

Method: Psychiatric assessment

Staff responsible: Psychiatrist

- Family

Goal 1: Maintain contact, relationships and information flow with his brothers and sisters

Method: Establish phone schedule for contact and arrange for opportunities for siblings to spend time doing activities together

Staff responsible: School Counselor

Goal 2: Establish visits with previous foster mother

Method: Establish phone schedule for contact and arrange to take him to foster home for visits and holidays

Staff responsible: School Counselor

Goal 3: Have an understanding of family living, normal growth and development, and basic child-care skills

Method: Enroll in individual and family development course; find practicum in child care center where he would work with staff person and spend part of weekend with a volunteer family so he can witness normal family life

Staff responsible: School Counselor

- Academic Education

Goal 1: Prepare for GED exam

Method: Ensure success by tutoring until he can take course, then enroll in GED class with educator staff present in the class to assist him

Staff responsible: Youth life educators

Goal 2: Expose to classic literature and demonstrate knowledge of themes and message

Method: watch movies such as *Of Mice & Men*; test through discussion and oral exam

Staff responsible: Youth life educators

Goal 3: Increase reading level to 8th grade level

Method: Hire reading tutor

Staff responsible: School Counselor

- Spirituality

Goal 1: Develop capacity to nurture and care for others

Method: Raise an animal of his choice from infancy and do volunteering in area of interest, e.g., explore retarded children (given his sister is retarded)

Staff responsible: Youth life educators

Goal 2: Identify with black struggle

Method: View civil rights tapes, Malcolm X, visit Black Museum, be exposed to film and story tapes about black history

Staff responsible: Youth life educators

Goal 3: Attend church of his choice regularly and be involved in religious education program

Method: Attend church camp, retreats, be involved in a church of his choice

Staff responsible: Youth life educators

Goal 4: Increase one level on moral development scale

Method: Watch movies once per day with value messages that challenge his existing mindset

Staff responsible: Youth life educators

Goal 5: Involve in adventure learning

Method: Ropes course, Outward Bound, wilderness experience such as caving, white water rafting, etc.

Staff responsible: Youth life educators

- Enrichment

Goal 1: Enhance art talent

Method: Enter cartooning class

Staff responsible: Youth life educators

Goal 2: Learn to cook

Method: Prepare his own meal two times per week

Staff responsible: Youth life educators

Goal 3: Learn principles of interior design

Method: Decorate his own room

Staff responsible: Youth life educators and interior decorator

Goal 4: Understand how to project image through dress, manners and language

Method: Image course, correct his English to make him aware of slang

Staff responsible: Youth life educators

- Careers

Goal 1: Awareness of his vocational interests and talents

Method: Vocational and interest testing

Staff responsible: School Counselor

Goal 2: Make Sam aware of career opportunities available given his talents

Method: Exposure to job sights and employers in his area of interest, visit sites and talk to those involved in the work at entry level and at senior level

Staff responsible: Youth life educators

Goal 3: Develop work ethic and skills

Method: Supervised house assignments or supervised volunteer job in community

Staff responsible: Youth life educators

- Cultural Arts

Goal 1: Expression of feelings through art and music

Method: Art and music therapy

Staff responsible: Clinician to purchase and coordinate therapy services from art and music therapist

- Citizenship

Goal: Register to vote

Method: Visit voting poll and cast mock ballot at every election and learn about issues through discussion so he knows where he stands

Staff responsible: Youth life educators

- Life Skills

   Goal 1: Attain independent living skills by 21st birthday

   Method: Administer independent living skills inventory and teach skills he is lacking

   Staff responsible: Youth life educators

   Goal 2: Obtain driver's license on 19th birthday

   Method: Enroll in private drivers' training course

   Staff responsible: Youth life educators

   Goal 3: Develop one lifelong leisure pursuit

   Method: Obtain recreation assessment, enroll in lessons, practice

   Staff responsible: Student Coordinator

SECTION V–PERMANCENCY/DISCHARGE PLAN

This component projects the ideal goal for the student, e.g., return to family, independent living, foster home, etc., as well as the criteria for discharge and the plan for the student immediately following discharge.

EXAMPLE: Sam's goal is to be able to develop his work ethic, gain sufficient control of his drinking, possess a career goal and develop the skills necessary for him to live independently in the community. He anticipates being discharged to supervised independent living on his 20th birthday. He expects to remain in supervised independent living until his 21st birthday.

SECTION VI–PROJECTED LENGTH OF STAY

The length of stay is determined by the staff's experience in serving students like Sam.

EXAMPLE: Sam has been in many foster homes and four residential treatment centers. It is anticipated he will spend three years in the therapeutic group home prior to discharge to independent living. The court recognizes this, as they are willing to support his placement until his 21st birthday.

SECTION VII–LEGAL STATUS

This component includes adjudicatory status; history of court oversight/involvement; civil and criminal status; forensic issues; treatment considerations, discharge/aftercare considerations; and identifies the student's legal guardian.

EXAMPLE: Sam's placement is under the direction of the Los Angeles Juvenile Court. He has several delinquency filings against him for breaking and entering, selling crack cocaine and being involved with a stolen car. However, the court viewed his actions as being the result of being molested by caretakers while in placements. The Los Angeles Department of Child Welfare knows of the molestations and they've done nothing to protect him since he was eight years old. They did not find him an adequate placement, which forced him to survive on the streets with no income. The court wishes to review his placement every six months. His attorney and advocate is Mrs. Francis Peters.

SECTION VIII—AFTERCARE PLAN

The aftercare plan is a compilation of the programs necessary to sustain the student's further growth and progress following placement.

EXAMPLE: Sam's Aftercare Plan is to remain in Kansas City, Kansas, as he feels it is much safer than returning to Los Angeles. He expects to be employed full time and will obtain supportive counseling on an as-needed basis from the Family Service Agency in Kansas City. He plans to maintain his relationship with his foster mother and his siblings by weekly phone calls and to visit them in Los Angeles during holidays.

SECTION IX—ASSESSMENT

This component identifies the measures and indicators that will be used to evaluate the agency's success in stimulating and motivating the student's growth and change.

EXAMPLE: The methods to determine Sam's growth are:

- *Percent of goals attained in growth plan*
- *Difference between pre- and post-tests on indicator of Healthy Person Scale and Independent Living Inventory*
- *Competencies gained in each of the curriculum areas*
- *Content of discharge summary*

The Growth Plan is designed in accordance with the Wisdom Principles, i.e., caring, contribution commitment, struggle, transformation, enlightenment, vision, courage and will. Sam will learn caring by having one-to-one coverage; getting his needs met; caring for himself, for his room and his possessions; and through the opportunities to be involved with volunteers, siblings and his foster mother. He will also be raising a pet from infancy, volunteering in the community and learning about African Americans and others who promoted a cause larger than themselves.

Sam learns contribution through his volunteer efforts at the Day Care Center where he is supervised in caring for infants and in his work with retarded children. He possesses a special spot in his heart for retarded children given his sister is retarded.

He will learn commitment through experiencing us being committed to him until he is 21, his foster mother and attorney's commitment to him and through his commitment to his employer, his pet and his volunteer assignments.

He will learn to struggle through his attempts to be self-disciplined, gain work skills, increase his reading level, overcome his alcohol problem and develop the competencies needed to be successful in independent living.

Sam will transform himself through the experiences he will have with our organization and its growth-producing culture and be enlightened by his adventure-based programming and African-American History lessons.

When he is ready to graduate, he will possess a vision of what is possible for himself and hopefully the courage and will to make the sacrifices necessary to achieve it. At the very least, he will experience a staff who demonstrate the courage and will to live through whatever problems he presents them, who will view his lack of progress not as failure or incompetence, but rather their failure to motive him or properly execute his Growth Plan.